M.A. Hugh Fraser

Principles And Practice Of The Law Of Libel And Slander

M.A. Hugh Fraser

Principles And Practice Of The Law Of Libel And Slander

ISBN/EAN: 9783741103612

Manufactured in Europe, USA, Canada, Australia, Japa

Cover: Foto ©ninafisch / pixelio.de

Manufactured and distributed by brebook publishing software (www.brebook.com)

M.A. Hugh Fraser

Principles And Practice Of The Law Of Libel And Slander

Principles and Practice

OF THE LAW OF

LIBEL AND SLANDER

WITH

SUGGESTIONS ON THE CONDUCT OF A CIVIL ACTION,

FORMS AND PRECEDENTS,

AND ALL STATUTES BEARING ON THE SUBJECT.

· BY

HUGH FRASER, M.A., LL.D.,

OF THE INNER TEMPLE AND NORTHERN CIRCUIT, BARRISTER-AT-LAW.

SOME-TIME LECTURER TO THE INCORPORATED LAW SOCIETY;
LATE SCHOLAR AND LAW STUDENT OF TRINITY HALL, CAMBRIDGE, AND HOLDER OF THE
INNS OF COURT STUDENTSHIP;

AUTHOR OF "THE LAW OF LIBEL IN ITS RELATION TO THE PRESS,"
AND "A COMPENDIUM OF THE LAW OF TORTS."

SECOND EDITION.

LONDON:
WILLIAM CLOWES AND SONS, LIMITED
27, FLEET STREET.
1897.

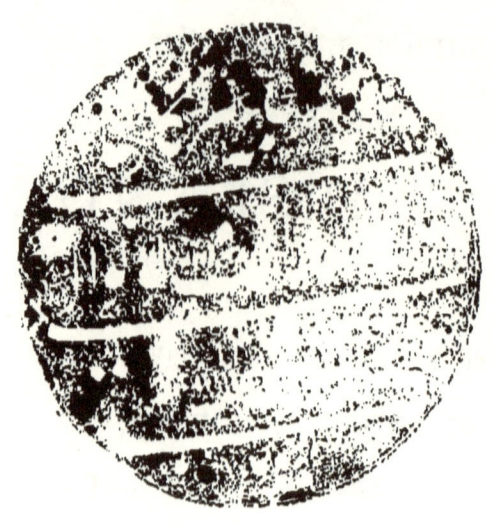

LONDON:
PRINTED BY WILLIAM CLOWES AND SONS, LIMITED,
STAMFORD STREET AND CHARING CROSS.

PREFACE TO THE SECOND EDITION.

IN preparing the present edition for the press, the book has been thoroughly revised and brought up to date. I have made no alteration in the plan or general arrangement of the work, and have endeavoured, as far as possible, not to increase its size.

I am indebted to my friend and former pupil Mr. G. M. HARRIS, M.A., Barrister-at-Law, for valuable assistance in the preparation of the present edition. I have also to thank my friends Mr. A. CLARKE WILLIAMS, LL.D., and Mr. J. D. HARWARD, M.A., Barristers-at-Law, for their kindness in revising the proof-sheets; and my thanks are especially due to Mr. HARWARD for the care and trouble which he has expended on the amplification and revision of the Index.

H. F.

4, ELM COURT, TEMPLE, E.C.,
May 3rd, 1897.

PREFACE TO THE FIRST EDITION.

The object of this work is to present to the reader the Principles and Practice of the Law of Libel and Slander in a concise form; and, considering the large and increasing number of actions of this kind with which the Courts are occupied, it is hoped that the book may prove useful to the Legal Profession. The Law is stated in the form of Propositions, followed by Explanatory Notes, in the preparation of which the original authorities have in every case been consulted. Several cases of importance which have been decided in the last few years have received special notice. Appendix A contains some practical suggestions on the conduct of a Civil Action, together with Forms and Precedents. In Appendix B will be found all the Statutes bearing on the Law of Libel and Slander, with references under each section to particular pages in the text.

I wish to express my obligations to my friend Mr. BLAKE ODGERS, the author of the well-known standard work on this subject, for occasional hints and kindly advice.

I have also to thank my friends Mr. A. CLARKE WILLIAMS, LL.D., and Mr. A. T. CARTER, D.C.L., Barristers-at-Law, for their kindness in revising the proof-sheets. For the copious Index I am indebted to my friend Mr. G. H. TAYLOR-WHITEHEAD, M.A., Barrister-at-Law.

H. F.

4, ELM COURT, TEMPLE, E.C.,
    April 3rd, 1893.

CONTENTS.

	PAGE
TABLE OF CASES...	xi
INDEX TO STATUTES CITED	xxxiii
LIST OF ABBREVIATIONS...	xxxv

PART I.

OF A CIVIL ACTION.

ARTICLE		PAGE
1.	Definition of libel and slander	1
2.	Construction	9
3.	No action without publication	13
4.	Action for libel maintainable without proof of special damage	18
5.	No action for slander without proof of special damage, except in four cases	19
6.	Intention immaterial	37
7.	Slander of title	38
8.	Slander of goods manufactured or sold by another	44
9.	Joinder of plaintiffs	51
10.	Joinder of defendants	53
11.	Joinder of causes of action	56
12.	Security for costs	58
13.	Liability in cases of joint publication; no right to contribution or indemnity from co-defendant...	59
14.	Principal and agent—master and servant	62
15.	Liability for repetition of libel or slander	66
16.	Married woman	68
17.	Husband's liability for wife's libel or slander	70
18.	Aliens—infants—lunatics—bankrupts	71
19.	Corporations and incorporated companies	77
20.	Defences to action for libel or slander	80

CONTENTS.

	PAGE
ARTICLE 21. Justification	81
22. Distinction between report and comment	86
23. Fair and *bonâ fide* comment on a matter of public interest	88
24. Privilege	96
25. Statements made in Parliament or in the course of judicial, naval, military, or State proceedings	101
26. Reports, &c., published by order of Parliament ...	106
27. Reports in a newspaper of proceedings in a Court of Justice	107
28. Other reports of judicial proceedings	113
29. Extracts from registers kept pursuant to Statute	118
30. Reports of proceedings in Parliament	120
31. Reports of proceedings of public meetings ...	121
32. Reports of vestry meetings, &c.	127
33. Notices and reports published at request of Government office or authority	130
34. Statements made in order to redress public grievances or punish crime	131
35. Statements made in order to protect interest of writer or speaker	133
36. Statements made in order to protect a common interest	136
37. Statements made in discharge of a duty	140
38. Malice	150
39. Defence of apology under sect. 2 of Lord Campbell's Act (6 & 7 Vict. c. 96)	156
40. Accord and satisfaction	157
41. Release	158
42. *Res judicata*	158
43. Statute of Limitations	159
44. Death of plaintiff or defendant	161
45. Evidence in aggravation of damages	163
46. Evidence in mitigation of damages	166
47. Consolidation of actions	171
48. Assessment of damages in a consolidated action ...	173
49. Injunctions	174
50. Costs	177
51. New trial	178

CONTENTS. ix

Part II.

OF CRIMINAL PROCEEDINGS.

		PAGE
Article 1.	Libel a crime	183
2.	Blasphemous, seditious, and obscene words, &c. ...	194
3.	Publication	197
4.	No prosecution for newspaper libel except by leave of judge	198
5.	Defences	200, 201
6.	Defence under sect. 6 of Lord Campbell's Act (6 & 7 Vict. c. 96)...	202
7.	Employer's criminal liability for libels published by his servants	203
8.	Libel or no libel, a question for the jury	205

Appendix A.
  On the conduct of a civil action, with forms and precedents 207

Appendix B.
  Statutes 241

INDEX 273

TABLE OF CASES.

	PAGE
Aberdein v. Macleay (1893), 9 Times L. R. 539	97, 99
Abrath v. N. E. Ry. Co. (1886), 11 App. Cas. 253, 254; 55 L. J. Q. B. 466 (H. L.)	77
Adams v Kelly (1824), Ry. & M. 157	17, 23, 64
Alexander v. Jenkins (1892), 1 Q. B. 797 (C. A.)	30, 31
Alexander v. N. E. Ry. Co. (1865), 34 L. J. Q. B. 152	83, 84
Allbutt v. General Council of Medical Education & Registration (1889), 23 Q. B. D. 400 (C. A.)	100, 146
Allcock v. Hall (1891), 1 Q. B. 444	182
Allen v. Eaton (1630), 1 Roll. Abr. 54	33
Allhusen v. Labouchere (1878), 3 Q. B. D. 654 (C. A.)	235
Allinson v. General Council of Medical Education (1892), 8 Times L. R. 784 (C. A.)	176
Allsop & wife v. Allsop (1860), 5 H. & N. 534; 29 L. J. Ex. 315	21
Amann v. Damm (1860), 8 C. B. N. S. 597; 8 W. R. 470	132, 147
Anderson v. Gorrie (1895), 1 Q. B. 668 (C. A.)	104
—— v. Hamilton (1816), 2 B. & B. 156, n.	213
—— v. Liebig's Extract of Meat Co., Ltd. (1882), 45 L.T. 757	174
Andrews v. Chapman (1853), 3 C. & K. 289	86, 116, 117
—— v. Nott Bower (1895), 1 Q. B. 888 (C. A.)	146
Annaly v. Trade Auxiliary Co., Ltd. (1890), 26 L. R. Ir. 394	118
Anon (1638) Cro. Jac. 516	33
Apollinaris Co.'s Trade Marks, In re (1891), 1 Ch. 1 (C. A.)	58
Armstrong and others v. Armit and others (1886), 2 Times L. R. 887	176
Ashley v. Harrison (1793), 1 Esp. 48; Peake, 256	165
Ashmore v. Borthwick (1885), 49 J. P. 792; 2 Times L. R. 113, 209	116
Astley (Sir John) v. Younge (1759), 2 Burr. 807	102
Atherley v. Harvey (1877), 2 Q. B. D. 524	235
Attorney-General v. Bradbury & Evans (1851), 21 L. J. Ex. 12; 7 Ex. 97	109

	PAGE
Austin (Sir J.) v. Culpepper (1684), 2 Show. 313; Skin. 123	3, 6
Australian Newspaper Co. v. Bennett (1894), App. Cas. 284	4, 9, 181
Ayre v. Craven (1834), 2 A. & E. 2	20
B— Re (1892), 1 Ch. 459	75
Baal v. Baggerley (1632), Cro. Car. 326	25
Bahama Islands, In re (1893), App. Cas. 138	87
Bainbridge v. Lax and others (1846), 9 Q. B. 819	157
Baker v. Carrick (1894), 1 Q. B. 838 (C. A.)	145
—— v. Morfue (1668), Sid. 327; 2 Keb. 202	33
—— and others v. Piper (1886), 2 Times L. R. 733	40
Baldwin v. Elphinston (1775), 2 W. Bl. 1037	15
Bankes v. Allen (1616), 1 Roll. Abr. 54	34
Banks v. Hollingsworth (1893), 1 Q. B. 442 (C. A.)	211
Bannister v. Kelly (1895), 59 J. P. 793	145
Barmund's case (1619), Cro. Jac. 473	21
Barnabas v. Traunter (1641), 1 Vin. Abr. 396	21
Barnes v. Bruddel (1669), 1 Vent. 4	21
—— v. Holloway (1799), 8 T. R. 150	35
Barnett v. Allen (1858), 3 H. & N. 376; 27 L. J. Ex. 412	10, 19, 26
Barrett v. Long (1851), 3 H. L. C. 395	154
Barrow v. Lewellin (1615), Hob. 62	13
Bayley v. Edmunds and others (1895), 11 Times L. R. 537 (C. A.)	186
Beamond v. Hastings (1610), Cro. Jac. 240	29
Beatson v. Skene (1860), 29 L. J. Ex. 430; 5 H. & N. 838	142, 213
Beauchamps (Lord) v. Sir R. Croft (1569), Dyer 285 a	102
Behrens v. Allen (1862), 3 F. & F. 135; 8 Jur. N. S. 118	85
Bellamy v. Burch (1847), 16 M. & W. 590	27
Bellerophon, H. M. S. (1874), 44 L. J. Ad. 5	213
Belt v. Lawes (1882), 51 L. J. Q. B. 359; (1884), 12 Q. B. D. 356 (C. A.)	46, 182, 212, 225
Bennetts v. McIlwraith & Co. (1896), 2 Q. B. 464 (C. A.)	52
Best v. Osborne & Co. (1896), 12 Times L. R. 419	224
Bill v. Neal (1662), 1 Lev. 52	29
Bishop v. Latimer (1861), 4 L. T. 775	8, 82, 118
Bittridge's case (1602), 4 Rep. 19 b	26
Blackburn v. Blackburn (1827), 4 Bing. 395; 3 C. & P. 146; 1 M. & P. 33, 63	37
Blackham v. Pugh (1846), 2 C. B. 611; 15 L. J. C. P. 290	133
Blagg v. Sturt (1846), 10 Q. B. 899; 16 L. J. Q. B. 39	7
Blake v. Pilfold (1832), 1 Moo. & Rob. 198	131
—— v. Stevens and others (1864), 11 L. T. 543; 4 F. & F. 232	8, 37, 38, 63, 83, 163
Bliss v. Stafford (1588), Owen, 37	43
Bloodworth v. Gray (1844), 7 M. & Gr. 334	27

	PAGE
Bond v. Douglas (1836), 7 C. & P. 626	17, 63
Bonnard v. Perryman (1891), 2 Ch. 269 (C. A.)	45, 174, 176
Boosey v. Wood (1865), 34 L. J. Ex. 65; 3 H. & C. 484	157, 158
Booth v. Arnold (1895), 1 Q. B. 571 (C. A.)	31
—— and another v. Briscoe (1877), 2 Q. B. D. 496 (C. A.)	79
Botterill and another v. Whytehead (1879), 41 L. T. 588	
	34, 83, 137, 139, 146, 148, 155
Bourke v. Warren (1826), 2 C. & P. 307	5
Bourn's (Sir John) case, Cro. Eliz. 497	5
Bowen v. Hall and others (1881), 6 Q. B. D. 333 (C. A.)	23
Boxsius v. Goblet Frères (1894), 1 Q. B. 842 (C. A.)	14, 100, 145
Boydell v. Jones (1838), 7 Dowl. 210; 1 Horn & H. 408; 4 M. & W. 446	6, 9, 118
Bradbury v. Cooper (1883), 12 Q. B. D. 94	221
Bradlaugh & Besant v. The Queen (1878), 3 Q. B. D. 607; 48 L. J. M. C. 5; 26 W. R. 410; 38 L. T. 118; 14 Cox, C. C. 68 (C. A.)	267
Bray v. Ford (1896), App. Cas. 44 (H. L.)	179
Brenon v. Ridgway (1887), 3 Times L. R. 592	91
Brett v. Watson (1872), 20 W. R. 723	155
Brine v. Bazalgette (1849), 18 L. J. Ex. 348; 3 Ex. 692	164
Brinsmead v. Harrison (1872), L. R. 7 C. P. 547	159
British & Foreign Contract Co. v. Wright (1884), 32 W. R. 413	236
Bromage v. Prosser (1825), 4 B. & C. 247	139, 212
Brook v. Rawl (1849), 4 Ex. 521; 19 L. J. Ex. 114	39, 40, 42, 43
Brown v. Croome (1817), 2 Stark. 297	139, 148
—— v. Smith (1853), 13 C. B. 596; 22 L. J. C. P. 151	20, 35
Browne v. Dunn (1893), 6 R. 67 (H. L.)	14, 103
Brunsden v. Humphrey (1884), 14 Q. B. D. 141 (C. A.)	59
Brunswick (Duke of) v. Harmer (1849), 19 L. J. Q. B. 20; 3 C. & K. 10; 14 Jur. 110; 14 Q. B. 185	15, 161
Bryce v. Rusden (1886), 2 Times L. R. 435	91
Bull v. Chapman (1853), 8 Ex. 104	60
Burdett v. Abbot (1811), 5 Dow, H. L. 165	2, 17, 63
Burnett v. Tak (1882), 45 L. T. 743	45, 174
Bursill v. Tanner (1884), 13 Q. B. D. 691	69
Burt v. Blackburn (1887), 3 Times L. R. 356 (C. A.)	75
Button v. Heyward (1722), 8 Mod. 24	25
Byrchley's case (1585), 4 Rep. 16	34
Cæsar v. Curseny (1593), Cro. Eliz. 305	29
Calder v. Halket (1839), 3 Moo. P. C. C. 28	105
Campbell v. Spottiswoode (1863), 3 B. & S. 769; 32 L. J. Q. B. 185; 8 L. T. 201	6, 66, 88, 89, 91, 92, 95

Capital & Counties Bank *v.* Henty & Sons (1882), 7 App. Cas.
  741; 5 C. P. D. 514; 52 L. J. Q. B. 232; 47 L. T. 662   9, 11, 12
Carr *v.* Duckett (1860), 5 H. & N. 783; 29 L. J. Ex. 468 . . 40
—— (Sir John) *v.* Hood (1808), 1 Camp. 355, n . . . 95
Carrol *v.* Bird (1800), 3 Esp. at p. 202 142
Carslake *v.* Mapledoram (1788), 2 T. R. 473 27
Carter *v.* Rigby (1896), 2 Q. B. 113 (C. A.) 52
Caulfield *v.* Whitworth (1868), 18 L. T. 527; 16 W. R. 936 82, 155
Chalmers *v.* Shackell (1834), 6 C. & P. 475 82
Chaloner *v.* Lansdown & Sons (1894), 10 Times L. R. 290 . 126
Chamberlain *v.* Boyd (1883), 11 Q. B. D. 407; 52 L. J. Q. B. 277 21, 43
Champion & Co., Ltd. *v.* Birmingham Vinegar Brewery Co., Ltd.
  (1893), 10 Times L. R. 164 176
Chance *v.* Beveridge & Freeman's Journal (1895), 11 Times
  L. R. 528 210
Charlton *v.* Watton (1834), 6 C. & P. 385 169
Chatterton *v.* Secretary of State for India in Council (1895),
  2 Q. B. 189 (C. A.) 106
Cheese *v.* Scales (1842), 10 M. & W. 488 7
Child *v.* Affleck & wife (1829), 9 B. & C. 403 . . . 143
Churchill *v.* Gedney (1889), 53 J. P. 471 10
—— (Lord) *v.* Hunt (1819), 2 B. & Ald. 685; 1 Chit. 480 . 6
Clark *v.* Freeman (1848), 11 Beav. 112; 17 L. J. Ch. 142; 12
  Jur. 149 8
—— *v.* Molyneux (1877), 3 Q. B. D. 237; 47 L. J. Q. B. 230;
  14 Cox. C. C. 10 (C. A.) . . 97, 138, 145, 150, 155, 180
Clarke *v.* Taylor (1836), 2 Bing. N. C. 654 83
Clarkson *v.* Lawson (1829-30), 6 Bing. 266, 587; 3 M. & P.
  605; 4 M. & P. 356 . . . . 8, 83
Clay *v.* Roberts (1863), 9 Jur. N. S. 580; 11 W. R. 649; 8
  L. T. 397 . . . . 7, 8
—— *v.* Yates (1856), 25 L. J. Ex. 237; 27 L. T. O. S. 126; 1
  H. & N. 73 60
Clement *v.* Lewis and others (1822), 3 Br. & Bing. 297; 7 Moore,
  200; 3 B. & Ald. 702 . . . . 8, 82, 118
Coats *v.* Chadwick (1894), 1 Ch. 347 87
Colburn *v.* Patmore (1834), 1 C. M. & R. 73 60
Colebrook *v.* Jones (1752), 1 Dick. 154 58
Collard *v.* Marshall (1892), 1 Ch. 571 176
Colledge *v.* Pike (1886), 56 L. T. 124 . . . . 60, 172
Collier (M.D.) *v.* Simpson (1831), 5 C. & P. 73 . . . 33
Commissioner for Railways *v.* Brown (1887), 13 App. Cas. 133. 181
Cook *v.* Field (1788), 3 Esp. 133 84
—— *v.* Ward (1830), 6 Bing. 409; 4 M. & P. 99 . . . 6, 37

TABLE OF CASES. xv

	PAGE
Cook v. Whellock (1890), 24 Q. B. D. 658 (C. A.)	77
Cooke v. Hughes (1824), Ry. & M. 115	197
—— and another v. Wildes (1855), 5 E. & B. 328; 24 L. J. Q. B. 367	135
Cooper v. Blackmore and others (1886), 2 Times L. R. 746	237
—— v. Lawson (1838), 8 A. & E. 746; 2 Jur. 919	91, 114, 117
Corcoran & wife v. Corcoran (1857), 7 Ir. L. R. N. S. 272	20
Coulson v. Coulson (1887), 3 Times L. R. 846	175
Coward v. Wellington (1836), 7 C. & P. 531	20, 134
Cox v. Cooper (1863), 12 W. R. 75; 9 L. T. 329	7
—— v. Feeney (1863), 4 F. & F. 13	94, 95
—— v. Lee (1869), L. R. 4 Ex. 284; 38 L. J. Ex. 219	6
Coxhead v. Richards (1846), 2 C. B. 569	100, 147
Crawfoot v. Dale (1675), 1 Vent. 263; 3 Salk. 327	35
Creevy v. Carr (1835), 7 C. & P. 64	68, 159, 170
Critchley v. Brown (1886), 2 Times L. R. 238	211
Croft v. King (1893), 1 Q. B. 419	210
Crown Bank, In re O'Malley, In re (1890), 44 Ch. D. 649; 59 L. J. Ch. 767	87
Cucks v. Starre (1633), Cro. Car. 285	33
Cumming v. Green (1891), 7 Times L. R. 409	231
Curry v. Walter (1796), 1 B. & P. 525; 1 Esp. 456	115

Daines and another v. Hartley (1848), 3 Ex. 200	10
Dalrymple v. Leslie (1881), 8 Q. B. D. 5	239
Darby v. Ouseley (1856), 25 L. J. Ex. 227; 1 H. & N. 1	163, 168
Davies v. Snead (1870), L. R. 5 Q. B. 611; 39 L. J. Q. B. 202	141, 147
—— and wife v. Solomon (1871), L. R. 7 Q. B. 112; 41 L. J. Q. B. 10	20
Davis v. Billing (1891), 8 Times L. R. 58 (C. A.)	226
—— v. Cutbush and others (1859), 1 F. & F. 487	67, 129, 140, 170
—— v. Duncan (1874), L. R. 9 C. P. 396; 43 L. J. C. P. 185; 30 L. T. 464	94
—— v. Gardiner (1593), 4 Rep. 16; 2 Salk. 694	20
—— & Sons v. Shepstone (1886), 11 App. Cas. 187	92
Davidson v. Duncan (1857), 26 L. J. Q. B. 104; 28 L. T. O. S. 265; 7 E. & B. 229	101, 129
Dawkins v. Paulet (Lord) (1869), L. R. 5 Q. B. 94; 39 L. J. Q. B. 53	106
—— v. Rokeby (Lord) (1875), L. R. 7 H. L. 744; 45 L. J. Q. B. 8	106
Day v. Bream (1837), 2 Moo. & R. 54	16, 66
—— v. Buller (1770), 3 Wils. 59	33
De Bernales v. New York Herald (1893), 2 Q. B. 97, n. (C. A.)	210

TABLE OF CASES.

	PAGE
De Crespigny v. Wellesley (1829), 5 Bing. 392; 2 M. & P. 695 . . . . 2, 65, 84, 163	
Defries v. Davis (1835), 7 C. & P. 112; 3 Dowl. 629 . . .	71
Delacroix v. Thevenot (1817), 2 Stark. 63	14
D'Hormusjee v. Grey (1882), 10 Q. B. D. 13	58
Desilla v. Schunks & Co. (1880), W. N. 96	55
Devereux v. Clarke (1891), 2 Q. B. 582	231
De Wahl v. Braune (1856), 1 H. & N. 178; 25 L. J. Ex. 343 .	74
Dibdin v. Swan & Bostock (1793), 1 Esp. 28	95
Dickson v. Wilton (The Earl of) (1859), 1 F. & F. 419 99, 150, 152	
Dixon v. Smith (1860), 29 L. J. Ex. 125; 5 H. & N. 450 .	144
Dodson v. Owen (1885), 2 Times L. R. 111	110
Doe v. Clifford (1847), 2 C. & Kir. 448	234
—— v. Ross (1840), 7 M. & W. 102	234
Donoghue v. Hayes (1831), Hayes, Ir. Ex. Rep. 265 . .	37, 38
Doyley v. Roberts (1837), 3 Bing. N. C. 835 . . .	28, 34
Drake v. Beckham (1849), 2 H. L. C. 579	76
Du Bost v. Beresford (1811), 2 Camp. 511	3
Duncombe v. Daniell (1837), 8 C. & P. 222; 2 Jur. 32; W. W. & H. 101 . . . . 67, 94, 129, 138, 170	
Dunn v. Devon & Exeter Constitutional Newspaper Co., Ltd. (1894), 10 Times L. R. 335; (1895), 1 Q. B. 211, n. . .	224
Dunne v. Anderson (1825), 3 Bing. 88; 10 Moore, 407; R. & M. 287	93
Duplany v. Davis (1887), 3 Times L. R. 184	96
Eastmead v. Witt (1856), 18 C. B. 544; 25 L. J. C. P. 294 .	133
Eastwood v. Holmes (1858), 1 F. & F. 347	5, 96
Eaton v. Johns (1842), 1 Dowl. N. S. 602	6
Ecklin v. Little (1890), 6 Times L. R. 366 . . .	23, 24
Eddison v. Dalziel (1893), 9 Times L. R. 334	173
Edsall v. Russell (1843), 12 L. J. C. P. 4; 6 Jur. 996 .	33, 85
Edwards v. Lowther (1876), 45 L. J. C. P. 417; 34 L. T. 255; 24 W. R. 434	210
—— v. Bell and others (1824), 1 Bing. 403	85
Elborow v. Allen (1623), Cro. Jac. 642	43
Ellisen, Ex parte, not reported, approved by Lush, J., in Reg. v. Carden (1879), 5 Q. B. D. 11, 13	190
Emmens v. Pottle & Sons (1885), 16 Q. B. D. 354 (C. A.). 2, 16, 65	
Evans v. Gwyn (1844), 5 Q. B. 844	32
—— v. Harlow (1844), 5 Q. B. 624; 13 L. J. Q. B. 120 .	8, 36
Eyre v. Garlick (1878), 42 J. P. 68	3
Fairman v. Ives (1822), 5 B. & Ald. 642	132

TABLE OF CASES.   xvii

	PAGE
Farrer v. Lowe & Co. & Medley (1889), 5 Times L. R. 234	211
Felkin v. Herbert (1863–4), 33 L. J. Ch. 294	92
Fernandez, Ex parte (1861), 30 L. J. C. P. 321	104
Fisher v. Owen (1878), 8 Ch. D. 645	235
Fleming v. Dollar (1889), 23 Q. B. D. 388; 58 L. J. Q. B. 548; 61 L. T. 230	86, 226
Fleming and others v. Newton (1848), 1 H. L. C. 343	118, 119
Forbes v. King (1833), 1 Dowl. 672; 2 L. J. Ex. 109	7
Ford v. Blest (1890), 6 Times L. R. 295	213
Forrester v. Tyrrell (1893), 9 Times L. R. 257 (C. A.)	17
Foster and others v. Lawson (1826), 3 Bing. 452	57
Foster v. Perryman (1891), 8 Times L. R. 115	231
Foulger v. Newcomb (1867), L. R. 2 Ex. 327; 36 L. J. Ex. 169	28, 36
Fowler and wife v. Homer (1812), 3 Camp. 294	132, 144
Francis v. Roose (1838), 3 M. & W. 191; 1 H. & H. 36	26
Frank v. Mainwaring (1839), 4 Beav. 37	74
Fraser v. Berkeley (1836), 7 C. & P. 621	95
Frescoe v. May (1860), 2 F. & F. 123	60, 159
Fryer v. Kinnersley (1863), 15 C. B. N. S. 422; 33 L. J. C. P. 96	139, 141, 148, 153

Gallagher v. Murton (1888), 4 Times L. R. 304	10
Gallwey v. Marshall (1853), 9 Ex. 294; 23 L. J. Ex. 78	32
Gardner v. Irvin (1878), 4 Ex. Div. 53	233
—— v. Slade (1849), 13 Q. B. 798; 18 L. J. Q. B. 336	143, 154
Gathercole v. Miall (1846), 15 L. J. Ex. 179; 10 J. P. 582; 10 Jur. 337; 15 M. & W. 319	95, 163
Gelen v. Hall (1857), 2 H. & N. 379	105
George v. Goddard (1861), 2 F. & F. 689	137
Gerard (Sir G.) v. Dickenson (1590), 4 Rep. 18; Cro. Eliz. 197	152
Gibson v. Evans (1889), 23 Q. B. D. 384; 58 L. J. Q. B. 621	236
Gilpin v. Fowler (1854), 9 Ex. 615; 23 L. J. Ex. 152; 18 Jur. 293	148, 152, 153
Glossop v. Spindler (1885), 29 Sol. Jour. 556	226
Goddart v. Haselfoot (1637), 1 Roll. Abr. 54	33
Godson v. Home (1819), 1 B. & B. 7; 3 Moore, 223	8
Goffin v. Donnelly (1881), 6 Q. B. D. 307; 50 L. J. Q. B. 303	101
Gompas v. White (1890), 54 J. P. 22	102
Goodall v. Little (1850), 1 Sim. N. S. 155	234
Gouraud v. Fitzgerald (1889), 37 W. R. 55	221, 222
Gourley v. Plimsoll (1873), L. R. 8 C. P. 362	233
Graham, Ex parte, Re Job (1870), 21 L. T. 802	76

… TABLE OF CASES.

	PAGE
Gray v. Bartholomew (1895), 1 Q. B. 209 (C. A.)	224
Great Australian, &c. Co. v. Martin (1877), 5 Ch. D. 1	71
Green v. Chapman (1837), 4 Bing. N. C. 92; 5 Scott, 340	95
Griffiths v. Lewis (1846), 7 Q. B. 61; 15 L. J. Q. B. 249	35, 134
Grimwade v. Dicks and others (1886), 2 Times L. R. 627	116
Gutsole v. Mathers (1836), 1 M. & W. 495; 5 Dowl. 69	40
Guy v. Gregory (1840), 9 C. & P. 587	164
Gwynn v. S. E. Ry. Co. (1868), 18 L. T. 738	83, 84
Halley, The (1868), L. R. 2 P. C. 193	73
Halsey v. Brotherhood (1880-1), 15 Ch. D. 523; 19 Ch. D. 386; 51 L. J. Ch. 233; 45 L. T. 640	39, 44, 47, 174
Hancock v. Case (1862), 2 F. & F. 711	136
Hannay and others v. Smurthwaite and others (1894), App. Cas. 494 (H. L.)	57
Harding v. Greening (1817), 8 Taunt. 42; 1 Moore 477; 1 Holt. N. P. 531	64
Hargrave v. Le Breton (1769), 4 Burr. 2422	40, 50, 135, 143
Harle v. Catherall and others (1866), 14 L. T. 801	91, 94, 95, 169
Harman v. Delany (1731), 2 Str. 898; Barnard 289; Fitz. 121	36, 49
Harper v. Beamond (1605), Cro. Jac. 56	29
Harris v. Thompson (1853), 13 C. B. 333	145
—— v. Warre (1879), 4 C. P. D. 125	212, 214
Harrison v. Bevington (1838), 8 C. & P. 708	57
—— v. Bush (1855), 5 E. & B. 344; 25 L. J. Q. B. 25	131
—— v. Fraser (1881), 29 W. R. 662	132
—— v. Pearce (1858), 32 L. T. O. S. 298; 1 F. & F. 567	59, 63
Hartley v. Herring (1799), 8 T. R. 130	20, 33
Haythorn v. Lawson (1827), 3 C. & P. 196	57
Hayward & Co. v. Hayward & Sons (1886), 34 Ch. D. 198; 56 L. J. Ch. 287	116, 174
Hebditch v. McIlwaine and others (1894), 2 Q. B. 54 (C. A.)	17, 99, 132, 133, 136, 139, 148
Hedley v. Barlow (1865), 4 F. & F. 224	92, 93
Helmore v. Smith (1886), 35 Ch. D. 449; 56 L. J. Ch. 145; 56 L. T. 72	162
Helsham v. Blackwood (1851), 20 L. J. C. P. 187; 11 C. B. 111; 15 Jur. 861	92
Hennessy v. Wright (1888), 57 L. J. Q. B. 594; 24 Q. B. D. 445 n. (C. A.)	231, 232, 235, 237, 239
—— v. Wright (1888), 36 W. R. 880	236
Henwood v. Harrison (1872), L. R. 7 C. P. 606; 41 L. J. C. P. 206; 26 L. T. 938; 20 W. R. 1000	93, 144
Heriot v. Stuart (1796), 1 Esp. 437	8, 95

TABLE OF CASES. xix

	PAGE
Hibbins v. Lee (1864), 11 L. T. 541; 4 F. & F. 243	92, 94
Hibbs v. Wilkinson (1859), 1 F. & F. 608	96
Hickinbotham v. Leach (1842), 10 M. & W. 363	231
Hicks' Case (1618), Hob. 215; Poph. 139	197
Highmore v. Earl and Countess of Harrington (1857), 3 C. B. N. S. 142	32
Hill v. Hart Davies (1882), 21 Ch. D. 798; 51 L. J. Ch. 845; 47 L. T. 82	175
Hindlip v. Mudford (1890), 6 Times L. R. 367	235
Hirst v. Goodwin (1862), 3 F. & F. 257	34, 166
Hoare v. Silverlock (1848), 12 Q. B. 624; 17 L. J. Q. B. 306	7, 138
Hodgson v. Scarlett (1818), 1 B. & Ald. 244	102
Hollis v. Briscow et ux. (1605), Cro. Jac. 58	29
Holwood v. Hopkins (1600), Cro. Eliz. 787	20
Hooper v. Truscott (1836), 2 Bing. N. C. 457; 2 Scott, 672	132, 152
Hopley v. Williams (1869), 6 Times L. R. 3; 53 J. P. 822	173
Hopwood v. Thorn (1850), 8 C. B. 293; 19 L. J. C. P. 94; 14 Jur. 87	19, 33, 135
Houlden v. Smith (1850), 14 Q. B. 841; 19 L. J. Q. B. 170	105
How v. Prinn (1702), 2 Salk. 694; 2 Lord Raym. 812; 7 Mod. 113; 1 Bro. P. C. 97	29, 30
Howard v. Crowther (1841), 8 M. & W. 601	76
Howe Machine Co., In re (1889), 41 Ch. D. 118	58
Hughes v. Merrett (1886), 17 Q. B. D. 273	178
—— v. Vargus (1893), 9 Times L. R. 551 (C. A.)	213
Hume v. Marshall (1878), 42 J. P. 136	34, 144
Humphreys v. Stanfield (1638), Cro. Car. 469	43
—— v. Stilwell (1861), 2 F. & F. 590	137
Humphries & Co. v. The Taylor Drug Co. (1888), 39 Ch. D. 693	238
Hunt v. Algar and others (1833), 6 C. & P. 245	171
—— v. Clarke, Re O'Malley (1889), 58 L. J. Q. B. 490; 61 L. T. 343	87
—— v. G. N. Ry. Co. (1891), 2 Q. B., 189 (C. A.)	136, 144
Hunter v. Sharpe (1866), 4 F. & F. 983; 15 L. T. 421	8, 96
Huntley v. Ward (1859), 1 F. & F. 552; 6 C. B. N. S. 514	37, 135
Ingram v. Lawson (1840), 9 C. & P. 333; 6 Bing. N. C. 212	4, 168
Ireland v. Champneys (1813), 4 Taunt. 884	162
Jackson v. Adams (1835), 2 Bing. N. C. 402	29
—— v. Hopperton (1864), 16 C. B. N. S. 829; 12 W. R. 913; 10 L. T. 529	152
Jacobs v. Schmaltz (1890), 62 L. T. 121; 6 Times L. R. 155	214
James v. Boston (1845), 2 C. & K. 4	131, 144
—— v. Rutlech (1599), 4 Rep. 17	5, 27

TABLE OF CASES.

PAGE

Jenkins v. Smith (1621), Cro. Jac. 586 33
Jenner and another v. A'Beckett (1871), L. R., 7 Q. B. 11; 41 L.
   J. Q. B. 14; 25 L. T. 464 96
Jenoure v. Delmege (1891), App. Cas. 73; 60 L. J. P. C. 11
                                                                  97, 150, 180
Jesson v. Hayes (1636), 1 Roll. Abr. 63 35
Johnson v. Evans (1800), 3 Esp. 32 132
—— v. Hudson (1836), 7 A. & E. 233, n. 63
Jones and another v. Broadhurst (1850), 9 C. B. 173 . . . 157
Jones v. Curling and another (1884), 13 Q. B. D. 262 (C. A.) . 178
—— v. Herne (1759), 2 Wils. 87 25
—— v. Richards (1885), 15 Q. B. D. 439 236
—— v. Thomas (1885), 34 W. R. 104; 53 L. T. 678; 2 Times
   L. R. 95 132
—— v. Williams (1885), 1 Times L. R. 572 . . 15, 132, 135

Kane v. Mulvany (1866), Ir. R., 2 C. L. 402 101
Kelly v. O'Malley and others (1889), 6 Times L. R. 62 . . 124
—— v. Sherlock (1866), L. R. 1 Q. B. 686; 35 L. J. Q. B. 209 93
—— v. Tinling (1865), L. R. 1 Q. B. 699; 35 L. J. Q. B. 231 94, 95
Kerr v. Gandy (1886), 3 Times L. R. 75 174
Kershaw v. Bailey (1848), 1 Ex. 743; 17 L. J. Ex. 129 . . 137
Keyzor and another v. Newcomb (1859), 1 F. & F. 559 . . 63
Kimber v. The Press Association (1892), 8 Times L. R. 671;
   (1893) 1 Q. B. 65 (C. A.) 115
Kine v. Sewell (1838), 3 M. & W. 297 . . . . 132, 134
King v. Lake (1672), 2 Ventr. 28 34
—— v. Watts (1838), 8 C. & P. 614 20
Kirby v. Simpson (1854), 10 Exch. 358 105
Kœnig v. Ritchie (1862), 3 F. & F. 413 . . . . 96, 134

Lake v. King (1680), 1 Saund. 131; 1 Lev. 240; 1 Mod. 58;
   Sid. 414 . . . . 101, 131
Lamb's case (1610), 9 Rep. fol. 60 . . . . . 2, 16, 17
Latimer v. Western Morning News Co. (1871), 25 L. T. 44 . 77
Laughton v. Bishop of Sodor and Man (1872), L. R. 4 P. C. 495;
   42 L. J. P. C. 11 . . . . 134, 138
Law v. Harwood (1628), Sir W. Jones, 196; Cro. Car. 140 . 42
Lawless v. Anglo-Egyptian Cotton and Oil Co. (1869), L. R. 4
   Q. B. 262; 10 B. & S. 226; 38 L. J. Q. B. 129 . . . 140
Lawrence v. Newberry (1891), 64 L. T. 797 5
Lay v. Lawson (1836), 4 A. & E. 795 148
Le Fanu and another v. Malcolmson (1848), 1 H. L. C. 637; 13
   L. T. O. S. 61 . . . . 5, 57

TABLE OF CASES. xxi

	PAGE
Lefroy v. Burnside (1879), 4 L. R. Ir., at p. 340	92
Lever v. Witty, unreported, tried at the Liverpool Assizes, July 26, 1893	6
Levi v. Milne (1827), 4 Bing. 195	5
Lewis v Levy (1858), 27 L. J. Q. B. 282; E. B. & E. 537	115, 118
—— v. Walter (1821), 4 B. & Ald. 605	84, 116
Leyman v. Latimer and others (1877–8), 3 Ex. D. 15, 352; 47 L. J. Ex. 470	83
Liebig's Extract of Meat Co., Ltd. v. Anderson (1882), 45 L. T. 757	174
Lilley v. Roney (1892), 8 Times L. R., 642	102
Littleboy v. Wright (1674), 1 Lev. 69; 1 Sid. 95	160
Littleton, ex parte (1888), 52 J. P. 264	192
Liverpool Household Stores Association v. Smith (1887), 37 Ch. D. 170 (C. A.)	176
London v. Eastgate (1619), 2 Rolle's Rep. 72	34
Lowden v. Blakey (1889), 23 Q. B. D. 332	234
Lowe v. Fox (1885), 15 Q. B. D. 667 (C. A.)	160
Lumby v. Allday (1831), 1 Cr. & J. 301	20
Lumley v. Gye (1853), 2 E. & B. 216; 22 L. J. Q. B. 463	23
Lynam v. Gowing (1880), 6 L. R. Ir. 259	104
Lynch v. Knight and wife (1861), 9 H. L. C. 577; 8 Jur. N. S. 724; 5 L. T. 291	20, 23, 166
M'Corquodale v. Bell and another (1876), W. N. 39	236
Macdougall v. Knight and Son (1890), L. R. 25 Q. B. D. 11; (1889), 14 App. Cas. 200	117
Mackay v. Ford (1860), 5 H. & N. 792; 29 L. J. Ex. 404	102
—— v. Manchester Press Co. (1889), 6 Times L. R. 16	224
Mackenzie v. Steinkopf (1890), 6 Times L. R. 141	236
Maclaren and Sons v. Davis and another (1890), 6 Times L. R. 372	180
Macleod v. Wakley (1828), 3 C. P. 311	95
M'Pherson v. Daniels (1829), 10 B. & C. 263; 5 M. & Rob. 251	66, 67, 81, 84
Malachy v. Soper and another (1836), 3 Bing. N. C. 371	4, 39, 41, 42
Mallon v. W. H. Smith & Son (1893), 9 Times L. R. 621	16, 65
Malone v. Fitzgerald (1886), 18 L. R. Ir. 187	239
Maloney v. Bartley (1812), 3 Camp. 210	65
Manby v. Witt (1856), 18 C. B. 544; 25 L. J. C. P. 294	133
Manning v. Avery (1674), 3 Keb. 153; 1 Vin. Abr. 553	43
Marks v. The Conservative Newspaper Co., Ltd. (1886), 3 Times L. R. 244	157, 158

	PAGE
Marriott v. Chamberlain (1886), 17 Q. B. D. 154 (C. A.)	238
Marshall v. Marshall (1888), 38 Ch. D. 330 (C. A.)	210
Marston v. Downes (1834), 1 A. & E. 31; 6 C. & P. 381	213, 234
Martin v. Strong (1836), 5 A. & E. 535	20, 138
—— et ux v. Trustees of British Museum & Thompson (1893), 10 Times L. R. 215; (1894), 10 Times L. R. 338	16, 237
Martyn v. Burlings (1597), Cro. Eliz. 589	34
Masham v. Bridges (1632), Cro. Car. 223	29
Masters v. Burgess (1886), 3 Times L. R. 96	144
Matthew v. Crass (1614), Cro. Jac. 323	20
May v. Brown (1824), 3 B. & C. 113; 4 D. & R. 670	7, 170
Mayor, &c., of Manchester v. Williams (1891), 1 Q. B. 94	77, 79
Mead v. Daubigny (1792), Peake, 168	154
—— v. Hughes and wife (1891), 7 Times L. R. 291	144
Mellin v. White (1895), App. Cas. 154	44, 47, 49, 176
Merivale and wife v. Carson (1887), 20 Q. B. D. 275 (C. A.)	88, 89, 90, 96
Merryweather v. Nixan (1799), 8 T. R. 186	60
Metropolitan Ry. Co. v. Wright (1886), 11 App. Cas. 152 (H. L.)	181
Metropolitan Saloon Omnibus Co. v. Hawkins (1859), 4 H. & N. 87	79
Mildmay et ux v. Standish (1584), 1 Rep. 177 b; Cro. Eliz. 34	41
Miller v. David (1874), L. R., 9 C. P. 118; 43 L. J. C. P. 84	28
Millington v. Loring (1880), 6 Q. B. D. 190 (C. A.)	214
Milissich v. Lloyds (1877), 46 L. J. C. P. 404; 36 L. T. 423; 13 Cox C. C. 575	111, 114, 116, 117
Mills v. Oddy (1834), 6 C. & P. 728	213, 234
Milman v. Pratt (1824), 2 B. & C. 486	42
Minet v. Morgan (1873), L. R., 8 Ch. 361	234
Mogul Steamship Co. v. M'Gregor (1892), App. Cas. 25; 61 L. J. Q. B. 295 (H. L.)	49
Monson v. Tussauds, Ltd. (1894), 1 Q. B. 671 (C. A.)	3, 175
Moor v. Foster (1606), Cro. Jac. 65	29
Moore v. Meagher (1807), 1 Taunt. 39; 3 Smith, 135	20
—— v. Terrell and others (1833), 4 B. & Ad. 870	8
Mordaunt v. Mordaunt (1870), 39 L. J. P. & M. 59	71
Morgan v. Morgan (1865), 11 Jur. N. S. 233	74
—— v. Lingen (1863), 8 L. T. 800	6
Morrison v. Belcher (1863), 3 F. & F. 614	96
Morrison and another v. Harmer and another (1837), 3 Bing. N. C. 759; 3 Hodges, 108; 4 Scott, 533	85, 96
Mountney v. Watton (1831), 2 B. & Ad. 673	82
Mulkern v. Ward (1872), L. R. 13 Eq. 622; 41 L. J. Ch. 464	93

TABLE OF CASES. xxiii

	PAGE
Mulligan *v.* Cole (1875), L. R. 10 Q. B. 549	9
Munster *v.* Lamb (1883), 11 Q. B. D. 588; 52 L. J. Q. B. 726 (C. A.)	102
Murdoch *v.* Funduklian (1885), 2 Times L. R. 215, 614	143, 155
Murfitt *v.* Smith (1887), 12 P. D. 116	240
Myers *v.* Defries, Times, July 23, 1877	114

Nelson *v.* Staff (1618), Cro. Jac. 422	20, 43
Nevill *v.* Fine Art and General Ins. Co. (1895), 2 Q. B. 156; (1897), App. Cas. 68 (H. L.)	9, 80, 154
Newman *v.* Zachary (1647), Aleyn, 3	42
Newton *v.* Chaplin (1850), 10 C. B. 356	213, 234
Nutt's Case (1727), 1 Barnard. K. B. 306; Fitz. 47	203

Oakey-Hall *v.* Bryce (1890), 6 Times L. R. 344 (C. A.)	231
O'Brien, *Ex parte* (1883), 12 L. R. Ir. 29; 15 Cox, C. C. 180	197, 202
—— *v.* Bryant (1846), 16 L. J. Ex. 77; 16 M. & W. 168	83
—— *v.* Clement (1846), 15 M. & W. 435; 15 L. J. Ex. 285	5
O'Connor *v.* The Star Newspaper Co. (1893), 9 Times L. R. 233 (C. A.)	178
Oddy *v.* Lord George Paulet (1865), 4 F. & F. 1009	153
Odger *v.* Mortimer (1873), 28 L. T. 472	94, 96
Onslow *v.* Horne (1771), 3 Wils. 177; 2 W. Bl. 750	29, 31
Oppenheim & Co. *v.* Sheffield (1893), 1 Q. B. 5 (C. A.)	235
O'Shea *v.* Wood (1891), L. R. P. D. 286	233, 234

Padmore *v.* Lawrence (1840), 11 A. & E. 380	132
Palmer *v.* Hummerston (1883), 1 Cab. & E. 36	134
Pankhurst *v.* Hamilton (1886), 2 Times L. R. 682; (1887), 3 Times L. R. 500	94, 168, 237
—— *v.* Sowler (1887), 3 Times L. R. 193	125, 127
Paris *v.* Levy (1860–1); 30 L. J. C. P. 11; 9 C. B. N. S. 342; 3 L. T. 324	96, 105
Parkes *v.* Prescott and another (1869), L. R. 4 Ex. 169	64
Parkins and wife *v.* Scott and wife (1862), 1 H. & C. 153; 31 L. J. Ex. 331	23, 165
Parmiter *v.* Coupland and another (1840), 9 L. J. Ex. 202; 6 M. & W. 105	9, 94
Parnell *v.* Walter (1890), 24 Q. B. D. 441	232, 236, 237
Parsons *v.* Surgey (1864), 4 F. & F. 247	188
Pater *v.* Baker (1847), 3 C. B. 831	39, 46
Pattison *v.* Jones (1828), 8 B. & C. 586; 3 C. & P. 387	142
Payne *v.* Beauwmorris (1669), 1 Lev. 248	20
Peacock *v.* Reynal (1612), 2 B. & G. 151	152

	PAGE
Peard v. Jones (1635), Cro. Car. 382	34

Pearson v. Lemaitre (1843), 5 M. & Gr. 700; 12 L. J. Q. B. 253;
   7 Jur. 748, 6 Scott, N. R. 607; 7 J. P. 336 . 154, 164, 169
Pedley v. May (1892), 8 Times L. R. 2 102
Pemberton v. Colls (1847), 10 Q. B. 461; 16 L. J. Q. B. 403 . 32
Penny v. Stubbs, unreported, tried in the Q. B. D., February
   19th, 1892. 168
Pennyman v. Rabanks (1595), Cro. Eliz. 427; 1 Vin. Abr. 551. 41
Penrhyn v. The Licensed Victuallers' Mirror (1890), 7 Times
   L. R. 1 227
Penruddock v. Hammond (1847), 11 Beav. 61 233
Peters and another v. Edwards and another (1887), 3 Times
   L. R. 423 157
Pfeiffer v. Midland Railway Co. (1886), 18 Q. B. D. 243 . . 240
Phillips v. Jansen (1798), 2 Esp. 624 . . . . 19, 34
—— v. L. and S. W. Railway Co. (1879), 5 Q. B. D. 78; 49
   L. J. Q. B. 833 (C. A.) 178, 181
Pinero v. Goodlake (1866), 15 L. T. 676 116
Pink v. Federation of Trades and Labour Unions (1892), 67
   L. T. 258 176
Pisani v. Lawson (1839), 6 Bing. N. C. 90. 71
Pitt v. Donovan (1813), 1 M. & S. 639 . . . . 40, 41
Pittard v. Oliver (1891), 1 Q. B. 474 (C. A.) 148
Popham v. Pickburn (1862), 31 L. J. Ex. 133; 5 L. T. 846 . 130
Poplett v. Stockdale (1825), Ry. & M. 337 60
Postlethwaite v. Rickman (1887), 35 Ch. D. 725 . . . 234
Praed v. Graham (1889), 24 Q. B. D. 53 (C. A.) . . 164, 181
Proctor v. Smiles (1886), 2 Times L. R. 474; 55 L. J. Q. B. 467
                                                                        233, 234, 238
—— v. Webster (1885), 16 Q. B. D. 112; 55 L. J. Q. B. 150;
   53 L. T. 765 132
Pulbrook, Ex parte (1892), 1 Q. B. 86 199
Pullman v. Hill & Co. (1891), 1 Q. B. 524 (C. A.) 2, 13, 14, 99, 141
Purcell v. Sowler (1877), 2 C. P. D. 218 (C. A.) . . 94, 95

Quartz Hill Gold Mining Co. v. Beall (1882), 20 Ch. D. 501;
   51 L. J. Ch. 874; 46 L. T. 746 (C. A.) . . 138, 174, 176

Rapkins v. Hall and others (1894), 10 Times L. R. 466 (C. A.). 63
Rassam v. Budge (1893), 9 Times L. R. 247; W. N. 52; 1
   Q. B. 571 226
Ratcliffe v. Evans (1892), 2 Q. B. 524 (C. A.)
                                   18, 21, 24, 41, 42, 44, 47, 50
Ravenhill v. Upcott (1869), 33 J. P. 299 . . . . 42, 157
Redford v. Birley and others (1822), 3 Stark. 103 . . . 126

	PAGE
Reg. v. Adams (1842), Trial of Holyoake, London, 1842 . .	195
—— v. Allison and others (1888), 59 L. T. 933 ; 53 J. P. 215 .	204
—— v. Bradlaugh and others (1883), 15 Cox, C. C. 217 . .	204
—— v. Brooke (1856), 7 Cox, C. C. 251	197
—— v. Carden (1879), 5 Q. B. D. 1 ; 49 L. J. M. C. 1 ; 41 L. T. 504 . . . . 187, 189	
—— v. Carlile (1845), 1 Cox, C. C. 229	194
—— v. Coghlan (1865), 4 F. & F. 316	7
—— v. Duffy (1870), 9 Ir. L. R. 329 ; 2 Cox, C. C. 45 . .	197
—— v. Ensor (1887), 3 Times L. R. 366	183
—— v. Gray (Andrew) (1861), 26 J. P. 663	116
—— v. Hicklin (1868), L. R. 3 Q. B. 360 ; 37 L. J. M. C. 89 ; 18 L. T. 398 . . . . 194, 196	
—— v. Holbrook and others (1877), 3 Q. B. D. 35 ; 37 L. T. 530 ; (1878), 4 Q. B. D. 42 ; 48 L. J. Q. B. 113 ; 39 L. T. 536	204
—— v. Labouchere (Lambri's case) (1880), 14 Cox, C. C. 419 .	85
—— v. Labouchere (Vallombrosa's Case) (1884), 12 Q. B. D. 320	183, 192
—— v. Munslow (1895), 1 Q. B. 758.	212
—— v. Payne (1896), 1 Q. B. 577 . . . . . 87, 177	
—— v. Ramsay and Foote (1883), 48 L. T. 733 ; 1 C. & E. 146 ; 15 Cox, C. C. 231 . . . . 195, 204	
—— v. Sullivan (1868), 11 Cox, C. C. 52	206
—— v. Veley (1867), 4 F. & F. 1117	134
—— v. Vincent (1838), 9 C. & P. 91, 109 . . .	126
—— v. Yates (1883), 11 Q. B. D. 750 ; 52 L. J. Q. B. 778 .	199
Reignald's Case (1640), Cro. Car. 563	36
Reiss v. Perry (1895), 11 Times L. R. 373	119
Republic of Costa Rica v. Erlanger (1876), 3 Ch. D. 62 . .	58
Rex v. Abingdon (1794), 1 Esp. 226	101
—— v. Almon (1770), 20 How. St. Tr., 851	198
—— v. Amphlit (1825), 4 B. & C. 35 ; 6 D. & R. 125 . .	15
—— v. Birt and others (1834), 5 C. & P. 154 . . .	126
—— v. Burdett (1820), 4 B. & Ald. 126 ; (1821), 4 B. & Ald. 314 . . . . 14, 195, 198	
—— v. Carlile (Mary) (1819), 3 B. & Ald. 167 . . 108, 194, 198	
—— v. Clement (1821), 4 B. & Ald. 218 ; 11 Price, 69 . .	108
—— v. Clerk (1728), 1 Barn. 304 . . . . . . 5, 65	
—— v. Creevey (1813), 1 M. & S. 273	101
—— v. Cuthell (1799), 27 How. St. Tr. 642	203
—— v. Darby (1687), 3 Mod. 139	183
—— v. Dodd (1736), 2 Sess. Cas. 33	203
—— v. Fursey (1835), 6 C. & P. 81	126

TABLE OF CASES.

	PAGE
Rex v. Garrett (1618), Hob. 215; Poph. 139	197
—— v. Gathercole (1838), 2 Lewin, C. C. 237	184
—— v. Gutch and others (1829), Moo. & Mal. 433	203
—— v. Higgins (1801), 2 East, 5	2, 185
—— v. Holt (1792), 5 T. R. 444	16
—— v. Hunt and others (1819), 3 B. & Ald. 566	126
—— v. Knell (1728), 1 Barn. 305	65
—— v. Osborne (1732), W. Kelynge, 230; 2 Barnard 138, 166	184
—— v. Peltier (1803), 28 Howell's State Trials, 617	71
—— v. Pocock (1741), 2 Strange, 1157	2
—— v. Shipley (Dean of St. Asaph) (1784), 4 Dougl. 73; 21 St. Tr. 1043; 3 T. R. 428, n.	205
—— v. Skinner (1772), Lofft, 55	104
—— v. Topham (1791), 4 T. R. 126	183
—— v. Walter (1799), 3 Esp. 21	203
—— v. Wegener (1817), 2 Stark. 245	197
—— v. Wilkes (1770), 4 Burr. 2527; 2 Wils. 151	194
—— v. Williams (1797), 26 How. St. Tr. 656; (1822), 2 B. & Ald. 595	184, 194
—— v. Wright (1799), 8 T. R. 293	128
Ridgway v. Smith & Son (1890), 6 Times L. R. 275	238
Riding v. Smith (1876), 1 Ex. D. 91; 45 L. J. Ex. 281	23
Risk Allah Bey v. Whitehurst and others (1868), 18 L. T. N. S. 615	163
Ritchie v. Sexton (1891), 64 L. T. 210; 55 J. P. 389	10
Roach v. Garvan (1742), 2 Atk. 469; 2 Dick. 794	5
Roberts v. Brown (1834), 10 Bing. 519; 6 C. & P. 757	92, 116
—— v. Camden (1807), 9 East, 93	25
—— and wife v. Roberts (1864), 5 B. & S. 384; 33 L. J. Q. B. 249	21
Robertson v. M'Dougall (1828), 4 Bing. 670; 3 C. & P. 259	136
Robinson v. Jones (1879), 4 L. R. Ir. 391	14
—— v. Marchant (1845), 7 Q. B. 918; 15 L. J. Q. B. 135	35, 57
Robshaw v. Smith (1878), 38 L. T. 423	141
Rogers v. Clifton (1803), 3 B. & P. 587	143, 152
Roselle v. Buchanan (1886), 16 Q. B. D. 656	221
Royal Aquarium, etc., Society v. Parkinson (1892), 1 Q. B. 431 (C. A.)	102, 105, 150
Rumney v. Walter (1891), 65 L. T. 757; 61 L. J. Q. B. 149; (1892), 8 Times L. R. 256	114
Rumsey v. Webb et ux. (1842), Car. & M. 104; 11 L. J. C. P. 129	20, 36, 137, 142
Russell v. Jackson (1851), 9 Hare 392	234
—— v. Notcutt (1896), 12 Times L. R. 195 (C. A.)	11
—— and another v. Webster (1874), 23 W. R. 59	12, 95

TABLE OF CASES.   xxvii

                                                                                          PAGE

Ryalls v. Leader and others (1865), L. R. 1 Ex. 296 ; 35 L. J. Ex.
    185 ; 14 L. T. 563 114
Sadler v. G. W. Ry. Co. (1895), 2 Q. B. 693 ; (1896), App.
    Cas. 450 (H. L.) 55
Salmon v. Isaac (1869), 20 L. T. 885 110
Salomons v. Knight (1891), 2 Ch. 294 (C. A.) 175
Sammons v. Bailey (1890), 24 Q. B. D. 727 235
Sandes and another v. Wildsmith and another (1893), 1 Q. B. 771   53, 58
Sands v. Child and others (1693), 3 Lev. 352 65
Saunders v. Mills (1829), 6 Bing. 213 ; 3 M. & P. 520 .   65, 169
Savile v. Jardine (1795), 2 H. Bl. 531 19
Saxby v. Easterbrook (1878), 3 C. P. D. 339 ; 27 W. R. 188 . 174
Saye & Sele v. Stephens (1628), cited Cro. Car. 535 ; Litt. 342 . 159
Scaife v. Kemp (1892), 2 Q. B. 319 237
Scarll v. Dixon (1864), 4 F. & F. 250 . . . .   144, 155
Scott v. Sampson (1882), 8 Q. B. D. 491 ; 51 L. J. Q. B. 380 ;
    46 L. T. 412 . . . .   67, 170
Seaman v. Bigg (1638), Cro. Car. 480 36
——— v. Netherclift (1876), 1 C. P. D. 540 ; 45 L. J. C. P. 798 . 104
Searles v. Scarlett (1892), 2 Q. B. 60 (C. A.) 119
Seroka v. Kattenburg and wife (1886), 17 Q. B. D. 177 ; 55 L. J.
    Q. B. 375 70
Seymour v. Butterworth (1862), 3 F. & F. 372 . . .   93, 94
Shackell v. Rosier (1836), 2 Bing. N. C. 634 60
Shepheard v. Whitaker (1875), L. R. 10 C. P. 502 ; 32 L. T. 402
                                                                         8, 37, 63
Shipley v. Todhunter (1836), 7 C. & P. 630 14
Sibthorpe's case (1628), W. Jones, 366 ; 1 Roll. Abr. 76 . . 32
Simmons v. Mitchell (1880), L. R. 6 App. Cas. 156 . . . 26
Simpson v. Robinson (1848), 12 Q. B. 511 ; 18 L. J. Q. B. 73   163, 225
Smith v. Harrison (1856), 1 F. & F. 565 163
——— v. Hodgeskins (1633), Cro. Car. 276 . . .   132, 152
——— v. Jeffreys (1846), 15 M. & W. 561 ; 15 L. J. Rep. Ex. 325   10
——— v. Mathews (1831), 1 Moo. & Rob. 151 135
——— v. Parker (1844), 14 L. J. Ex. 52 ; 13 M. & W. 459 . 83
——— v. Richardson (1737), Willes, 20 168
——— v. Scott (1847), 2 C. & K. 580 . . . .   114, 169
——— v. Spooner (1810), 3 Taunt. 246 40
——— v. Wood (1813), 3 Camp. 323 135
Smurthwaite and others v. Hannay and others (1893), 2 Q. B.
    412 ; (1894), App. Cas. 494 (H. L.) . . .   51, 52, 54
Snag v. Gray (1571), 1 Roll. Abr. 57 34
Soane v. Knight (1827), Moo. & Mal. 74 96

TABLE OF CASES.

	PAGE
Société Anonyme des Manufactures de Glaces v. Tilghman's Patent Sand Blast Co. (1883), 25 Ch. D. 1; 53 L. J. Ch. 1; 49 L. T. 451 (C. A.)	174
Société Générale de Paris v. Dreyfus Brothers (1887), 37 Ch. D. 215	74
Solomons and others v. Medex (1816), 1 Stark. 191	57
Somers v. House (1694), Holt, 39; Skin. 364	25
Somerville v. Hawkins (1851), 10 C. B. 583; 20 L. J. C. P. 131; 16 L. T. O. S. 283	133, 143
South Hetton Coal Co., Ltd. v. Proprietors of North Eastern News Association (1894), 1 Q. B. 133 (C. A.)	18, 78, 79, 88, 90, 96
Southee v. Denny (1848), 1 Ex. 196; 17 L. J. Ex. 151	33
Speck v. Phillips (1839), 5 M. & W. 279; 8 L. J. Ex. 277	168
Speight v. Gosnay (1891), 60 L. J. Q. B. 231; 55 J. P. 501	23, 165
Spencer v. Amerton (1835), 1 Moo. & Rob. 470	137
Spill v. Maule (1869), L. R. 4 Ex. 232; 38 L. J. Ex. 138	138, 153
Stace v. Griffith (1869), L. R. 2 P. C. 420; 20 L. T. 197	144, 213
Stanhope v. Blith (1585), 4 Rep. 15	19
Stanley v. Boswell (1598), 1 Roll. Abr. 55	20
Steele v. Brannan (1872), L. R. 7 C. P. 261; 41 L. J. M. C. 85; 26 L. T. 509	108, 127
Sterry v. Foreman (1827), 2 C. & P. 592	20
Stevens v. Sampson (1879), 5 Ex. D. 53; 49 L. J. Ex. 120 (C. A.)	110
Steward v. Young (1870), L. R. 5 C. P. 122; 39 L. J. C. P. 85	40, 135
Stiles v. Nokes (1806), 7 East, 493	118
Stockdale v. Hansard (1839), 9 A. & E. 1, 243; 7 C. & P. 731	107, 163
Storey v. Challands (1837), 8 C. & P. 234	20, 144
Strauss v. Francis (1866), 15 L. T. 674; 4 F. & F. 939, 1107	95
Strode v. Holmes (1651), Styles, 338; 1 Roll. Abr. 58	29
Stuart v. Bell (1891), 2 Q. B. 341 (C. A.) . 46, 99, 100, 141, 147, 150	
—— v. Lovell (1817), 2 Stark. 93	95, 154
Stubbs v. Marsh (1866), 15 L. T. 312	8, 162
Sutton v. Plumridge (1867), 16 L. T. 741	144

Tabart v. Tipper (1808), 1 Camp. 350	4
Talbutt v. Clark and another (1840), 2 M. & Rob. 312	65, 169
Tangyes v. Inman & Co. (1889), 88 L. T. Jo. 32	236
Tarpley v. Blabey (1836), 2 Bing. N. C. 437; 7 C. & P. 395	3, 17, 64, 170
Tasburgh v. Day (1618), Cro. Jac. 484	42
Taylor v. Hall (1742), 2 Str. 1189	27

	PAGE
Taylor v. How (1601), Cro. Eliz. 861.	29
—— v. Perkins (1607), Cro. Jac. 144; 1 Rolle's Abr. 44	27
Tempest v. Chambers (1815), 1 Stark. 67.	26
Thomas v. Jackson (1825), 3 Bing. 104	35
—— v. Williams (1880), 14 Ch. D. 864; 49 L. J. Ch. 605; 43 L. T. 91	175
Thompson v. Bernard (1807), 1 Camp. at p. 48.	26
—— v. Shackell (1828), 1 Moo. & Mal. 187	96
Thorley v. Lord Kerry (1812), 4 Taunt. 355; 3 Camp. 214, n.	6
Thorley's Cattle Food Co. v. Massam (1880), 14 Ch. D. 781; 42 L. T. 851 (C. A.)	174
Thurman v. Wild and another (1840), 11 A. & E. 453	157
Todd v. Hawkins (1837), 8 C. & P. 88; 2 M. & Rob. 20	138
Tomlinson v. Brittlebank (1833), 4 B. & Ad. 630	25
Tompson v. Dashwood (1883), 11 Q. B. D. 43; 52 L. J. Q. B. 425; 48 L. T. 943	17, 155
Toogood v. Spyring (1834), 1 C. M. & R. 181	138, 148, 149
Tozier v. Hawkins (1885), 15 Q. B. D. 680 (C. A.)	210
Trollope v. London Building Trades Federation (1895), 11 Times L. R. 228	176
Trotman v. Dunn (1815), 4 Camp. 211	104
Tucker v. Lawson (1886), 2 Times L. R. 593	60, 169, 172
Turnbull v. Bird (1861), 2 F. & F. 508	93
Tuson v. Evans (1840), 12 A. & E. 733	136
Tutty v. Alewin (1770), 11 Mod. 221	33
Twycross v. Grant and others (1878), 4 C. P. D. 40; 47 L. J. Q. B. 676; 39 L. T. 618	162
Underwood v. Parks (1744), 2 Strange, 1200	168, 231
Usill v. Hales (1878), 3 C. P. D. 319; 47 L. J. C. P. 323; 38 L. T. 65	115
Vaughan v. Ellis (1609), Cro. Jac. 213	42, 43
Villers v. Monsley (1769), 2 Wils. 403	6, 19, 27
Vine, Ex parte, In re Wilson (1878), 8 Ch. D. 364; 47 L. J. Bank. 116; 38 L. T. 327, 730	71, 76
Vines v. Serell (1835), 7 C. & P. 163.	163
Wakley v. Cooke and Healey (1849), 19 L. J. Ex. 91; 4 Ex. 511	83
—— v. Healey (1848-9), 7 C. B. 591; 18 L. J. C. P. 241	8
—— v. Johnson (1826), Ry. & M. 422	170
Walker v. Brogden (1865), 19 C. B. N. S. 65; 13 W. R. 809; 12 L. T. 495	8

TABLE OF CASES.

PAGE

Waller *v.* Loch (1881), 7 Q. B. D. 621; 51 L. J. Q. B. 274 (C. A.)
                141, 142, 145
Ward *v.* Marshall (1887), 3 Times L. R. 578 233
—— *v.* Smith (1830), 4 C. & P. 302 14
—— *v.* Weeks (1830), 7 Bing. 211; 4 M. & P. 796 . . 19, 23, 24
Warman *v.* Hine (1837), 1 Jur. 820 . . . . . 7, 85
Warren *v.* Warren (1834), 1 C. M. & R. 250 . . 14, 140, 148
Wason *v.* Walter (1868), L. R. 4 Q. B. 73; 38 L. J. Q. B. 34
                  93, 94, 120
Watkin *v.* Hall (1868), L. R. 3 Q. B. 396; 37 L. J. Q. B. 125
                25, 66, 67, 84
Watson *v.* Reynolds (1826), Moo. & Mal. 1 135
—— *v.* Walter (1868), L. R. 4 Q. B. 95; 38 L. J. Q. B. 42 . 101
Watts *v.* Fraser and another (1835), 6 L. J. K. B. 226; 7
 Ad. & E. 223; 7 C. & P. 369; 1 Jur. 671 . . 15, 63, 170
Weatherston *v.* Hawkins (1786), 1 T. R. 110 135
Weaver *v.* Lloyd (1824), 2 B. & C. 678; 1 C. & P. 295 . . 85
Webb *v.* Beavan (1883), 11 Q. B. D. 609; 52 L. J. Q. B. 544;
 49 L. T. 201; 47 J. P. 488 . . . . 19, 25, 26, 214
Weldon *v.* De Bathe (1884), 33 W. R. 328; 54 L. J. Q. B. 113;
 53 L. T. 520 21
Wells *v.* Webber (1862), 2 F. & F. 715 8
Wenman *v.* Ash (1853), 13 C. B. 836; 22 L. J. C. P. 190. . 15
Wennhak *v.* Morgan (1888), L. R. 20 Q. B. D. 635 . . . 15
Western Counties Manure Co. *v.* Lawes Chemical Manure Co.
 (1874), L. R. 9 Ex. 218, 222; 43 L. J. Ex. 171 . . 44, 45, 46
White and others *v.* Batey & Co., Ltd. and another (1892),
 8 Times L. R. 698 . . . . 138, 145
White *v.* Mellin (1895), App. Cas. 154 (H. L.) . . 44, 47, 49, 176
Whiteley *v.* Adams (1863), 15 C. B. N. S. 392; 33 L. J. C. P. 89
               100, 135, 137, 144
Whitfield and others *v.* S. E. Railway Co. (1858), E. B. & E.
 115; 27 L. J. Q. B. 229 . . . . . . 2, 14, 77
Whitney and others *v.* Moignard (1890), 24 Q. B. D. 630 . 164, 214
Whittaker *v.* Scarborough Post Newspaper Co. (1896), 2 Q. B.
 148 237
Whittington *v.* Gladwin (1825), 5 B. & C. 180; 2 C. & P. 146 . 85
Wilby *v.* Elston (1849), 18 L. J. C. P. 320, 1 Str. 471; 1 Vin.
 Abr. 396 36
Wild *v.* Tomkinson (1826), 5 L. J. K. B. 265 71
Williams *v.* Cartwright (1895), 1 Q. B. 142 (C. A.) . . . 210
—— *v.* Morris (1894), 10 Times L. R. 603 211
—— *v.* Quebrada Railway, etc., Co. (1895), 2 Ch. 751 . . 234
—— *v.* Ramsdale (1888), 36 W. R. 125 222

TABLE OF CASES.   xxxi

	PAGE
Williams v. Smith (1888), L. R. 22 Q. B. D. 134	119
Williamson v. Freer (1874), L. R. 9 C. P. 393	14
Willmett v. Harmer and another (1839), 8 C. & P. 695	83, 84
Wilson v. Reed and others (1860), 2 F. & F. 149	93
—— v. Rastall (1792), 4 T. R. 753	234
—— v. Thornbury (1874), 17 Eq. 517	236
Wilton v. Brignall (1875), W. N. 239	236
Wood v. Cox (1888–9), 4 Times L. R. 550; 5 Times L. R. 272 (C. A.)	67, 170, 178
—— v. Durham (1888), 21 Q. B. D. 501; 57 L. J. Q. B. 547; 57 L. T. 770; 4 Times L. R. 556	67, 170, 226
Woodard v. Dowsing (1828), 2 M. & Ry. 74	7
Woodgate v. Ridout (1865), 4 F. & F. 202	8, 93, 116
Woodward v. Lander (1834), 6 C. & P. 548	131
Worcester, etc., Banking Co. v. Firbank, Pauling & Co. (1894), 1 Q. B. 784 (C. A.)	72
Wright v. Moorhouse (1694), Cro. Eliz. 358	29
—— v. Woodgate (1835), 2 C. M. & R. 573	145, 153
Yarborough v. Bank of England (1812), 16 East, 6	77
Yates v. The Queen (1885), 14 Q. B. D. 648; 54 L. J. Q. B. 258; 52 L. T. 305 (C. A.)	199
Yorkshire Provident Life Insurance Co. v. Gilbert and Rivington (1895), 2 Q. B. 148 (C. A.)	233
Zierenberg v. Labouchere (1893), 2 Q. B. 183	231, 232, 233

INDEX TO STATUTES CITED.

	PAGE
1 Edw. 6, c. 1, s. 1	194
2 & 3 Edw. 6, c. 1, ss. 2, 3	194
1 Eliz. c. 2, ss. 2, 3	194
13 Eliz. c. 12, s. 2	194
21 Jac. 1, c. 19, s. 7	160
13 Car. 2, c. 5	126
14 Car. 2, c. 4, s. 1	194
1 Will. & M., sess. 2, c. 2	126
4 Will. & Mary, c. 18, s. 1	192
9 Will. 3, c. 35	194
4 & 5 Anne, c. 3 [al. c. 16], s. 19	160
32 Geo. 3, c. 60 (Fox's Act)	205, 241, 242
39 Geo. 3, c. 79, s. 28	242
s. 29	208, 242
53 Geo. 3, c. 160	194
57 Geo. 3, c. 19, s. 23	126
60 Geo. 3 & 1 Geo. 4, c. 8	194, 195, 244, 245
3 & 4 Will. 4, c. 42, s. 7	160
6 & 7 Will. 4, c. 76, s. 19	245, 246
2 & 3 Vict. c. 12, ss. 1, 2	208, 246, 247
ss. 3, 4	246
3 & 4 Vict. c. 9	107, 131, 247, 248, 249
6 & 7 Vict. c. 96 (Lord Campbell's Act), *Text of Act*	249-252
s. 1	167, 249
s. 2	156, 250
s. 4	183, 190, 251
s. 5	183, 251
s. 6	189, 200, 202, 251
s. 7	201, 203, 204, 252
s. 8	252
8 & 9 Vict. c. 75	156, 224, 253, 254

INDEX TO STATUTES CITED.

	PAGE
9 & 10 Vict. c. 33	108, 243, 254, 255
11 & 12 Vict. c. 12, s. 3	255, 256
c. 42, s. 1	187
19 & 20 Vict. c. 97, s. 10	160
s. 12	160
20 & 21 Vict. c. 83	196, 256–258
22 & 23 Vict. c. 17	190
30 & 31 Vict. c. 35, s. 3	187
32 & 33 Vict. c. 24, Sch. II.	243, 246, 247, 255
42 & 43 Vict. c. 59 (Civil Procedure Acts Repeal Act, 1879), Schedule. Part ii.	254
44 & 45 Vict. c. 60 (Newspaper Libel and Registration Act, 1881), *Text of Act*	259–264
s. 1	109, 259, 260
s. 4	188, 190, 260
s. 5	190, 260, 261
s. 6	190, 261
s. 8	209, 261
s. 9	209, 261, 262
s. 11	262
s. 13	209, 261, 262, 263
s. 14	209, 263
s. 15	209, 263
45 & 46 Vict. c. 75 (Married Woman's Property Act, 1882), s. 1, subs. 2	68
s. 14	70
51 & 52 Vict. c. 41 (Local Government Act, 1888)	128
c. 43 (County Courts Act, 1888), ss. 56, 64	18
s. 66	58, 77, 211
c. 64 (Law of Libel Amendment Act, 1888), *Text of Act*	265–268
s. 1	109, 112, 200, 265
s. 3	108, 110, 111, 265
s. 4	108, 109, 121–130, 265, 266
s. 5	54, 171–174, 266
s. 6	61, 167, 171, 266, 267
s. 8	187, 191, 198, 267
52 & 53 Vict. c. 18 (Indecent Advertisements Act, 1889)	197, 268, 269
53 Vict. c. 5 (Lunacy Act, 1890), s. 108	74
53 & 54 Vict. c. 44 (Supreme Court of Judicature Act, 1890), s. 1	182
54 & 55 Vict. c. 51 (Slander of Women Act, 1891)	19, 36, 37, 269
54 & 55 Vict. c. 65 (Lunacy Act, 1891)	75
58 & 59 Vict. c. 40 (Corrupt and Illegal Practices Prevention Act, 1895)	177, 185, 186, 270, 271

LIST OF ABBREVIATIONS.

A. & E.	Adolphus and Ellis.
Al.	Aleyn's Reports.
App. Cas.	Appeal Cases (L. R.).
(1891) (1892) &c., App. Cas.	(1891) (1892) &c., Law Reports, Appeal Cases.
Atk.	Atkyns.
B. & A. or Barn. & Ald.	Barnewell and Alderson.
B. & Ad. or Barn. & Adol.	Barnewell and Adolphus.
Barn.	Barnardiston.
B. & B.	Broderip and Bingham.
B. & G.	Brownlow and Goldsborough.
B. & S.	Best and Smith.
Bl.	Blackstone.
Bro. P. C.	Brown's Parliamentary Cases.
Burr.	Burrow.
C. A.	Court of Appeal.
C. B.	Common Bench.
C. B. N. S.	Common Bench, New Series.
C. L. R.	Common Law Reports.
C. & M.	Crompton and Meeson.
Car. & M.	Carrington and Marshman.
C. M. & R.	Crompton, Meeson and Roscoe.
C. P.	Common Pleas.
Cab. & El.	Cababé and Ellis.
Camp.	Campbell.
Car. & Kir.	Carrington and Kirwan.
Car. & P.	Carrington and Payne.
Ch. D.	Chancery Division (L. R.).
(1891) (1892) &c., 1, 2, &c., Ch.	(1891) (1892) &c., Law Reports, 1, 2, &c., Chancery Division.
Cox Cr. Ca.	Cox's Criminal Cases.
Cr. and J.	Crompton and Jervis.
Cro. (1, 2, 3)	Croke's Reports (temp. Eliz. Jam. Cha.).

D. & R.	Dowling and Ryland.
Dick.	Dickens.
Doug.	Douglas.
Dow, H. L.	Dow's Reports, House of Lords.
Dowl. N. S.	Dowling's Practice Reports, New Series.
Dy.	Dyer.
East	East.
El. & Bl.	Ellis and Blackburn.
El. B. & E.	Ellis, Blackburn and Ellis.
Esp.	Espinasse.
Ex.	Exchequer Reports.
Ex. Div.	Exchequer Division (L. R.).
F. & F.	Foster and Finlason.
Fitz.	Fitzgibbon.
H. & C.	Hurlstone and Coltman.
H. & H.	Horn and Hurlstone.
H. & N.	Hurlstone and Norman.
H. L. R.	Clark's House of Lords Reports.
H. Bl.	Henry Blackstone.
Harg. St. Tr.	Hargreave's State Trials.
Hawk.	Hawkins' Pleas of the Crown.
Hayes' Ir. Ex. Rep.	Hayes' Irish Exchequer Reports.
Hob.	Hobart.
Hodg.	Hodges.
Holt.	Holt's (Sir John) Reports.
Holt N. P.	Holt's Nisi Prius Reports.
How.	Howell's State Trials.
I. C. L. R.	Irish Common Law Reports.
Ir. C. Law & Ch.	Irish Common Law and Chancery Reports.
Ir. L. R.	Irish Law Reports.
J. P.	Justice of the Peace.
J. W.	Jones' (Sir William) Reports.
Jur.	Jurist.
Jur. N. S.	Jurist, New Series.
Keb.	Keble's Reports.
L. J.	Law Journal.
L. J. B.	Law Journal, Bankruptcy.
L. J. Ch.	Law Journal, Chancery.
L. J. C. P.	Law Journal, Common Pleas.
L. J. Ex.	Law Journal, Exchequer.
L. J. H. L.	Law Journal, House of Lords.
L. J. I.	Law Journal (Ireland).
L. J. M. C.	Law Journal, Magistrates' Cases.

LIST OF ABBREVIATIONS.

L. J. P. & M.	Law Journal, Probate and Matrimonial.
L. T.	Law Times.
L. T. (N. S.)	Law Times (New Series).
L. T. (O. S.)	Law Times (Old Series).
Lev.	Levinz.
Lew.	Lewis's Crown Cases.
Lit.	Littleton.
Lofft	Lofft.
M. & P.	Moore and Payne.
M. P. C. C.	Moore's Privy Council Cases.
M. & S.	Maule and Selwyn.
M. & W.	Meeson and Welsby.
Man. & G.	Manning and Granger.
Man. & Ry.	Manning and Ryland.
Mod.	Modern Reports.
Moo. & M.	Moody and Malkin.
Moo. & S.	Moore and Scott.
Ow.	Owen.
Pea.	Peake.
Poph.	Popham.
Pr.	Price.
Q. B.	Queen's Bench Reports; Queen's Bench (L. R. and L. J.).
Q. B. D.	Queen's Bench Division (L. R.).
(1891) (1892) &c., 1, &c., Q. B.	(1891) (1892) &c., Law Reports, 1, &c., Queen's Bench Division.
R.	The Reports.
Raym. (Ld.).	Lord Raymond's Reports.
Rep. 1, 2, &c.	Coke's Reports, 1, 2, &c.
Roll. R. & Roll. Abr.	Rolle's Reports and Rolle's Abridgment.
Ry. & M.	Ryan and Moody.
Salk.	Salkeld.
Scott	Scott.
Show.	Shower.
Sid.	Siderfin.
Skinn.	Skinner.
Smith	Smith.
Sol. J.	Solicitors' Journal.
Stark.	Starkie.
Stra.	Strange.
St. Tr.	State Trials.
Sty.	Styles.
T. L. R.	Times Law Reports.

LIST OF ABBREVIATIONS.

T. R.	Term Reports (Durnford and East).
Taun.	Taunton.
Vent.	Ventris.
Vin. Abr.	Viner's Abridgment.
W. N.	Weekly Notes.
W. R.	Weekly Reporter.
Willes	Willes' Reports.
Wils.	Wilson.
W. Bl.	William Blackstone.
W. W. & H.	Willmore, Wollaston and Hodges.

Principles and Practice

OF THE

LAW OF LIBEL AND SLANDER.

———•———

PART I.—OF A CIVIL ACTION.
  „ II.—OF CRIMINAL PROCEEDINGS.

Part I.—OF A CIVIL ACTION.

Art. 1.—Definition of libel and slander.

A defamatory statement is a statement concerning any person which exposes him to hatred, ridicule, or contempt, or which causes him to be shunned, or avoided, or which has a tendency to injure him in his office, profession, or trade. Such a statement, if in writing, printing, or other permanent form, is a libel; if in spoken words or significant gestures a slander (a).

NOTE 1.—The distinction between libel and slander carries with it, as will be hereafter seen, many important consequences. Thus, libel is both a civil wrong and a criminal offence: while slander is a civil wrong only, though the words may happen to come within the criminal law as

(a) Objection may be taken to the above definition, on the ground that it contains no reference to publication. But careful consideration has led the author to think that it tends to accuracy of expression and clearness of thought to omit all such reference. Moreover, this course is justified by the language of the judges in the cases touching publication—

being blasphemous, seditious, or obscene (*b*), or as being a solicitation to commit a crime (*c*), or as being a contempt of court (*d*). Again, where a defamatory statement is written or printed, the law assumes that of necessity the person defamed has suffered damage, and, in the absence of legal justification or excuse, the publication of such a statement is wrongful (*e*). On the other hand, spoken words are actionable only when they produce, as a natural consequence, the loss of some definite temporal advantage (or, as it is called, special damage), or when they impute to the defamed person charges of a certain kind (*f*).

It is sometimes said that libel can be distinguished from slander by the fact that the former is addressed to the eye, the latter to the ear. This is no doubt true as a general rule, but there

---

e.g., *per* Lord Coke, in *John Lamb's case* (1610), 9 Rep. fol. 60; Lord Erskine, in *Burdett* v. *Abbot* (1817), 5 Dow, H. L. at p. 201; Best, C. J., in *De Crespigny* v. *Wellesley* (1829), 5 Bing. at p. 402; Lord Campbell, C. J., in *Whitfield* v. *S. E. Rail. Co.* (1858), 27 L. J. Q. B. at p. 231; Lord Esher, M. R., in *Emmens* v. *Pottle* (1885), 16 Q. B. D. at p. 357, *Pullman* v. *Hill & Co.* (1891), 1 Q. B. at p. 527, *Hebditch* v. *McIlwaine and others* (1894), 2 Q. B. at pp. 58, 59, 61; A. L. Smith, L. J., *ibid.* at pp. 62, 63; Davey, L. J., *ibid.* at p. 64—where such phrases as "the publication of a libel," "where any one publishes a libel," are of constant occurrence, showing clearly that the term libel is used in accordance with the meaning ascribed to it in the above definition.

(*b*) See p. 194, *infra*.
(*c*) *Rex* v. *Higgins* (1801), 2 East, 5.
(*d*) *Rex* v. *Pocock* (1741), 2 Strange, 1157.
(*e*) See p. 18, *infra*.
(*f*) See p. 19, *infra*.

LIBEL AND SLANDER EXPLAINED.

appears to be at least one exception to it—the case of a defamatory statement communicated by significant gestures, *e.g.*, the finger language of the deaf and dumb. Such a case, so far as can be discovered, has never arisen, but it is submitted that it would be governed by the same rules as spoken words, and would, therefore, come under the description of slander.

It is submitted that the real distinction is this—that, in the case of libel, the defamatory matter is in some permanent form; and usually, though not necessarily, in writing or printing. For instance, a statue (g), caricature (h), effigy (i), chalk marks on a wall (k), "signs or pictures, as by fixing up a gallows against a man's door, or by painting him in a shameful or ignominious manner" (l) may constitute a libel (m). Slander, on the other hand, is in its nature transient, and is always in the form of spoken words or significant gestures.

NOTE 2.—*Concerning any person.* In order to be defamatory the words complained of must

(g) Hawkins' Pleas of the Crown, 8th ed. vol. 1, 542.
(h) *Austin* v. *Culpepper* (1684), 2 Show. 313; Skin. 123; *Du Bost* v. *Beresford* (1811), 2 Camp. 511.
(i) 5 Rep. 125. See also the judgment of Henn Collins, J., in *Monson* v. *Tussauds Limited* (1894), 1 Q. B. at p. 678.
(k) *Tarpley* v. *Blabey* (1836), 7 C. & P. 395.
(l) *Eyre* v. *Garlick* (1878), 42 J. P. 68.
(m) Since the publication of this passage in the first edition of this work, the well-known case of *Monson* v. *Tussauds Limited* (1894), 1 Q. B. 671, has been decided by the Court of Appeal, and the observations made by Lopes, L. J., in his judgment in that case at p. 692, show that the above passage correctly summarises the law.

concern the plaintiff himself. They must affect his character, or touch him in the way of his office, profession, or trade. If they are directed solely at the plaintiff's goods, or his title to property, though an action may lie therefor, it is not an action of libel or slander, but "an action on the case for special damage sustained by reason of the speaking or publication." (*n*).

In some cases, however, an attack on a man's goods or title to property may also injuriously affect his reputation. Thus it is libellous to write and publish of a bookseller that he sells immoral poems (*o*); and to say of a wine merchant that his wine is poisoned, or of a tea dealer that his tea is made green by drying it on copper, is a slander upon him in the way of his trade (*p*). So, too, "offensive language applied to a newspaper may cast a reflection, and be understood as casting a reflection, upon persons connected with the newspaper. . . . Whether it is an imputation which would attach to any individual, and, if so, to whom, must depend in each case upon the language used and upon the circumstances." (*q*).

In order to be defamatory the words must refer to some particular individual, and the plaintiff must prove that he is that particular individual.

(*n*) *Per* Tindal, C. J., in *Malachy* v. *Soper* (1836), 3 Bing. N. C. at p. 384.

(*o*) *Tabart* v. *Tipper* (1808), 1 Camp. 350.

(*p*) *Per* Coltman, J., in *Ingram* v. *Lawson* (1840), 6 Bing. N. C. at p. 216.

(*q*) *Per curiam*, in *Australian Newspaper Co.* v. *Bennett* (1894), App. Cas. at p. 288.

"If a man wrote that all lawyers were thieves, no particular lawyer could sue him, unless there is something to point to the particular individual" (*r*). And provided that the plaintiff can satisfy the jury that he was especially referred to, it is sufficient (*s*), whether the words complained of describe him by his own name, or its initial letter (*t*), or by asterisks (*u*), or by a fictitious name (*x*), or by the name of somebody else (*y*), or merely refer to a definite body of persons of which he is a member, for "if those who look on know well who is aimed at, the very same injury is inflicted, the very same thing is in fact done, as would be done if his name and Christian name were ten times repeated" (*z*).

But where it is uncertain whether the plaintiff was the particular individual aimed at, no action lies, *e.g.*, where after the trial of an action at which there were three witnesses, the defendant said, "One of you three is perjured," it was held that no action lay, as there was nothing to show that the plaintiff was the particular witness referred to (*a*).

(*r*) *Per* Willes, J., in *Eastwood* v. *Holmes* (1858), 1 F. & F. 349.
(*s*) *Lawrence* v. *Newberry* (1891), 64 L. T. 797.
(*t*) *Roach* v. *Garvan* (1742), 2 Atk. 469; 2 Dick. 794; *O'Brien* v. *Clement* (1846), 15 M. & W. 435; 15 L. J. Ex. 285.
(*u*) *Bourke* v. *Warren* (1826), 2 C. & P. 307.
(*x*) *Rex* v. *Clerk* (1728), 1 Barn. 304.
(*y*) *Levi* v. *Milne* (1827), 4 Bing. 195.
(*z*) *Per* Lord Campbell, C. J., in *Le Fanu and another* v. *Malcolmson* (1848), 1 H. L. C. at p. 668.
(*a*) *Sir John Bourn's* case, cited Cro. Eliz. 497. See also *James* v. *Rutlech* (1599), 4 Rep. 17.

NOTE 3.—*Which exposes him to hatred, ridicule, or contempt, or which causes him to be shunned or avoided.*—Thus it has been held libellous (*b*) to write of a man that he is a man of straw (*c*), a hypocrite (*d*), a rascal (*e*), a devil of devils (*f*), an impostor (*g*), that he is dishonest (*h*), ungrateful (*i*), impecunious (*j*), insane (*k*), and even, in one case, that his conduct had been unfeeling (*l*). So, too, it has been held libellous to publish in a newspaper a story in which the plaintiff is made to appear ridiculous, even though he has told it himself in the first instance (*m*); and ironical praise may amount to a libel (*n*).

On the other hand it has been held not libellous to write of a man that he endeavoured to discourage sedition in Ireland, for this would not

(*b*) For examples of slander under this head, see pp. 19, 25–27, *infra*, and note the rule as to the necessity of proving special damage in certain cases of slander, Article 5, p. 19, *infra*.

(*c*) *Eaton* v. *Johns* (1842), 1 Dowl. N. S. 602.
(*d*) *Thorley* v. *Lord Kerry* (1812), 4 Taunt. 355; 3 Camp. 214, n.
(*e*) *Villiers* v. *Monsley* (1769), 2 Wils. 403.
(*f*) Per Kennedy, J., in *Lever* v. *Witty*, unreported, tried at the Liverpool Assizes, July 26th, 1893.
(*g*) *Campbell* v. *Spottiswoode* (1863), 3 B. & S. 769; 32 L. J. Q. B. 185.
(*h*) *Austin* v. *Culpepper* (1684), Skin. 123; 2 Show. 313.
(*i*) *Cox* v. *Lee* (1869), L. R. 4 Ex. 284; 38 L. J. Ex. 219.
(*j*) *Eaton* v. *Johns* (1842), 1 Dowl. N. S. 602.
(*k*) *Morgan* v. *Lingen* (1863), 8 L. T. 800.
(*l*) *Churchill* v. *Hunt* (1819), 2 B. & Ald. 685; 1 Chit. 480.
(*m*) *Cook* v. *Ward* (1830), 6 Bing. 409; 4 M. & P. 99.
(*n*) *Boydell* v. *Jones* (1838), 4 M. & W. 446; 7 Dowl. 210.

injure him in the opinion of good citizens and respectable people (*o*); or that he sued his mother-in-law in a County Court, for he may have properly done so (*p*); or that he owes money, for this does not imply that he cannot, or will not, pay his debts (*q*); or that he is " man Friday " (*r*), " for the man Friday, as we all know, was a respectable man, although a black man " (*s*).

NOTE 4.—*Or which has a tendency to injure him in his office, profession, or trade.*—To impute to any one who holds an office or profession that he is unfit therefor, or that he has acted improperly therein, is libellous (*t*); *e.g.*, to write of a guardian of the poor that he is a defaulter in his accounts (*u*), or of a parish overseer that he is dishonest as such (*v*), or is oppressive towards the poor (*x*). So it is libellous to accuse a magistrate's clerk of corruption (*y*), or a vestry clerk of misapplying the parish monies (*z*); to write of a clergyman that his conduct is enough to make infidels of his

(*o*) *Clay* v. *Roberts* (1863), 9 Jur. N. S. 580; 11 W. R. 649; 8 L. T. 397.
(*p*) *Cox* v. *Cooper* (1863), 12 W. R. 75; 9 L. T. 329.
(*q*) Per Bramwell, B., in *Reg.* v. *Coghlan* (1865), 4 F. & F. 316.
(*r*) *Forbes* v. *King* (1833), 1 Dowl. 672; 2 L. J. Ex. 109.
(*s*) Per Lord Denman, C. J., in *Hoare* v. *Silverlock* (1848), 12 Q. B. at p. 626.
(*t*) For examples of slander, see pp. 27–36.
(*u*) *Warman* v. *Hine* (1837), 1 Jur. 820.
(*v*) *Cheese* v. *Scales* (1842), 10 M. & W. 488.
(*x*) *Woodard* v. *Dowsing* (1828), 2 M. & Ry. 74.
(*y*) *Blagg* v. *Sturt* (1846), 10 Q. B. 899; 16 L. J. Q. B. 39.
(*z*) *May* v. *Brown* (1824), 3 B. & C. 113.

parishioners (*a*); of a solicitor that he has been guilty of disgraceful (*b*), shameful (*c*), unscrupulous (*d*) or unprofessional (*e*) conduct; or of a barrister that he is an impostor and a quack lawyer (*f*).

It is libellous to write of a medical man that he is a quack (*g*), or that he prepares quack medicines (*h*); but not that he has met homœopathists in consultation (*i*).

Similarly, it is libellous to write of a merchant or tradesman that he is dishonest or fraudulent in his business (*k*), or that he is insolvent (*l*).

If the action be for libel it is sufficient for the plaintiff to prove that he has *at any time* held such

(*a*) *Walker* v. *Brogden* (1865), 19 C. B. N. S. 65; 13 W. R. 809; 12 L. T. 495.

(*b*) *Moore* v. *Terrell and others* (1833), 4 B. & Ad. 870.

(*c*) *Clement* v. *Lewis* (1820), 3 B. & B. 297; 3 B. & Ald. 702; 7 Moore, 200.

(*d*) *Godson* v. *Home* (1819), 1 B. & B. 7; 3 Moore, 223.

(*e*) *Clarkson* v. *Lawson* (1829), 6 Bing. 266, 587; 3 M. & P. 605; 4 M. & P. 356; *Bishop* v. *Latimer* (1861), 4 L. T. 775; *Blake* v. *Stevens and others* (1864), 4 F. & F. 232; 11 L. T. 543; *Woodgate* v. *Ridout* (1865), 4 F. & F. 202.

(*f*) *Wakley* v. *Healey* (1848–49), 7 C. B. 591; 18 L. J. C. P. 241.

(*g*) *Wells* v. *Webber* (1862), 2 F. & F. 715; *Hunter* v. *Sharpe* (1866), 4 F. & F. 983; 15 L. T. 421.

(*h*) *Clark* v. *Freeman* (1848), 11 Beav. 112; 17 L. J. Ch. 142; 12 Jur. 149.

(*i*) *Clay* v. *Roberts* (1863), 9 Jur. N. S. 580; 11 W. R. 649; 8 L. T. 397.

(*k*) *Heriot* v. *Stuart* (1796), 1 Esp. 437; *Evans* v. *Harlow* (1844), 5 Q. B. 624; 13 L. J. Q. B. 120.

(*l*) *Stubbs* v. *Marsh* (1866), 15 L. T. 312; *Shepheard* v. *Whitaker* (1875), L. R. 10 C. P. 502; 32 L. T. 402.

office or practised such profession or trade; but if he sue for slander he must prove strictly that *at the time the words were spoken* he held such office or practised such profession or trade (*m*).

Art. 2.—Construction.

In order to determine whether a statement is defamatory, it must first be construed in its natural and ordinary meaning; if not defamatory in such meaning, it must be construed in the special meaning, if any, in which it was understood by the persons by and to whom it was published (*n*).

NOTE.—It is for the judge to say whether the words are reasonably capable of a defamatory meaning, but for the jury to say whether, under the circumstances of the case, they in fact bear that meaning (*o*). In the recent case of *Nevill v. Fine Art and General Insurance Co.* (*p*), in the House of Lords, it was pointed out by Lord Halsbury, L. C., that in order to justify the judge in leaving the case to the jury " the words must be susceptible of a libellous meaning in this sense,

---

(*m*) *Boydell* v. *Jones* (1838), 4 M. & W. 446; *Parmiter* v. *Coupland* (1840), 9 L. J. Ex. 202; 6 M. & W. 105.

(*n*) *Capital and Counties Bank* v. *Henty* (1882), 7 App. Cas. 741; 52 L. J. Q. B. 232; 47 L. T. 662; *Russell* v. *Notcutt* (1896), 12 Times L. R. 195.

(*o*) Ibid. See also *Mulligan* v. *Cole* (1875), L. R. 10 Q. B. 549; *Australian Newspaper Co.* v. *Bennett* (1894), App. Cas. at p. 287; *Nevill* v. *Fine Art and General Insurance Co.* (1897), App. Cas. 68.

(*p*) (1897) App. Cas. at pp. 76–77.

that a reasonable man could construe them unfavourably in such a sense as to make some imputation upon the person complaining." "It is not enough to say that by some person or another the words *might* be understood in a defamatory sense" (*q*). Where words are reasonably capable of an innocent and a defamatory meaning, it is a question of fact for the jury in what meaning they were actually understood (*r*). And in every case the burden of proof is on the party who alleges that the words were understood in a meaning other than their natural and ordinary meaning. "If the word is an ordinary English word, then the Court will construe it in its natural meaning, unless some other is shown to have been given it. If the word is a cant expression or a commercial term (*s*), then the meaning may depend upon the circumstances in evidence (*t*). But where the words complained of are ordinary English and *primâ facie* quite intelligible, witnesses cannot be called to state what they understood the words to mean unless it is first shown that the words did not on this occasion bear their ordinary English meaning (*u*).

It is important to notice that where the words

(*q*) (1897) App. Cas. at p. 73.

(*r*) *Churchill* v. *Gedney* (1889), 53 J. P. 471; *Ritchie* v. *Sexton* (1891), 64 L. T. 210; 55 J. P. 389.

(*s*) *Smith* v. *Jeffreys* (1846), 15 M. & W. 561; 15 L. J. Ex. 325.

(*t*) Per Bramwell, B., in *Barnett* v. *Allen* (1858), 27 L. J. Ex. at pp. 414, 415.

(*u*) *Daines* v. *Hartley* (1848), 3 Ex. 200; see also *Gallagher* v. *Murton* (1888), 4 Times L. R. 304.

are not defamatory in their natural and ordinary sense, the plaintiff must be prepared to satisfy the jury that there were facts known both to the person publishing the defamatory matter, and to the person to whom it was published, which would naturally lead the latter to understand the words in a defamatory sense (*v*). As was pointed out by Brett, L. J., in the well-known case of *Capital and Counties Bank* v. *Henty* (*x*), "the first question for the jury is whether the document would be read in a defamatory sense by persons of ordinary reason in the position of those to whom it is published. If, in the opinion of the jury, it would not be so read according to the *primâ facie* meaning of the language, then there is a further question (if there is any evidence upon which it can be raised) whether there were facts known both to the person who framed the alleged libel, and to the persons to whom it was published, which would lead the latter reasonably to put upon the document the construction that, having a second defamatory sense, it was issued ironically or otherwise than in the primary sense of the language." In that case Messrs. Henty, brewers at Chichester, issued to their tenants a circular containing the following words:—" Messrs. Henty & Sons hereby give notice that they will not receive in payment any cheques drawn on any of the branches of the

(*v*) *Capital and Counties Bank* v. *Henty & Sons* (1880), 5 C. P. D. 514; (1882), 7 App. Cas. 741; *Russell* v. *Notcutt* (1896), 12 Times L. R. 195.

(*x*) (1880), 5 C. P. D. at p. 539.

Capital and Counties Bank." The issue of this circular caused a run upon the bank, who thereupon brought an action of libel against Messrs. Henty. It was, however, held that the words in their natural and ordinary meaning were not libellous; that therefore it was for the plaintiffs to prove that, by reason of the special circumstances of the case, they were understood in a special libellous sense ; and that, in the absence of any such evidence, there was no case to go to the jury, and there must therefore be judgment for the defendants.

Moreover, where the words are not *primâ facie* defamatory, and where the plaintiff therefore intends to maintain that the words were defamatory by reason of their being understood in a special sense, he must be careful to insert in his Statement of Claim an averment specifying the defamatory meaning of the words complained of, and showing how they come to have that meaning, and how they relate to the plaintiff (*y*). Such an averment is called an *innuendo*. No innuendo is necessary where the words complained of are defamatory in their ordinary meaning (*z*).

(*y*) *Per* Lord Selborne, in *Capital and Counties Bank* v. *Henty* (1882), 7 App. Cas. at p. 748.
(*z*) *Russell and another* v. *Webster* (1874), 23 W. R. 59.

ART. 3.—**No action without publication.**

No action can be maintained for libel or slander unless there be publication, i.e., a communication by the defendant of the words complained of to some person other than the plaintiff.

NOTE.—*A communication to some person other than the plaintiff.*—Thus there is no publication, and therefore no action will lie, if the defamatory matter be communicated only to the plaintiff himself. This was expressly decided in *Barrow* v. *Lewellin* (a), where the defendant despatched a sealed letter through the post to the plaintiff. As the present Master of the Rolls said, in the recent case of *Pullman* v. *Hill & Co.* (b), " if the statement is sent straight to the person of whom it is written, there is no publication of it, for you cannot publish a libel of a man to himself. If a letter is not communicated to any one but the person to whom it is written, there is no publication of it."

On the other hand, "if the writer of a letter shows it to any person other than the person to whom it is written, he publishes it" (b); for example, if he shows it to his own clerk, or places it in the hands of a type-writer in order that such clerk or type-writer may copy it for him, there is a publication

(a) (1615), Hob. 62.
(b) (1891), 1 Q. B. at p. 527.

of the letter (*d*). Similarly it has been held that there is a publication if the libel be on a postcard (*e*), or contained in a telegram (*f*), for in each case "it is necessarily communicated to all the clerks through whose hands it passes" (*g*). And there is evidence of publication if it can be proved that the defendant knew, when he posted the letter containing the libel, that it would probably be opened by some person other than the plaintiff, for example, his clerk (*h*).

So, too, "if a letter is sent by the post, it is *primâ facie* proof, until the contrary is proved, that the party to whom it is addressed received it in due course" (*i*). "The moment a man delivers a libel from his hands, his control over it is gone; he has shot his arrow, and it does not depend upon him whether it hits the mark or not" (*k*). There is, however, no publication if the person into whose hands the libellous communication has come has never read it (*l*).

(*d*) *Pullman* v. *Hill & Co.*, *supra*. See also *Boxsius* v. *Goblet Frères* (1894), 1 Q. B. 842.

(*e*) *Robinson* v. *Jones* (1879), 4 L. R. Ir. 391.

(*f*) *Whitfield* v. *S. E. Rail. Co.* (1858), E. B. & E. 115; *Williamson* v. *Freer* (1874), L. R. 9 C. P. 393.

(*g*) *Per* Brett, J., in *Williamson* v. *Freer* (1874), L. R. 9 C. P. at p. 395.

(*h*) *Delacroix* v. *Thevenot* (1817), 2 Stark. 63.

(*i*) *Per* Parke, B., in *Warren* v. *Warren* (1834), 1 C. M. & R. at p. 252. See also *Ward* v. *Smith* (1830), 4 C. & P. 302; *Shipley* v. *Todhunter* (1836), 7 C. & P. 630.

(*k*) *Per* Best, J., in *Rex* v. *Burdett* (1820), 4 B. & Ald. at p. 126.

(*l*) *Per* Lord Herschell, L. C., in *Browne* v. *Dunn* (1893), 6 R. at p. 74.

In accordance with the common law principle that husband and wife are one person, "the uttering of a libel by a husband to his wife is no publication" (*m*). "For many purposes they are," however, "essentially distinct and different persons, and, amongst others, for the purpose of having the honour and feelings of the husband assailed and injured by acts or communications made to the wife" (*n*). Thus it has been held that sending a defamatory letter to a wife about her husband is sufficient publication (*o*).

Where the libel is contained in a newspaper, the sale of each copy of the newspaper containing the libel is *primâ facie* a publication thereof (*p*), rendering the distributor as well as his principal responsible for the libel. So, too, is the delivery of a libellous manuscript to the printer (*q*), and it would seem even the delivery of the newspaper to a government official as required by law (*r*). But in all these cases it is open to the defendant

(*m*) *Per* Huddleston, B., in *Wennhak* v. *Morgan* (1888), L. R. 20 Q. B. D. at p. 637.

(*n*) *Per* Maule, J., in *Wenman* v. *Ash* (1853), 13 C. B. at pp. 844, 845.

(*o*) *Wenman* v. *Ash* (1853), 13 C. B. 836; 22 L. J. C. P. 190; *Jones* v. *Williams* (1885), 1 Times L. R. 572.

(*p*) *Duke of Brunswick* v. *Harmer* (1849), 19 L. J. Q. B. 20; 14 Q. B. 185.

(*q*) *Baldwin* v. *Elphinston* (1775), 2 W. Bl. 1037; *Watts* v. *Fraser and another* (1835), 6 L. J. K. B. 226; 7 Ad. & E. 223; 7 C. & P. 369; 1 Jur. 671.

(*r*) *Rex* v. *Amphlit* (1825), 4 B. & C. 35; 6 D. & R. 125.

to show that he did not in fact publish the libel, which he can do by proving that he did not know that the paper contained or was likely to contain a libel, and that he ought not to have known it, having used reasonable care (*s*). Thus he is not liable where he has carried the libel in a newspaper (*t*) or pamphlet (*u*) or parcel (*x*) which he does not know contains libellous matter, and which he had no reason to suppose was likely to contain such matter. "A newspaper is not like a fire; a man may carry it about without being bound to suppose that it is likely to do an injury. It seems to me that the defendants are no more liable than any other innocent carrier of an article which he has no reason to suppose likely to be dangerous" (*y*).

There is also a *primâ facie* case of publication against the defendant where the manuscript from which the libel was printed is shown to be in his handwriting, there being no necessity to prove

(*s*) *Per* Lord Esher, M. R., in *Emmens* v. *Pottle and Son* (1885), 16 Q. B. D. p. 357. See also *John Lamb's case* (1610), 9 Rep. fol. 60; *Martin et ux* v. *The Trustees of the British Museum and Thompson* (1894), 10 Times L. R. 338.

(*t*) *Emmens* v. *Pottle* (1885), 16 Q. B. D. 354; *Mallon* v. *W. H. Smith & Son* (1893), 9 Times L. R. 621. See also the observations of Lord Kenyon, C. J., in *Rex* v. *Holt* (1793), 5 T. R. at p. 444.

(*u*) *Martin et ux* v. *The Trustees of the British Museum and Thompson* (1894), 10 Times L. R. 338.

(*x*) *Day* v. *Bream* (1837), 2 Moo. & R. 54.

(*y*) *Per* Bowen, L. J., in *Emmens* v. *Pottle* (1885), 16 Q. B. D. at p. 358.

that he expressly ordered or authorized the printing (*z*).

It was formerly held that if A., intending to send a letter to B., which if so sent would be privileged, by mistake sends it to C., A. is not liable (*a*). It has, however, been recently decided by the Court of Appeal that this is incorrect in principle, and that A. is liable as having published the matter to C., in respect of whom there is no privilege (*b*).

The same act may amount to a publication both of libel and slander, *e.g.*, if any one knowing that a document contains a libel upon another reads it to a third person, he publishes a libel and also a slander to such third person (*c*).

It is for the jury to find whether the facts on which it is endeavoured to prove publication are true, but for the judge to decide whether the facts as proved constitute a publication.

(*z*) Per Lord Erskine in *Burdett* v. *Abbot* (1811), 5 Dow, H. L. at p. 201; *Adams* v. *Kelly* (1824), Ry. & M. 157; *Tarpley* v. *Blabey* (1836), 2 Bing. N. C. 437; 7 C. & P. 395; *Bond* v. *Douglas* (1836), 7 C. & P. 626.

(*a*) *Tompson* v. *Dashwood* (1883), 11 Q. B. D. 43.

(*b*) *Hebditch* v. *McIlwaine & Others* (1894), 2 Q. B. 54, overruling *Tompson* v. *Dashwood*, *supra*, which, it was submitted by the author in the first edition of this work, was wrongly decided.

(*c*) *John Lamb's case* (1610), 9 Rep. fol. 60; *Forrester* v. *Tyrrell* (1893), 9 Times L. R. 257 (C. A.).

ART. 4.—**Action for libel maintainable without proof of special damage.**

For every libel an action for damages will lie even though no special damage can be proved (d).

NOTE.—In this respect there is a remarkable difference between libel and slander. In the case of libel, *i.e.*, where the defamatory statement is in writing, printing, or other permanent form, the law assumes that of necessity the person defamed has suffered damage, and therefore he is entitled to maintain an action, even though he does not and cannot prove that he has suffered any definite temporal loss, or, as it is technically called, special damage (e).

On the other hand, in the case of slander, *i.e.*, where the defamatory statement is merely spoken, or made by gesture, the plaintiff cannot succeed without proof of special damage, except in the four cases which are dealt with in the next Article.

(d) No action for libel can be brought in the County Court, except by consent (51 & 52 Vict. c. 43, ss. 56, 64), although such an action begun in the High Court may, under certain circumstances (as to which see pp. 58, 211, *infra*) be remitted to the County Court.

(e) *Per cur.* in *Ratcliffe* v. *Evans* (1892), 2 Q. B. at p. 529, and *per* Kay, L. J., in *South Hetton Coal Co., and N. E. News Association* (1894), 1 Q. B. at p. 144.

ART. 5.—**No action for slander without proof of special damage, except in four cases.**

No action for slander will lie without proof of special damage, except (1) *where the words charge the plaintiff with having committed a criminal offence* (f); *or* (2) *where they impute that he has a contagious disease of a particular kind* (g); *or* (3) *where they are spoken of him in relation to his office, profession, or trade* (h); *or* (4) *where they impute unchastity or adultery to any woman or girl* (i).

NOTE 1.—Except in the four cases mentioned above (in which the words are said to be actionable *per se*), no action for slander will lie, unless the plaintiff can prove that in consequence of the words complained of he has suffered some special damage. Thus, in the absence of such proof, it is not actionable to call anyone a cheat (k), a rogue (l), a swindler (m), or a villain (n), nor, unless it touches him in his office, profession, or trade (o),

(f) *Webb* v. *Beavan* (1883), 11 Q. B. D. 609; 52 L. J. Q. B. 544; 49 L. T. 201; 47 J. P. 488.
(g) *Villers* v. *Monsley* (1769), 2 Wils. 403; and see p. 27, *infra*.
(h) *Phillips* v. *Jansen* (1798), 2 Esp. 624.
(i) Slander of Women Act, 1891 (54 & 55 Vict. c. 51), s. 1.
(k) Per Pollock, C. B., in *Barnett* v. *Allen* (1858), 27 L. J. Ex. at p. 414.
(l) *Stanhope* v. *Blith* (1585), 4 Rep. 15; *Hopwood* v. *Thorn* (1850), 8 C. B. 293; 19 L. J. C. P. 94; 14 Jur. 87.
(m) *Savile* v. *Jardine* (1795), 2 H. Bl. 531; *Ward* v. *Weeks* (1830), 7 Bing. 211; 4 M. & P. 796.
(n) *Stanhope* v. *Blith*, *supra*.
(o) See Note 4, p. 27, *infra*.

is it actionable to verbally accuse a man of immoral or profligate conduct (*q*).

In order to maintain an action of slander where the words are not actionable *per se*, the plaintiff must therefore prove some definite temporal loss; *e.g.*, the loss of a client (*r*) or customer (*s*), or the loss (*t*) or refusal (*u*) of some appointment or employment (*x*), or, unless indeed it be merely a device to maintain the action (*y*), the loss of a gift whether pecuniary (*z*) or otherwise (*a*), or of gratuitous hospitality (*b*), for a dinner at a friend's expense is a thing of some temporal value (*c*). So too the loss of a marriage (*d*) or of the consortium of one's husband is enough (*e*); but *not* strained

(*q*) *Lumby* v. *Allday* (1831), 1 Cr. & J. 301; *Ayre* v. *Craven* (1834), 2 A. & E. 2.
(*r*) *King* v. *Watts* (1838), 8 C. & P. 614; *Brown* v. *Smith* (1853), 22 L. J. C. P. 151.
(*s*) *Storey* v. *Challands* (1837), 8 C. & P. 234.
(*t*) *Payne* v. *Beuwmorris* (1669), 1 Lev. 248.
(*u*) *Sterry* v. *Foreman* (1827), 2 C. & P. 592.
(*x*) *Martin* v. *Strong* (1836), 5 A. & E. 535; *Rumsey* v. *Webb et ux.* (1842), 11 L. J. C. P. 129.
(*y*) *Coward* v. *Wellington* (1836), 7 C. & P. 531.
(*z*) *Corcoran* v. *Corcoran* (1857), 7 Ir. L. R. N. S. 272.
(*a*) *Hartley* v. *Herring* (1799), 8 T. R. 130.
(*b*) *Moore* v. *Meagher* (1807), 1 Taunt. 39; 3 Smith, 135; *Lynch* v. *Knight* (1861), 9 H. L. C. 577; 8 Jur. N. S. 724; 5 L. T. 291.
(*c*) *Davies and Wife* v. *Solomon* (1871), L. R. 7 Q. B. 112; 41 L. J. Q. B. 10.
(*d*) *Davis* v. *Gardiner* (1593), 4 Rep. 16; 2 Salk. 694; *Holwood* v. *Hopkins* (1600), Cro. Eliz. 787; *Matthew* v. *Crass* (1614), Cro. Jac. 323; *Nelson* v. *Staff* (1618), Cro. Jac. 422.
(*e*) Per Lord Campbell in *Lynch* v. *Knight and Wife* (1861), 9 H. L. C. at p. 589.

relations and the probability of a divorce (*f*), nor the loss of friends (*g*), nor mental pain or distress or bodily illness (*h*), for "bodily pain or suffering cannot be said to be the natural result in all persons" (*i*), nor even expulsion from a religious society (*k*). "The risk of temporal loss is not the same as temporal loss" (*l*), and therefore no action will lie for speaking disparaging words of a candidate of a club, in consequence of which the majority of the club refuse to change the rules in such a way as to improve the chances of his election (*m*).

It used to be thought that the loss of general business, as distinct from the loss of specific custom, was not admissible in evidence as special damage to support an action for words not actionable *per se*. Having regard, however, to the decision of the Court of Appeal in *Ratcliffe* v. *Evans* (*n*), it would now appear to be the law

(*f*) *Barmund's case* (1619), Cro. Jac. 473.
(*g*) *Barnes* v. *Bruddel* (1669), 1 Vent. 4; *Weldon* v. *De Bathe* (1884), 33 W. R. 328; 54 L. J. Q. B. 113; 53 L. T. 520.
(*h*) *Allsop and Wife* v. *Allsop* (1860), 5 H. & N. 534; 29 L. J. Ex. 315.
(*i*) Per Pollock, C. B., in *Allsop and Wife* v. *Allsop* (1860), 29 L. J. Ex. at p. 317.
(*k*) *Roberts* v. *Roberts* (1864), 5 B. & S. 384; 33 L. J. Q. B. 249; but see *Barnabas* v. *Traunter* (1641), 1 Vin. Abr. 396.
(*l*) Per Bowen, L. J., in *Chamberlain* v. *Boyd* (1883), 11 Q. B. D. at p. 416.
(*m*) *Chamberlain* v. *Boyd* (1883), 11 Q. B. D. 407; 52 L. J. Q. B. 277. It was also held in this case that the damage was too remote.
(*n*) (1892), 2 Q. B. 524.

that where the statement complained of " in its very nature is intended, or reasonably likely to produce, and in the ordinary course of things does produce, a general loss of business, as distinct from the loss of this or that known customer, evidence of such general decline of business is admissible " (*o*), and is sufficient to support an action for slander.

In the same case (*p*) the Court laid down the following general rules as to special damage:— " The necessity of alleging and proving actual temporal loss with certainty and precision in all cases of the sort has been insisted upon for centuries. In all actions accordingly on the case, where the damage actually done is the gist of the action, the character of the acts themselves which produce the damage, and the circumstances under which the acts are done, must regulate the degree of certainty and particularity with which the damage done ought to be stated and proved. As much certainty and particularity must be insisted on, both in pleading and proof of damage, as is reasonable, having regard to the circumstances and to the nature of the acts themselves by which the damage is done. To insist upon less would be to relax old and intelligible principles; to insist upon more would be the vainest pedantry. . . . The nature and circumstances of the publication of the falsehood may accordingly require the admission of evidence of general loss

---

(*o*) (1892), 2 Q. B. at p. 533.
(*p*) *Ibid.* at pp. 532, 533.

of business as the natural and direct result produced, and perhaps intended to be produced."

Moreover, the special damage must be the natural and probable result of the words complained of (*q*); and therefore a person is not liable for damage caused by the repetition of slanders of which he himself was the originator, unless such repetition was the natural and probable result of such original publication, or was expressly or impliedly authorized by him (*r*).

Thus, if A. utters a slander affecting B. to C., and C. repeats it to D., who repeats it to E., then, subject to the two exceptions just mentioned, A. is not liable for damage caused by the repetition of the slander by C. to D., or by D. to E.

In *Speight* v. *Gosnay* (*s*), the defendant uttered a slander consisting of a false imputation upon the chastity of the plaintiff, an unmarried woman (*t*), in the presence of the plaintiff's mother. The mother repeated it to the plaintiff, who repeated it to the man to whom she was

(*q*) *Lumley* v. *Gye* (1853), 2 E. & B. 216; 22 L. J. Q. B. 463; *per* Lord Wensleydale, in *Lynch* v. *Knight and Wife* (1861), 9 H. L. C. at p. 600; *Bowen* v. *Hall* (1881), 6 Q. B. D. 333.

(*r*) *Adams* v. *Kelly* (1824), Ry. & Moo. 157; *Ward* v. *Weeks* (1830), 7 Bing. 211; 4 M. & P. 796; *Parkins et ux.* v. *Scott et ux.* (1862), 1 H. & C. 153; 31 L. J. Ex. 331; *Riding* v. *Smith* (1876), 1 Ex. D. 91; 45 L. J. Ex. 281; *Ecklin* v. *Little* (1890), 6 Times L. R. 366; *Speight* v. *Gosnay* (1891), 60 L. J. Q. B. 231; 55 J. P. 501.

(*s*) (1891), 60 L. J. Q. B. 231; 55 J. P. 501.

(*t*) Such an imputation would now be actionable without proof of special damage. See pp. 36, 37, *infra*.

engaged to be married, and he broke off the engagement. There being no evidence that the defendant authorized or intended the repetition of the slander, or that he knew of the plaintiff's engagement, it was held by the Court of Appeal that an action of slander could not be maintained against the defendant.

"Verbal defamatory statements may, indeed, be intended to be repeated, or may be uttered under such circumstances that their repetition follows in the ordinary course of things from their original utterance. Except in such cases, the law does not allow the plaintiff to recover damages which flow not from the original slander, but from its unauthorized repetition" (*u*). In *Ward* v. *Weeks* (*x*), Tindal, C. J., thus explained the reason for this rule : " Every man must be taken to be answerable for the necessary consequences of his own wrongful acts, but such a spontaneous and unauthorized communication cannot be considered as the necessary consequence of the original uttering of the words." The result of this is, that where the words are not actionable *per se*, the originator of the slander frequently escapes all liability.

It is no excuse, though it may be evidence in mitigation of damages (*y*), that the person repeating a slander mentions that he has heard it

(*u*) Per cur. in *Ratcliffe* v. *Evans* (1892), 2 Q. B. at p. 530. See also *Ecklin* v. *Little* (1890), 6 Times L. R. 366.

(*x*) (1830), 7 Bing. at p. 215.

(*y*) See pp. 169, 170, *infra*.

from A. B., naming his informant, or adds that he does not, of course, believe it (*z*).

NOTE 2.—*Where the words charge the plaintiff with having committed a criminal offence.*—" The distinction seems a natural one, that words imputing that the plaintiff has rendered himself liable to the mere infliction of a fine are not slanderous, but that it is slanderous to say that he has done something for which he has been made to suffer corporally " (*a*). Prior to *Webb* v. *Beavan* (*b*), it used to be thought that the offence charged must be not merely criminal, but also indictable. It was, however, expressly laid down in that case that it is sufficient to charge the plaintiff with having committed a criminal offence; for many offences which were formerly indictable are not so now, but merely punishable on summary conviction.

It is, of course, actionable, without proof of special damage, to charge the plaintiff with the commission of any definite criminal offence. *e.g.*, burglary (*c*), forgery (*d*), larceny (*e*), murder (*f*), perjury (*g*).

(*z*) *Watkin* v. *Hall* (1868), L. R. 3 Q. B. 396; 37 L. J. Q. B. 125.
(*a*) *Per* Pollock, B., in *Webb* v. *Beavan* (1883), 11 Q. B. D. at p. 610.
(*b*) (1889), 11 Q. B. D. 609; 52 L. J. Q. B. 544.
(*c*) *Somers* v. *House* (1694), Holt, 39; Skin. 364.
(*d*) *Baal* v. *Baggerley* (1632), Cro. Car. 326; *Jones* v. *Herne* (1759), 2 Wils. 87.
(*e*) *Tomlinson* v. *Brittlebank* (1833), 4 B. & Ad. 630.
(*f*) *Button* v. *Heyward* (1722), 8 Mod. 24.
(*g*) *Roberts* v. *Camden* (1807), 9 East, 93.

It is not, however, necessary that any specific crime be charged; it is enough if there be a general accusation of crime. Thus, where the words complained of were, "I will lock you up in Gloucester gaol next week; I know enough to put you there," and the innuendo was, "meaning thereby that the plaintiff had been and was guilty of having committed some criminal offence or offences," it was held that this disclosed a cause of action (*h*).

On the other hand, without proof of special damage, words which "convey in their natural and ordinary sense suspicion, and suspicion only, ... would not support an action for slander" (*i*). And if the defendant can satisfy the jury that the words complained of were merely understood as words of heat and vulgar abuse, and not as imputing a criminal offence, the plaintiff will fail unless he can prove special damage (*k*); thus, to call a man a thief is not actionable where that expression is accompanied with other words which clearly denote that the speaker did not intend to impute felony to the party charged (*l*).

(*h*) *Webb* v. *Beavan*, *supra*; see also *Tempest* v. *Chambers* (1815), 1 Stark. 67; *Francis* v. *Roose* (1838), 3 M. & W. 191; 1 H. & H. 36.

(*i*) *Per cur.* in *Simmons* v. *Mitchell* (1880), L. R. 6 App. Cas. at p. 162.

(*k*) *Barnett* v. *Allen* (1858), 3 H. & N. 376; 27 L. J. Ex. 412.

(*l*) See *per* Lord Ellenborough in *Thompson* v. *Bernard* (1807), 1 Camp. at p. 48; see also *Bittridge's case* (1602), 4 Rep. 19 b.

NOTE 3.—*Where the words impute that the plaintiff has a contagious disease of a particular kind.*—To come within the rule, the disease must be either leprosy (*n*), the plague (*o*), or venereal disease (*p*). To say of anyone that he has small-pox is, it would seem, not actionable (*q*).

Moreover, the imputation must be that the plaintiff was suffering from the disease at the time the words were spoken. " Charging another with having had a contagious disorder is not actionable, for unless the words spoken impute a continuance of the disorder at the time of speaking them, the gist of the action fails; for such a charge cannot produce the effect which makes it the subject of an action, namely, his being avoided by society " (*m*).

NOTE 4.—*Where the words are spoken of the plaintiff in relation to his office, profession, or trade.*—In order to succeed without proof of special damage, the plaintiff must prove (1) that at the time the words were spoken he held such office or carried on such profession or trade (*r*); and (2) that the words tend to prejudice him in such

(*m*) Per Ashurst, J., in *Carslake* v. *Mapledoram* (1788), 2 T. R. at p. 475; see also *Taylor* v. *Hall* (1742), 2 Str. 1189.
(*n*) *Taylor* v. *Perkins* (1607), Cro. Jac. 144; 1 Rolle's Abr. 44.
(*o*) *Villers* v. *Monsley* (1769), 2 Wils. 403.
(*p*) *Bloodworth* v. *Gray* (1844), 7 M. & Gr. 334.
(*q*) *James* v. *Rutlech* (1599), 4 Rep. 17 b; *Villers* v. *Monsley* (1769), 2 Wils. 403.
(*r*) *Bellamy* v. *Burch* (1847), 16 M. & W. 590.

office, profession, or trade (*s*). An action will not therefore lie for every saying of a depreciatory or contemptuous nature concerning the holder of an office, a professional man, or a trader. The words complained of must *touch* or *affect* him in such office, profession, or trade (*t*). Thus, it is not actionable to call a stonemason a ringleader of the nine hours' system, since this is not an imputation which relates to his capacity or conduct as a stonemason (*u*).

It is immaterial what is the nature of the plaintiff's calling, provided that it is lawful. As was laid down by the Court in *Foulger* v. *Newcomb* (*x*), "the rule as to words spoken of a man in his office or trade is not necessarily confined to offices and trades, of the nature and duties of which the Court can take judicial notice. The only limitation . . . is that it does not apply to illegal callings."

Further, it is obvious that words which would be injurious to a man in one kind of office, profession, or trade would not necessarily be so in another. Thus, merely to impute want of ability to a justice of the peace is not actionable without proof of special damage, for ability is not an essential for that office; but to accuse a barrister

(*s*) *Per cur.* in *Foulger* v. *Newcomb* (1867), L. R. 2 Ex. at p. 330.

(*t*) Com. Dig. Action for Defamation, D. 27; *per* **Tindal,** C. J., in *Doyley* v. *Roberts* (1837), 3 Bing. N. C. at p. 840.

(*u*) *Miller* v. *David* (1874), L. R. 9 C. P. 118; 43 L. J. C. P. 84.

(*x*) (1867), L. R. 2 Ex. at p. 330.

or doctor of incapacity in the discharge of his professional duties is actionable without proof of special damage.

Further illustration is afforded by the following cases :—

Persons holding an Office.

To accuse a justice of the peace of corruption (*y*), or of disgraceful or dishonourable conduct, or anything which, if true, would be good ground for removal from office (*z*), is actionable without proof of special damage. Similarly, to say of a clerk to a city company (*a*), churchwarden (*b*), officer of a court of justice (*c*), or constable (*d*), that he is unworthy of or has cheated in his office, is actionable without proof of special damage.

On the other hand, it is not actionable without proof of special damage to say of a justice of the peace that he is stupid (*e*), or of a member of Parliament that he is insincere (*f*).

(*y*) *Cæsar* v. *Curseny* (1593), Cro. Eliz. 305; *Beamond* v. *Hastings* (1610), Cro. Jac. 240; *Masham* v. *Bridges* (1632), Cro. Car. 223.

(*z*) *Harper* v. *Beamond* (1605), Cro. Jac. 56; *How* v. *Prinn* (1702), 2 Salk. 694; 2 Lord Raym. 812.

(*a*) *Wright* v. *Moorhouse* (1694), Cro. Eliz. 358.

(*b*) *Strode* v. *Holmes* (1651), Styles, 338; 1 Roll. Abr. 58; *Jackson* v. *Adams* (1835), 2 Bing. N. C. 402.

(*c*) *Stanley* v. *Boswell* (1598), 1 Roll. Abr. 55; *Moor* v. *Foster* (1606), Cro. Jac. 65.

(*d*) *Taylor* v. *How* (1601), Cro. Eliz. 861.

(*e*) *Bill* v. *Neal* (1662), 1 Lev. 52; *Hollis* v. *Briscow et ux.* (1605), Cro. Jac. 58.

(*f*) *Onslow* v. *Horn* (1771), 3 Wils. 177; 2 W. Bl. 750.

It should be noticed that "there is a distinction between that which is actionable in the case of *offices of honour or credit* as compared with the case of an *office of profit*" (*g*). "In offices of profit, words that impute either defect of understanding, of ability, or integrity, are actionable; but in those of credit, words that impute want only of ability are not actionable, as of a justice of the peace: 'He is a justice of the peace! He is an ass, and a beetle-headed justice.' *Ratio est*, because a man cannot help his want of ability, as he may his want of honesty; otherwise where words impute dishonesty or corruption, as in this case, where the office is an office of credit, and the party charged with inclinations and principles which show him unfit, and that he ought to be removed, which is a disgrace" (*h*).

In the recent case of *Alexander* v. *Jenkins* (*i*), in the Court of Appeal, Lord Herschell pointed out that "the ground upon which the action has been said to be maintainable" in the case of offices of honour or credit "would seem to be this, that the language used has been such as, if true, would show that the man ought to be deprived of his office, and therefore involves a risk of exclusion from that office" (*k*). In the course of his judg-

---

(*g*) *Per* Lord Herschell, in *Alexander* v. *Jenkins* (1892), 1 Q. B. at pp. 801, 802.

(*h*) *Per cur.* in *How* v. *Prinn* (1702), 2 Salk. at p. 694. Judgment for the plaintiff affirmed in the House of Lords, 7 Mod. 113; 1 Bro. P. C. 97.

(*i*) (1892), 1 Q. B. 797.

(*k*) (1892), 1 Q. B. at p. 802.

ment (*l*) Lord Herschell laid down the rule "that where the imputation is an imputation *not of misconduct in an office*, but of unfitness *for* an office, and the office for which the person is said to be unfit is not an office of profit, but one merely of what has been called honour or credit, the action will not lie, unless the conduct charged be such as would enable him to be removed or deprived of that office." It was accordingly held that, without proof of special damage, no action lay where the plaintiff had been elected to the office of town councillor for a borough, and the words complained of were: "He is never sober, and is not a fit man for the council. On the night of the election he was so drunk that he had to be carried home"; for the office of town councillor was not one of profit, and the charges if true afforded no ground for dismissing the plaintiff from his office (*m*).

In the case of *Alexander* v. *Jenkins* cited above, the words complained of did not impute misconduct in, but only unfitness for, office; and the question whether words imputing misconduct in office would be actionable without proof of special damage was expressly reserved by the Court of Appeal in giving judgment. This question has, however, been since decided in the case of *Booth* v. *Arnold* (*n*), where it was held by the Court of

(*l*) (1892), 1 Q. B. at p. 802.
(*m*) *Alexander* v. *Jenkins, supra;* see also *Onslow* v. *Horne* (1771), 2 W. Bl. 750.
(*n*) (1895), 1 Q. B. 571.

Appeal that an action of slander will lie without proof of special damage for words imputing misconduct in an office, although the office is not one of profit, and whether there is a power of removal from the office for such misconduct or not.

The Learned Professions.

THE CHURCH.

It is actionable without proof of special damage to say anything defamatory of a clergyman who "was beneficed or was in the actual receipt of professional temporal emolument as a preacher, lecturer, or the like at the time of the speaking of the words . . . (provided that) the charge, if true, would have been a cause of deprivation of the benefice in the first case, and also of degradation from orders, and consequently of the loss of the emoluments, in the other cases" (*o*). Thus it is actionable without proof of special damage to accuse a beneficed clergyman of preaching false doctrine (*p*), or to impute to him immorality (*q*), or misappropriation of the sacrament money (*r*); but to charge him with fraud (*s*),

(*o*) Per Pollock, C. B., in *Gallwey* v. *Marshall* (1853), 9 Ex., at p. 299.

(*p*) *Dr. Sibthorpe's case* (1628), W. Jones, 366; 1 Roll. Abr. 76.

(*q*) *Evans* v. *Gwyn* (1844), 5 Q. B. 844; *Gallwey* v. *Marshall* (1854), 9 Ex. 294; 23 L. J. Ex. 78; *Highmore* v. *Countess of Harrington* (1857), 3 C. B. N. S. 142.

(*r*) *Highmore* v. *Countess of Harrington, supra.*

(*s*) *Pemberton* v. *Colls* (1847), 10 Q. B. 461; 16 L. J. Q. B. 403.

or intemperance (*t*), is not actionable without proof of special damage, unless such charge affects him in his professional character.

On the other hand, where the plaintiff does not hold a benefice or office from which he might be removed, an action will not lie without proof of special damage (*u*).

MEDICINE.

To impute to any medical man that he is professionally ignorant (*x*), unskilful (*y*), or negligent (*z*) in the discharge of his professional duties, or to say that he is a quack (*a*), is actionable *per se*.

THE LAW.

It is actionable, without proof of special damage, to accuse a solicitor of cheating in his profession (*b*), or of being grossly ignorant of law (*c*), or

(*t*) *Cucks* v. *Starre* (1638), Cro. Car. 285.
(*u*) *Hartley* v. *Herring* (1799), 8 T. R. 130; *Hopwood* v. *Thorn* (1850), 8 C. B. 293; 19 L. J. C. P. 94.
(*x*) *Tutty* v. *Alewin* (1770), 11 Mod. 221; *Collier* v. *Simpson* (1831), 5 C. & P. 73.
(*y*) *Southee* v. *Denny* (1848), 1 Ex. 196; 17 L. J. Ex. 151.
(*z*) *Edsall* v. *Russell* (1843), 12 L. J. C. P. 4.
(*a*) *Allen* v. *Eaton* (1630), 1 Roll. Abr. 54; *Goddart* v. *Haselfoot* (1637), 1 Roll. Abr. 54.
(*b*) *Jenkins* v. *Smith* (1621), Cro. Jac. 586; *Anon.* (1638), Cro. Jac. 516.
(*c*) *Baker* v. *Morfue* (1668), Sid. 327; 2 Keb. 202; *Day* v. *Buller* (1770), 3 Wils. 59.

of betraying his client's secrets (*d*), or of acting unprofessionally (*e*); but not of cheating persons who are not his clients on occasions in no way connected with his business (*f*).

So to say of a barrister that he knows no law (*g*), or is not fit to be a lawyer (*h*), or gives bad advice (*i*), or has deceived his client and revealed the secrets of his cause (*k*), is actionable *per se* (*i*).

Other Professions.

Similarly, to impute incapacity to an architect (*l*), a land agent or surveyor (*m*), journalist, schoolmaster (*n*), or veterinary surgeon (*o*), is actionable *per se*.

(*d*) *Martyn* v. *Burlings* (1597), Cro. Eliz. 589.
(*e*) *Byrchley's case* (1585), 4 Rep. 16; *Phillips* v. *Jansen* (1798), 2 Esp. 624.
(*f*) *Doyley* v. *Roberts* (1837), 3 Bing. N. C. 835. It must of course be remembered that if the words complained of amount to an accusation of a criminal offence they will be actionable *per se* apart altogether from the question whether or not they were spoken of the plaintiff in the way of his profession. *See* pp. 25, 26, *supra*.
(*g*) *Bankes* v. *Allen* (1616), 1 Roll. Abr. 54.
(*h*) *Peard* v. *Jones* (1635), Cro. Car. 382.
(*i*) *King* v. *Lake* (1672), 2 Ventr. 28.
(*k*) *Snag* v. *Gray* (1571), 1 Roll. Abr. 57.
(*l*) *Botterill and another* v. *Whytehead* (1879), 41 L. T. 588.
(*m*) *London* v. *Eastgate* (1619), 2 Rolle's Rep. 72.
(*n*) *Hume* v. *Marshall* (1878), 42 J. P. 136.
(*o*) *Hirst* v. *Goodwin* (1862), 3 F. & F. 257.

Merchants and Tradesmen.

To accuse a merchant or tradesman of fraud or dishonesty in the way of his business (*p*)—*e.g.* to say that he adulterates his goods (*q*), or uses false weights or measures (*r*)—is actionable without proof of special damage. "Such would be the case with any words which imputed to a man fraudulent conduct in the business whereby he gained his bread" (*s*).

Also "words imputing insolvency to a person in the way of his trade are actionable, without proof of special damage" (*t*). So, too, are words which impute that a merchant or tradesman is in financial difficulty (*u*). In short, "whatever hurts a man in his business is actionable" (*x*).

Where, however, the words complained of do not amount to a charge against the plaintiff personally, but are merely an attack on the goods he

---

(*p*) *Crawfoot* v. *Dale* (1675), 1 Vent. 263; 3 Salk. 327; *Thomas* v. *Jackson* (1825), 3 Bing. 104.

(*q*) *Jesson* v. *Hayes* (1636), 1 Roll. Abr. 63.

(*r*) *Griffiths* v. *Lewis* (1846), 7 Q. B. 61; 15 L. J. Q. B. 249.

(*s*) Per Best, C. J., in *Thomas* v. *Jackson* (1825), 3 Bing. at p. 105.

(*t*) Per Lord Denman, C. J., in *Robinson* v. *Marchant* (1845), 15 L. J. Q. B. at p. 136.

(*u*) *Barnes* v. *Holloway* (1799), 8 T. R. 150; *Whittington* v. *Gladwin* (1825), 5 B. & C. 180; 2 C. & P. 146; *Brown* v. *Smith* (1853), 13 C. B. 596; 22 L. J. C. P. 151.

(*x*) Per Bayley, J., in *Whittington* v. *Gladwin* (1825), 2 C. & P. at p. 148.

sells, no action will lie without proof of special damage (*y*).

CLERKS, SERVANTS, ETC.

It is actionable, without proof of special damage, to impute to a clerk or servant that he cheats or swindles his employers (*z*), or that he is unfit for his place (*a*), or to accuse him of conduct which is inconsistent with a proper discharge of his duties; *e.g.*, to say, of a gamekeeper, that he trapped foxes (*b*).

NOTE 5.—*Where the words impute unchastity or adultery to any woman or girl.*

Prior to the passing of the Slander of Women Act, 1891 (54 & 55 Vict. c. 51) (*c*), no action lay, without proof of special damage, for words imputing unchastity or adultery to a woman (*d*).

(*y*) *Harman* v. *Delany* (1731), 2 Str. 898; Fitz. 121; and see Article 8, p. 44, *infra*; *Evans* v. *Harlow* (1844), 5 Q. B. 624; 13 L. J. Q. B. 120.

(*z*) *Seaman* v. *Bigg* (1638), Cro. Car. 480; *Reignald's case* (1640), Cro. Car. 563.

(*a*) *Rumsey* v. *Webb* (1842), 11 L. J. C. P. 129.

(*b*) *Foulger* v. *Newcomb* (1867), L. R. 2 Ex. 327; 36 L. J. Ex. 169.

(*c*) Set out on p. 269, *infra*.

(*d*) *Wilby* v. *Elston* (1849), 18 L. J. C. P. 320. Theoretically, there was one exception to this, where the action was brought for words spoken in the City of London or Bristol, or the borough of Southwark, but there is no report of any such action within the last hundred years, and the custom upon the existence and proof of which such action depended has long been obsolete, see 1 Str. 471, 555; 1 Vin. Abr. 396.

This Act, however, introduced the much-needed reform, and enabled a woman or girl to maintain such an action without proof of special damage. It should be noticed that the Act specially provides that "the plaintiff shall not recover more costs than damages, unless the judge shall certify that there was reasonable ground for bringing the action" (*e*).

Art. 6.—Intention immaterial.

Except in cases of qualified privilege (f), the intention with which the words complained of were published is immaterial (g), and the defendant will not be excused on the ground that he published them by accident or mistake (h), or in jest (i), or with an honest belief in their truth (k).

Note.—Thus the defendant was held liable in *Cook* v. *Ward* (*l*), where the plaintiff told some friends an absurd story about himself, and the

(*e*) Slander of Women Act, 1891 (54 & 55 Vict. c. 51), s. 1.
(*f*) See pp. 97, 98, *infra*.
(*g*) *Cook* v. *Ward* (1830), 6 Bing. 409; 4 M. & P. 99.
(*h*) *Blake* v. *Stevens and others* (1864), 11 L. T. 543; 4 F. & F. 232; *Shepheard* v. *Whitaker* (1875), L. R. 10 C. P. 502; 32 L. T. 402.
(*i*) 9 Rep. 59; and *Donoghue* v. *Hayes* (1831), Hayes, Ir. Ex. Rep. 265.
(*k*) *Blackburn* v. *Blackburn* (1827), 4 Bing. 395; 3 C. & P. 146; 1 M. & P. 33, 63; *Huntley* v. *Ward* (1859), 6 C. B. N. S. 514; 1 F. & F. 552.
(*l*) (1830), 6 Bing. 409; 4 M. & P. 99.

defendant published it in his newspaper, simply for the purpose of amusing his readers, and believing that the plaintiff would not object. And in *Blake* v. *Stevens and others* (m), the plaintiff obtained 100l. damages against the defendants for the publication of a libellous statement, which had been inserted by mistake in a law book of which they were the publishers.

Similarly it is no defence that the defendant uttered the words complained of in jest (n), " for jests of this kind are not to be endured, and the injury to the reputation of the party grieved is no way lessened by the merriment of him who makes so light of it " (o).

Art. 7.—**Slander of title.**

Slander of title is a false malicious statement in writing, printing, or by word of mouth injurious to any person's title to property and causing special damage to such person. For the publication of such statement an action will lie (p).

Note 1.—Strictly speaking, the subject-matter of this and the succeeding Article has no place in a work on libel and slander. There is no wrong

(m) (1864), 11 L. T. 543; 4 F. & F. 232.
(n) 9 Rep. 59; and *Donoghue* v. *Hayes, supra.*
(o) Hawkins, Pleas of the Crown, 8th ed. Vol. I. 546.
(p) As to what amounts to publication, see Article 3, p. 13, *supra.*

to the reputation—no defamation—and the action is not for libel or slander, but "an action on the case for special damage sustained by reason of the speaking or publication of the slander of the plaintiff's title" (*q*). Moreover, the rules of law which govern this so-called "slander of title" are wholly different to those relating to libel and slander. Nevertheless, for the sake of convenience, it seems desirable to deal shortly with the subject.

In order to succeed in an action of this kind, the plaintiff must prove three things:—

(1) That the statement is false.
(2) That it is malicious.
(3) That it has caused him special damage.

"Unless he shows falsehood and malice and an injury to himself, the plaintiff shows no case to go to the jury" (*r*). "In order to maintain an action of this kind, there must be malice and falsehood, and special damage must ensue therefrom" (*s*).

NOTE 2.—*Malicious.* The malice here spoken of is want of good faith, or any corrupt or wrong motive (*t*). "Acting maliciously means acting

(*q*) *Per* Tindal, C. J., in *Malachy* v. *Soper* (1836), 3 Bing. N. C. at p. 384.
(*r*) *Per* Maule, J., in *Pater* v. *Baker* (1847), 3 C. B. at p. 831.
(*s*) *Per* Parke, B., in *Brook* v. *Rawl* (1849), 19 L. J. Ex. at p. 115.
(*t*) See Article 38, p. 150, *infra*, and *Halsey* v. *Brotherhood* (1881), 19 Ch. D. 386; 51 L. J. Ch. 233.

from a bad motive" (*u*). Thus no action lies if the defendant made the representation *bonâ fide* for the purpose of protecting the actual or imaginary rights of himself (*x*), or his connections or relatives (*y*); similarly where the defendant has *bonâ fide* made the representation in his capacity of agent or solicitor for the purpose of protecting the rights of his principal or client (*z*).

Even though there was apparently no reasonable and probable cause for the statement complained of, it does not always follow that the defendant was acting in bad faith (*a*). "The question here is not what judgment a sensible and reasonable man would have formed, but whether the defendant did or did not entertain the opinion he communicated" (*b*). "The *bonâ fides* of the communication, and not whether a man of rational understanding would have done so and so, is the question to be canvassed. A man of intemperate passions, or of weak understanding, or a man acting under an erroneous

(*u*) *Per* Parke, B., in *Brook* v. *Rawl* (1849), 19 L. J. Ex. at p. 115.

(*x*) *Smith* v. *Spooner* (1810), 3 Taunt. 246; *Carr* v. *Duckett* (1860), 5 H. & N. 783; 29 L. J. Ex. 468.

(*y*) *Pitt* v. *Donovan* (1813), 1 M. & S. 639; *Gutsole* v. *Mathers* (1836), 1 M. & W. 495; 5 Dowl. 69.

(*z*) *Hargrave* v. *Le Breton* (1769), 4 Burr. 2422; *Steward* v. *Young* (1870), L. R. 5 C. P. 122; 39 L. J. C. P. 85; *Baker and others* v. *Piper* (1886), 2 Times L. R. 733.

(*a*) *Pitt* v. *Donovan* and *Steward* v. *Young*, *supra*.

(*b*) *Per* Bailey, J., in *Pitt* v. *Donovan* (1813), 1 M. & S. at p. 649.

impression, may be carried further than a man of more mature judgment; but still he would not be liable to an action of slander of this sort" (c).

The law will, however, presume malice where the defendant is himself in no way concerned or interested in the property (d).

NOTE 3.—*In writing, printing, or by word of mouth.* "It makes no difference whether the falsehood is oral or in writing" (e). "The circumstance of the slander of title being conveyed in a letter or other publication appears to us to make no other difference than that it is more widely and permanently disseminated, and the damages in consequence more likely to be serious, than where the slander of title is by words only; but that it makes no difference whatever in the legal ground of action" (f).

NOTE 4.—*Injurious to any person's title to property.* It is immaterial what is the nature of the property in question, or what is the estate or interest which is attacked. The property may be real or personal. The estate or interest therein

(c) *Per* Lord Ellenborough in *Pitt* v. *Donovan* (1813), 1 M. & S. at p. 648.
(d) *Mildmay et ux.* v. *Standish* (1584), 1 Rep. 177 b; Cro. Eliz. 34; *Pennyman* v. *Rabanks* (1595), Cro. Eliz. 427; 1 Vin. Abr. 551.
(e) *Per cur.* in *Ratcliffe* v. *Evans* (1892), 2 Q. B. at p. 532.
(f) *Per* Tindal, C. J., in *Malachy* v. *Soper* (1836), 3 Bing. N. C. at p. 386.

may be vested or contingent, in possession or remainder (*g*).

NOTE 5.—*And causing special damage to such person*—*i.e.*, actual temporal loss. " The necessity of alleging and proving actual temporal loss with certainty and precision in all cases of this sort has been insisted on for centuries " (*h*).

Such special damage is usually proved by showing that in consequence of the words complained of the plaintiff has been unable to sell (*i*) or let the property in question.

As the Court observed in *Law* v. *Harwood* (*k*), " the action is not maintainable without showing special prejudice. . . . Slandering of one's title does not import in itself loss, without showing particularly the cause of loss by reason of the speaking the words, as that he could not sell or let the said lands."

It has been held enough to prove that in consequence of the words complained of the property was wrongfully seized by a third party (*l*), or that it had depreciated in value (*m*), or been rendered unsaleable (*n*) or that an intending

(*g*) *Vaughan* v. *Ellis* (1609), Cro. Jac. 213.
(*h*) Per cur. in *Ratcliffe* v. *Evans* (1892), 2 Q. B. at p. 532.
(*i*) *Tasburgh* v. *Day* (1618), Cro. Jac. 484; *Law* v. *Harwood* (1628), Sir W. Jones, 196; Cro. Car. 140.
(*k*) (1628), Cro. Car. at p. 141.
(*l*) *Newman* v. *Zachary* (1647), Aleyn, 3.
(*m*) *Milman* v. *Pratt* (1824), 2 B. & C. 486; *Brook* v. *Rawl* (1849), 4 Ex. 521; 19 L. J. Ex. 114.
(*n*) *Malachy* v. *Soper and another* (1836), 3 Bing. N. C. 371; *Ravenhill* v. *Upcott* (1869), 33 J. P. 299.

purchaser refused to sign (*o*) or complete (*p*) a contract for the purchase of it, or that the plaintiff was compelled to incur costs in defending his title (*q*).

There is, however, no special damage where there is only a probability that intending purchasers will be deterred from buying (*r*), or the plaintiff has no estate or interest in the property, but only an expectancy (*s*), for " the risk of temporal loss is not the same as temporal loss " (*t*).

And the plaintiff must prove that the special damage is caused by the words complained of. Thus, "if a person makes a statement which is partly *bonâ fide* and partly *malâ fide*, and it occasions injury to another, that other is not entitled to recover damages unless he can trace the injury to that part of the statement which is made *malâ fide*" (*u*).

(*o*) *Bliss* v. *Stafford* (1588), Owen, 37.
(*p*) *Vaughan* v. *Ellis* (1609), Cro. Jac. 213.
(*q*) *Elborow* v. *Allen* (1623), Cro. Jac. 642.
(*r*) *Manning* v. *Avery* (1674), 3 Keb. 153; 1 Vin. Abr. 553.
(*s*) *Nelson* v. *Staff* (1618), Cro. Jac. 422; *Humphreys* v. *Stanfield* (1638), Cro. Car. 469.
(*t*) Per Bowen, J., in *Chamberlain* v. *Boyd* (1883), 11 Q. B. D. at p. 416.
(*u*) Per Parke, B., in *Brook* v. *Rawl* (1849), 19 L. J. Ex. at p. 115.

Art. 8.—**Slander of goods manufactured or sold by another.**

Slander of goods is a false statement in writing, printing, or by word of mouth, made maliciously, or without lawful occasion, disparaging the goods of any person, and causing such person special damage (x). For the publication of such statement an action will lie (y).

Note 1.—As already pointed out, the subject matter of this and the preceding Article ought not properly to be dealt with in a work on libel and slander. It is not part of the law of defamation, and is governed by wholly different rules. Nevertheless, convenience appears to demand some notice of the subject. " Such an action is not one of libel or of slander, but an action on the case for damage wilfully and intentionally done without just occasion or excuse, analogous to an action for slander of title. To support it, actual damage must be shown, for it is an action which only lies in respect of such damage as has actually occurred " (z).

To constitute this wrong it is not necessary that the matter complained of should be injurious

(x) Per Bramwell, B., in *Western Counties Manure Co.* v. *Lawes Chemical Manure Co.* (1874), L. R. 9 Ex. 218, 222; 43 L. J. Ex. 171; see also *Halsey* v. *Brotherhood* (1881), 19 Ch. D. 386; 51 L. J. Ch. 233; *Ratcliffe* v. *Evans* (1892), 2 Q. B. at p. 524; *White* v. *Mellin* (1895), App. Cas. 154.

(y) As to what constitutes publication, see Art. 3, pp. 13–17, *supra*.

(z) Per cur. in *Ratcliffe* v. *Evans* (1892), 2 Q. B. at p. 527.

to the plaintiff's reputation, nor that the defendant should know at the time he made the statement that it was false (a).

In order to succeed, the plaintiff must prove (1) that the statement is false; (2) that it was made maliciously or without lawful occasion; and (3) that it has caused him special damage.

NOTE 2.—*A false statement.* It is by no means clear that the *onus* of proving that the words are false lies upon the plaintiff. The case usually cited in support of this proposition is *Burnett* v. *Tak* (b), where it was held that in order to obtain an interim injunction to restrain the publication of statements disparaging the plaintiff's goods, the plaintiff must prove that the words are false. This decision is, however, not conclusive. For a motion for an interim injunction is a very special and technical application (c), and it by no means follows that because the plaintiff on such an application is required to prove that the words are false, he would therefore be required to do so at the trial of an action for publishing disparaging statements of this kind.

In the few reported cases on this branch of the law, it appears to have been proved by the plaintiff, or admitted by the defendant, that the words complained of were false. But there is no decision either way.

(a) *Western Counties Manure Co.* v. *Lawes Chemical Manure Co., supra.*
(b) (1882), 45 L. T. 743.
(c) See *Bonnard* v. *Perryman* (1891), 2 Ch. 269 (C. A.).

In an ordinary action for libel the falsity of the charge is presumed in the plaintiff's favour (*d*), and there seems to be no satisfactory reason why it should not also be presumed in actions of this kind.

NOTE 3.—*Made maliciously or without lawful occasion.* It is not altogether clear what degree of malice a plaintiff is expected to prove in such an action as this. The old cases were precise that "malice in fact" must be proved. Thus, Wilde, C. J., said in *Pater* v. *Baker* (*e*), "It seems to have been admitted, and indeed it could not well have been denied, that proof of actual malice was requisite to sustain the action." Even if this were the law now, still it must be remembered that "malice in fact is not confined to personal spite and ill-will, but includes every unjustifiable intention to inflict injury on the person defamed, or in the words of Brett, L. J., every wrong feeling in a man's mind" (*f*).

But in later cases it has been laid down that it is not necessary for the plaintiff in an action of this kind to prove actual malice; it is sufficient if the statement be made "without lawful occasion" (*g*).

(*d*) See the observations of Field, J., and Huddleston, B., in *Belt* v. *Lawes* (1882), 51 L. J. Q. B. at p. 361.

(*e*) (1847), 3 C. B. at p. 831.

(*f*) *Per* Lindley, L. J., in *Stuart* v. *Bell* (1891), 2 Q. B. at p. 351, quoting with approval the definition of malice given by Brett, L. J., in *Clark* v. *Molyneux* (1877), 3 Q. B. D. at p. 247.

(*g*) *Per* Lord Bramwell, in *Western Counties Manure Co.* v. *Lawes Chemical Manure Co.* (1874), L. R. 9 Ex. at p. 222.

In *Halsey* v. *Brotherhood* (*h*), Jessel, M. R., in the Court of first instance, said, " The plaintiff must make out, if he wants to maintain an action for damages, that the defendant has not been acting *bonâ fide*." On the case coming before the Court of Appeal (*i*), Lord Coleridge held that " there must be also the element of *malâ fides* and a distinct intention to injure the plaintiff, apart from the honest defence of the defendant's own property." But Baggallay, L. J., in the same case (*k*) appears to regard it as sufficient if the statements " were made without what is ordinarily expressed as reasonable and probable cause; " whilst Lindley, L. J. (*l*), again, required that the statements should be made " dishonestly."

In *Ratcliffe* v. *Evans* (*m*), the Court of Appeal, consisting of Lord Esher, M. R., and Bowen and Fry, L. JJ., in a considered judgment, describe such an action as "an action on the case for damage wilfully and intentionally done *without just occasion or excuse*, analogous to an action for slander of title," and the most recent case, *White* v. *Mellin* (*n*), does not alter the law on the subject.

It is noticeable, however, that in delivering judgment in the House of Lords in the last-

(*h*) (1880), 15 Ch. D. at p. 523.
(*i*) In *Halsey* v. *Brotherhood* (1881), 19 Ch. D. at p. 389.
(*k*) *Ibid.* at pp. 389, 390.
(*l*) *Ibid.* at p. 392.
(*m*) (1892), 2 Q. B. at p. 527.
(*n*) (1895), App. Cas. 154.

mentioned case, Lord Herschell, L. C., said (*o*), "in the view of Lindley, L. J. (in the Court of Appeal), it was necessary, in order to the maintenance of the action, that three things should be proved: that the defendant had disparaged the plaintiff's goods; that such disparagement was false; and that damage had resulted or was likely to result. . . . Lopes, L. J., adds the word *maliciously*, that 'it is actionable to publish maliciously without lawful occasion a false statement disparaging the goods of another person.' By that it may be intended to indicate that the object of the publication must be to injure another person, and that the advertisement is not published *bonâ fide* merely to sell the advertiser's own goods, or, at all events, that he published it with a knowledge of its falsity. One or other of those elements, it seems to me, must be intended by the addition of the word *maliciously*."

It was not necessary for the decision of the case for the Court to decide which of these views was correct. Lord Herschell, L. C., and Lords Macnaghten and Morris, did not discuss the question. Lords Watson and Shand, however, both adopted the view of the law taken by Lindley, L. J., in the Court of Appeal.

In determining whether a statement is made without lawful occasion, it must be remembered that trade competition is in itself no ground of

---

(*o*) *Ibid.* at pp. 158, 160.

action, no matter what damage it causes (*q*). A trader may, if he likes, puff his own goods, and advertise that they are as good as any others in the trade; and if he does so no action will lie against him (*r*). Otherwise, as Lord Herschell, L. C., pointed out in *White* v. *Mellin* (*s*), " the Courts would always be occupied in trying the merits of rival productions, and be turned into a machinery for advertising rival productions by pronouncing judicial decisions on their merits." In that case (*t*) the defendant sold the plaintiff's " Infants' Food," affixing to the plaintiff's wrappers a label containing the following words: " The public are recommended to try Dr. Vance's prepared food for infants and invalids, it being far more nutritious and healthful than any other preparation yet offered." At the trial of the action, Romer, J., held that the label was merely the puff of a rival trader, and dismissed the action with costs, and his decision was subsequently upheld by the House of Lords.

If, however, there is any imputation of fraud or dishonesty in the plaintiff's conduct of his trade or business, then an ordinary action for defamation will lie. For such an imputation is not a mere statement disparaging the plaintiff's goods; it is an attack upon the plaintiff's character. And

(*q*) *Mogul Steamship Co.* v. *McGregor* (1892), App. Cas. 25; 61 L. J. Q. B. 295.
(*r*) *Harman* v. *Delany* (1731), 2 Str. 898; 1 Barnard. 289; Fitz. 121.
(*s*) (1895) App. Cas. at p. 165.
(*t*) *Ibid*. p. 154.

E

it would amount to a libel upon the plaintiff if in writing, and to a slander upon him in the way of his trade or business if spoken, so that in either case it would be actionable without proof of special damage (*u*).

NOTE 4.—*And causing such person special damage.* As to what constitutes "special damage," see pp. 20–25, *supra;* and note that under certain circumstances a general loss of business, as distinct from loss of specific customers, is admissible in evidence, and is sufficient special damage to maintain an action of this kind.

What those circumstances are has been recently explained by the Court of Appeal (*x*), as follows: —"In an action for falsehood producing damage to a man's trade, which in its very nature is intended or reasonably likely to produce, and which, in the ordinary course of things does produce, a general loss of business, as distinct from the loss of this or that known customer, evidence of such general decline of business is admissible. In *Hargrave* v. *Le Breton* (*y*), it was a falsehood openly promulgated at an auction. In the case before us to-day, it is a falsehood openly disseminated through the press, probably read and possibly acted on by persons of whom the plaintiff never heard. To refuse, with reference to such a subject-matter, to admit such general evidence,

(*u*) See pp. 7, 8, 35, *supra.*
(*x*) In *Ratcliffe* v. *Evans* (1892), 2 Q. B., at pp. 533, 534.
(*y*) (1769), 4 Burr. 2422.

would be to misunderstand and warp the meaning of old expressions; to depart from, and not to follow, old rules; and, in addition to all this, would involve an absolute denial of justice and of redress for the very mischief which was intended to be committed."

ART. 9.—**Joinder of plaintiffs.**

All persons may be joined in one action as plaintiffs, in whom any right to relief in respect of or arising out of the same transaction or series of transactions is alleged to exist, whether jointly, severally, or in the alternative, where if such persons brought separate actions any common question of law or fact would arise; provided that, if upon the application of any defendant it shall appear that such joinder may embarrass or delay the trial of the action, the Court or a judge may order separate trials, or make such other order as may be expedient (a).

NOTE.—The above Article follows verbatim the words of the first paragraph of Ord. XVI., Rule 1, which came into operation on October 26, 1896, and which adopts the principle suggested by Lord Esher, M. R., in *Smurthwaite* v. *Hannay* (b), and the suggestion of Lord Russell, L. C. J., in *Carter*

(a) Rules of the Supreme Court, Ord. XVI., r. 1.
(b) (1893), 2 Q. B. at pp. 422, 424.

v. *Rigby* (c); " and judgment may be given for such one or more of the plaintiffs as may be found to be entitled to relief, for such relief as he or they may be entitled to, without any amendment. But the defendant, though unsuccessful, shall be entitled to his costs occasioned by so joining any person who shall not be found entitled to relief unless the Court or a judge in disposing of the costs shall otherwise direct (d)."

It must be borne in mind that Ord. XVI., Rule 1, from which the above Article is taken, deals merely with the joinder of *parties* to an action, and has no reference to the joinder of *causes of action* (e). The joinder of causes of action is dealt with by Ord. XVIII., and forms the subject of Article 11, *infra*, p. 56.

In *Booth* v. *Briscoe* (f), decided under the old rule, which has been replaced by the rule cited in the above Article, eight persons who were trustees of certain charities brought an action for a libel commenting on the management of the charities by " the trustees," and it was held that the persons in question were rightly joined as plaintiffs. This case, it is submitted, would be followed at the present day.

Where, however, two or more persons have separate and distinct causes of action against

(c) (1896), 2 Q. B. at p. 118.
(d) Rules of the Supreme Court, Ord. XVI., r. 1.
(e) *Smurthwaite* v. *Hannay* (1894), App. Cas. 494. See also *Bennetts* v. *McIlwraith & Co.* (1896), 2 Q. B. 464 (C. A.).
(f) (1877), 2 Q. B. D. 496.

another person, they cannot join as co-plaintiffs, and this would appear to be so even though the causes of action could be conveniently tried together. Thus, in *Sandes* v. *Wildsmith* (g), where a writ was issued by two persons claiming damages for slander, and the Statement of Claim alleged separate and distinct slanders, some of which were alleged to have been spoken of one plaintiff only, and some of the other plaintiff only, it was held that such persons could not be properly joined as plaintiffs.

ART. 10.—**Joinder of defendants.**

All persons may be joined as defendants against whom the right to any relief is alleged to exist, whether jointly, severally, or in the alternative. And judgment may be given against such one or more of the defendants as may be found to be liable according to their respective liabilities without any amendment (h).

NOTE.—The plaintiff is not, however, compelled to join as defendants in the same action every person who is concerned in, and liable for, the publication complained of. But if he brings separate actions against such persons, two

(g) (1893), 1 Q. B. 771.
(h) Rules of the Supreme Court, 1883, Ord. XVI., r. 4.

or more of them may apply to have the actions consolidated, and at the trial of such consolidated action the damages and costs shall be separately apportioned as against the different defendants (*i*).

The above article follows verbatim the words of Ord. XVI., Rule 4. This order, as has been already pointed out (*j*), deals merely with the joinder of *parties* to an action, and has no reference to the joinder of *causes of action* (*k*). The joinder of causes of action is dealt with by Ord. XVIII., and forms the subject of Art. 11, *infra*, p. 56.

The meaning of Ord. XVI., Rule 4, was much discussed in the House of Lords in *Smurthwaite* v. *Hannay* (*l*), and it may now be taken as settled that the rule does not mean that any number of persons charged on distinct grounds of liability can be joined as defendants in the same action. What it means is that only those persons can be joined as defendants in one action who are persons against whom not any right to relief, but *the* right to any relief is alleged to exist (*m*).

(*i*) Sect. 5 of the Law of Libel Amendment Act, 1888; and see Article 47, p. 171, *infra*.
(*j*) See p. 52, *supra*.
(*k*) *Smurthwaite* v. *Hannay* (1894), App. Cas. 494.
(*l*) (1894) App. Cas. 494.
(*m*) See particularly the judgments of Bowen, L. J., in *Hannay* v. *Smurthwaite* (1893), 2 Q. B. at pp. 424, 425; and of Lord Russell in *Smurthwaite* v. *Hannay* (1894), App. Cas. at pp. 504, 505. Note also that in the subsequent

Thus, where two firms connected in business write to each other letters containing libels of the same class concerning the plaintiff, and each firm circulates the letter of the other, they may be joined as defendants in one action (*n*). On the other hand, where two persons independently publish separate libels on the plaintiff, such persons cannot be joined as defendants in an action for damages for libel (*o*), for "you cannot bring plaintiffs—and by parity of reasoning you cannot bring defendants—before the Court, where the causes of action vested in the different plaintiffs or the causes of action that exist against the different defendants are separate" (*p*).

It is not necessary that every defendant shall be interested as to all the relief prayed for, or as to every cause of action included in any proceeding against him; but the Court or a judge may make such order as may appear just to prevent any defendant from being embarrassed or put to expense, by being required to attend any proceedings in which he may have no interest (*q*).

case of *Sadler* v. *G. W. R. Co.* (1895), 2 Q. B. at p. 693, A. L. Smith, L. J., said, "As I read *Smurthwaite* v. *Hannay*, the question of the joinder of two plaintiffs applies equally to joinder of two defendants."

(*n*) *Desilla* v. *Schunks & Co.* (1880), W. N. 96.
(*o*) *Sadler* v. *G. W. R. Co.* (1896), App. Cas. 450.
(*p*) Per Rigby, L. J., in *Sadler* v. *G. W. R. Co.* (1895), 2 Q. B. at p. 696. See also the observations of Lord Davey in the same case in the House of Lords (Law Reports (1896), App. Cas. at p. 456).
(*q*) Rules of the Supreme Court, 1883, Ord. XVI., r. 5.

Art. 11.—Joinder of causes of action.

The plaintiff may unite in the same action for libel or slander several causes of action; but if it appear to the Court or a judge that any such causes of action cannot be conveniently tried or disposed of together, the Court or judge may order separate trials of any of such causes of action to be had, or may make such other order as may be necessary or expedient for the separate disposal thereof (r).

Claims by plaintiffs jointly may be joined with claims by them or any of them separately against the same defendant (s).

Note.—This Article is taken from Ord. XVIII., Rules 1 and 6. It has been decided by the House of Lords in *Smurthwaite* v. *Hannay* (t) that this order relates only to joinder of *causes of action.* The order assumes that the action has been rightly constituted under Ord. XVI., Rule 1; it only provides, where parties have been rightly joined under that rule, what may be done by them as to joining separate causes of action.

The rules of practice on this subject are somewhat obscure; but it is submitted that, subject to the power of the Court to intervene when considerations of convenience justify it, the following rules as to joinder of causes of action apply :—

(r) Rules of the Supreme Court, 1883, Ord. XVIII., r. 1.
(s) *Ibid.*, r. 6.
(t) (1894), App. Cas. 494.

(1) Where there is identity of parties, any number of causes of action may be joined;

(2) Where there is identity of the subject-matter, *i.e.* where every cause of action included in the action arises out of the same set of facts, any number of causes of action may be joined, even though there be not identity of parties (*u*).

For instance, a statement may be a libel both on a firm and on an individual partner of a firm, as, *e.g.*, where it is alleged that one of the partners in the firm is insolvent. In such a case the partner and the firm have separate causes of action (*v*) which may be properly joined. And, generally speaking, it is wise, in an action by a firm for libel or slander, for both the firm and the individual partners to sue where possible; for, if the firm alone sues, it cannot recover any special damage sustained by one of the partners in consequence of the libel (*w*); nor, if one of the partners sue alone, can he in such an action recover any special damage sustained by the firm in consequence of the libel (*x*).

It is submitted that even where the imputations are not identical, provided that they are substantially the same, a firm, and one or more of the

(*u*) *Smurthwaite* v. *Hannay* (1894), App. Cas. 494; and see Art. 9, *supra*, p. 51.

(*v*) *Foster and others* v. *Lawson* (1826), 3 Bing. 452; *Harrison* v. *Bevington* (1838), 8 C. & P. 708.

(*w*) *Haythorn and another* v. *Lawson* (1827), 3 C. & P. 196; *Le Fanu* v. *Malcolmson* (1848), 1 H. L. C. 637; 13 L. T. O. S. 61.

(*x*) *Solomons and others* v. *Medex* (1816), 1 Stark. 191; *Robinson* v. *Marchant* (1845), 7 Q. B. 918; 15 L. J. Q. B. 135.

partners thereof, may sue in the same action for libel or slander. In such circumstances any separate damage sustained by one of the plaintiffs will be separately assessed and recovered.

But where there are separate claims by different plaintiffs in respect of different libels or slanders, such claims cannot be joined in one action (*y*).

ART. 12.—**Security for costs.**

A plaintiff ordinarily resident out of the jurisdiction may be ordered to give security for costs (*z*), *unless he resides in Scotland or Ireland* (*a*), *or is abroad in an official capacity on the public service* (*b*), *or has property within the jurisdiction which would be available for costs* (*c*), *or unless there is a co-plaintiff resident in England* (*d*). *Further, if a plaintiff has no visible means of paying the defendant's costs, an order will be made remitting the action to the County Court, unless the plaintiff gives security for costs or satisfies the Court that he has a cause of action more fit to be presented in the High Court than in the County Court* (*e*).

NOTE.—The fact that the plaintiff, though

(*y*) *Sandes* v. *Wildsmith* (1893), 1 Q. B. 771.
(*z*) *Republic of Costa Rica* v. *Erlanger* (1876), 3 Ch. D. 62.
(*a*) *Re Howe Machine Co.* (1889), 41 Ch. D. 118.
(*b*) *Colebrook* v. *Jones* (1752), 1 Dick. 154.
(*c*) *Re Apollinaris Co.'s Trade Marks* (1891), 1 Ch. 1.
(*d*) *D'Hormusjee* v. *Grey* (1882), 10 Q. B. D. 13.
(*e*) County Courts Act, 1888 (51 & 52 Vict. c. 43), s. 66; and see p. 211, *infra*, and the cases there cited.

ordinarily resident abroad, is temporarily resident within the jurisdiction, will not of itself prevent an order for security for costs being made (*f*).

ART. 13.—**Liability in cases of joint publication; no right to contribution or indemnity from co-defendant.**

Where there has been a joint publication of the libel by two or more persons each of them is liable for all the ensuing damage, and has no claim to contribution or indemnity against the other or others, even though before publication there has been an express promise to that effect; but judgment in an action against one of such persons is a bar to an action against the other or others (*g*).

On the other hand, where the same libel has been published by different persons upon different occasions, a defendant who was responsible for the first publication, but in no way concerned with the second, would not be liable for any damage which he could prove was solely caused by the second publication, and in no way the result of the first; but the fact that one of such persons has been sued, and damages recovered against him, is no defence (*h*) *to an action brought against any of the others in respect of the same libel* (*i*).

(*f*) Rules of the Supreme Court, 1883, Ord. LXV., r. 6 a.
(*g*) *Brunsden* v. *Humphrey* (1884), 14 Q. B. D. 141.
(*h*) See, however, Arts. 46, 47, pp. 166–173, *infra*, as to evidence in mitigation of damages and consolidation of actions under the Law of Libel Amendment Act, 1888.
(*i*) *Harrison* v. *Pearce* (1858), 32 L. T. O. S. 298; 1 F.

Note 1.—*Joint publication . . . no claim to contribution.* The first clause of this Article is merely a particular application of the well-known rule that there is no contribution between tort feasors (*k*). The effect of it is, that the proprietor of a newspaper sued jointly with his negligent editor and the author of the libel cannot obtain compensation from either of them in respect of the damages which he has been obliged to pay to the plaintiff (*l*); nor will the fact, that there has been an express promise to indemnify him if he will publish the libel, in any way improve his position, for such a promise is void, the consideration for it being illegal (*m*). A printer cannot maintain an action for his charges for printing a libel (*n*); and if he agrees to print a book for a certain price, and finds in the course of his work that the book contains libellous matter, he may refuse to proceed, and can sue for that part of the work which is not libellous in an action for work and labour performed, and materials provided, or, as it is called, on a *quantum meruit* (*o*).

& F. 567; *Frescoe* v. *May* (1860), 2 F. & F. 123; *Colledge* v. *Pike* (1886), 56 L. T. 124; *Tucker* v. *Lawson* (1886), 2 Times L. R. 593.

(*k*) *Merryweather* v. *Nixan* (1799), 8 T. R. 186. See Article 48, p. 173, *infra*.

(*l*) *Colburn* v. *Patmore* (1834), 1 C. M. & R. 73.

(*m*) *Shackell* v. *Rosier* (1836), 2 Bing. N. C. 634.

(*n*) *Poplett* v. *Stockdale* (1825), Ry. & M. 337; *Bull* v. *Chapman* (1853), 8 Ex. 104.

(*o*) *Clay* v. *Yates* (1856), 25 L. J. Ex. 237; 27 L. T. O. S. 126; 1 H. & N. 73.

NOTE 2.—*Judgment in an action against one of such persons is a bar to an action against the other or others.* Thus, where a libel appears in a newspaper, and judgment is recovered against the proprietor who turns out to be insolvent, the plaintiff cannot maintain an action against the publishers or the editor of the paper. Neither, on the same principle, can he in such a case sue the author for the publication in the newspaper, for this is the same cause of action; but he can, if he likes, sue the author for the publication of the libel to the editor, for this is a different publication and a separate cause of action.

NOTE 3.—*Where the same libel has been published on different occasions.* The most common example of this kind which is met with in practice is the case of a libel which has been published in the first instance by one newspaper, and which has been subsequently copied by other newspapers. Under such circumstances, the fact that one of such newspapers has been sued and damages recovered against it is no defence, though admissible in mitigation of damages (*p*).

Where a libel has been published in a newspaper, the proprietor, publisher, editor, printer, author, and any one who utters, gives, sells, or lends a copy of the newspaper containing the libel may be proceeded against. But it must be

(*p*) Law of Libel Amendment Act, 1888 (51 & 52 Vict. c. 64), s. 6; and see Arts. 46, 47, pp. 166–167, 171, *infra*.

remembered, as has been pointed out (*q*), that where there has been a joint publication by two or more of such persons, judgment in an action against one of them is a bar to an action in respect of the same publication against the other or others.

ART. 14.—**Principal and agent—master and servant.**

A principal or master is liable for any slander or libel published with his authority or consent by his agent or servant. The agent or servant is liable for publishing the slander; he is also liable for publishing the libel unless he can prove that he did not know, and ought not to have known, that he was publishing a libel.

NOTE 1.—*Liability of principal or master.* The principal or master is liable, where the words complained of are published with his authority or consent. Such authority or consent may be express or implied. It will be implied in the case of a libel, where such libel has been published in pursuance of the general orders of the principal or master. So far as liability to an action is concerned, the position of the defendant is in no way altered by the fact that the publication was without his knowledge or in his absence. That is no answer to a *civil action* though, as will be seen, it affords a defence to *criminal proceed-*

(*q*) Note 2, p. 61, *supra*.

ings (*r*). Thus the proprietor (*s*), publisher (*t*), editor (*u*), and printer (*v*) of a newspaper are civilly liable for an accidental slip caused by the printer's man in setting up the type, and for a libellous advertisement inserted without their knowledge.

In *Watts* v. *Fraser and Moyes* (*x*), both editor and printer were held liable for a libellous illustration, although they had never seen it, on the ground that the illustration was referred to in the accompanying letter-press, which had been printed by their servants.

The author or actual composer of any libel which is published in a newspaper is liable for the damage caused by such publication, if it can be proved that he requested, procured, or authorized the same (*y*). But it is not necessary that there should be an express request to publish; it is sufficient to prove that defendant sent his manuscript to the editor (*z*), or spoke the words complained of under such circumstances that

(*r*) See p. 203, *infra*.
(*s*) *Shepheard* v. *Whitaker* (1875), L. R. 10 C. P. 502; *Harrison* v. *Pearce* (1858), 32 L. T. O. S. 298; 1 F. & F. 567; *Rapkins* v. *Hall and others* (1894), 10 Times L. R. 466 (C. A.).
(*t*) *Blake* v. *Stevens and others* (1864), 11 L. T. 543; 4 F. & F. 232.
(*u*) *Per* Pollock, C. B., in *Keyzor and another* v. *Newcomb* (1859), 1 F. & F. at p. 562.
(*v*) *Johnson* v. *Hudson* (1836), 7 A. & E. 233 n.
(*x*) (1835), 6 L. J. K. B. 226; 7 Ad. & E. 223; 7 C. & P. 369.
(*y*) *Per* Lord Erskine in *Burdett* v. *Abbot* (1811), 5 Dow, H. L. at p. 201.
(*z*) *Bond* v. *Douglas* (1836), 7 C. & P. 626.

he must have intended them to be published (*a*). He will be equally liable even though the editor has cut up his manuscript and merely published part of it (*b*), or has not inserted the exact words made use of by the defendant, provided that the sense and substance is the same (*c*).

In *Harding* v. *Greening* (*d*), the defendant, a tradesman, was in the habit of employing his daughter to draw out his bills and write his letters of business. A customer, to whom a bill written by the daughter had been sent by the daughter, being advised by the plaintiff that the charge was too high, sent it back. Thereupon the bill was returned to the customer, enclosed in a letter also written by the defendant's daughter, which contained a libel upon the plaintiff. Upon proof of these facts, Gibbs, C. J., held that there was no evidence to go to the jury, and non-suited the plaintiff; and his decision was upheld by the Court of Common Pleas. It is respectfully submitted that this decision would not, however, be upheld at the present day.

NOTE 2.—*Liability of agent or servant.* It is no defence that in publishing the words complained of the defendant was merely acting as the agent or servant of another, "for the warrant of no

(*a*) *Adams* v. *Kelly* (1824), Ry. & Moo. 157.
(*b*) *Tarpley* v. *Blabey* (1836), 2 Bing N. C. 437; 7 C. & P. 395.
(*c*) Per Montague Smith, J., in *Parkes* v. *Prescott* (1869), L. R. 4 Ex. at p. 179.
(*d*) (1817), 8 Taunt 42; 1 Moore 477; 1 Holt N. P. 531.

man, not even of the king himself, can excuse the doing of an illegal act "(e). Thus a printer's man whose sole duty it was to clap down the press has been held liable (*f*); so too has a compositor for setting up the type of a libel (*g*).

In accordance with the above principles, "if a man receives a letter with authority from the author to publish it, the person receiving it will not be justified, if it contains libellous matter, in inserting it in the newspapers. No authority from a third person will defend a man against an action brought by a person who has suffered from an unlawful act" (*h*). Neither is it any defence that the libel was copied from another newspaper, and was stated to be so (*i*).

But in the case of libel it will be a good defence for the defendant to prove that he did not know that the paper contained or was likely to contain a libel, and that he ought not to have known it, having used reasonable care (*j*). Thus, he is not liable if he prove that he carried the

(*e*) *Per cur. in Sands* v. *Child and others* (1693), 3 Lev. 352; *Maloney* v. *Bartley* (1812), 3 Camp. 210.

(*f*) *Rex* v. *Clerk* (1728), 1 Barn. 304.

(*g*) *Rex* v. *Knell* (1728), 1 Barn. 305.

(*h*) *Per* Best, C. J., in *De Crespigny* v. *Wellesley* (1829), 5 Bing. at pp. 404, 405.

(*i*) *Saunders* v. *Mills* (1829), 6 Bing. 213; 3 M. & P. 520; *Talbutt* v. *Clark* (1840), 2 M. & Rob. 312.

(*j*) *Per* Lord Esher, M. R., in *Emmens* v. *Pottle and Son* (1885), 16 Q. B. D. at p. 357; and *per* Bowen, L. J., *ibid.* at p. 358. See also *Mallon* v. *W. H. Smith and Son* (1893), 9 Times L. R. 521.

libel in a parcel (*k*), or newspaper (*l*), or pamphlet (*m*), which he did not know contained libellous matter, and which he had no reason to suppose was likely to contain such matter.

Art. 15.—**Liability for repetition of libel or slander.**

It is no defence to an action for libel or slander that the defendant published it by way of repetition or hearsay (n); or that he stated his authority for the words complained of (o); or, except when the occasion is privileged (p), that he believed the words to be true (q).

Note 1.—That some other person has previously published the same charges against the plaintiff, and that the defendant is therefore merely repeating what has already been stated by someone else, is no defence, nor is it generally admissible

---

(*k*) *Day* v. *Bream* (1837), 2 M. & Rob. 54.

(*l*) *Emmens* v. *Pottle* (1885), 16 Q. B. D. 354; *Mallon* v. *W. H. Smith & Son* (1893), 9 Times L. R. 621. See also the observations of Lord Kenyon, C. J. in *Rex* v. *Holt* (1793), 5 T. R. at p. 144.

(*m*) *Martin et ux* v. *The Trustees of the British Museum and Thompson* (1894), 10 Times L. R. 338.

(*n*) *Watkin* v. *Hall* (1868), L. R. 3 Q. B. 396; 37 L. J. Q. B. 125.

(*o*) *M'Pherson* v. *Daniels* (1829), 10 B. & C. 263.

(*p*) See Articles 28–37, pp. 97, 98, 113–149, *infra*.

(*q*) *Per* Blackburn, J., in *Campbell* v. *Spottiswoode* (1863), 32 L. J. Q. B. at p. 202.

REPETITION.

as evidence in mitigation of damages. "As great an injury may accrue from the wrongful repetition as from the first publication of slander; the first utterer may have been a person insane, or of bad character. The person who repeats it gives greater weight to the slander" (r). If, however, the defamatory statement appears on the face of it to be copied from a certain newspaper, or communicated by a particular person, the defendant may prove in mitigation of damages that a paragraph to the same effect did appear in that newspaper, or that the statement complained of was in fact communicated to him by such person (s). And it would seem that general evidence of bad reputation is admissible in mitigation of damages (t), although evidence of rumours to the same effect as the words complained of is inadmissible (u). If, however, defendant can prove that in copying the libel, or (semble) in repeating the slander, he omitted certain parts which referred in very adverse terms to the plaintiff, the fact that he did so is admissible as evidence to prove absence of malice, and this allows the admission in evidence

---

(r) Per Littledale, J., in *M·Pherson* v. *Daniels* (1829), 10 B. & C. at p. 272, cited with approval by Blackburn, J., in *Watkin* v. *Hall* (1868), L. R. 3 Q. B. at p. 401.

(s) *Duncombe* v. *Daniell* (1837), 8 C. & P. 222; per Wightman, J., in *Davis* v. *Cutbush* (1859), 1 F. & F. 487.

(t) *Scott* v. *Sampson* (1882), 8 Q. B. D. 491; 51 L. J. Q. B. 380; 46 L. T. 412; *Wood* v. *Durham* (1888), 21 Q. B. D. 501; 57 L. J. Q. B. 547; 57 L. T. 770. See also *Wood* v. *Cox* (1888), 4 Times L. R. 550.

(u) *Scott* v. *Sampson, supra.*

of the original libel or slander (*v*). It not unfrequently happens in cases of slander when the words are not actionable *per se*, that the person repeating the slander is in a worse position than the person from whom he heard it; for in such a case, if the special damage necessary to support the action flows from the repetition and not from the original publication of the words, as a general rule the person repeating is alone liable (*x*).

Similarly, the fact that the defendant at the time he made the statement *bonâ fide* believed it to be true, will not, except in the cases dealt with under the head of qualified privilege (*y*), afford him any defence, though it may be given in evidence in mitigation of damages (*z*).

Art. 16.—**Married woman.**

A married woman can sue or be sued for libel or slander in all respects as if she were a feme sole. *Damages or costs, if recovered by her in such action, are her separate property; and if recovered against her, are payable out of her separate property* (a).

Note.—This is the effect of sect. 1, sub-sect. (2), of the Married Women's Property Act, 1882; by

(*v*) *Creevey* v. *Carr* (1835), 7 C. & P. 64.
(*x*) See pp. 165, 166, *infra*.
(*y*) pp. 97, 98, *infra*.
(*z*) See p. 169, *infra*.
(*a*) Married Women's Property Act, 1882 (45 & 46 Vict. c. 75), s. 1, sub-s. 2.

which it is also expressly provided that the husband need not be joined with his wife as plaintiff or defendant, or be made a party to any action or other legal proceeding brought by or taken against her. Generally speaking, it is, however, still desirable to join the husband as co-plaintiff in any action brought by his wife, for by that means whatever damages either may have suffered will be recovered in one action.

So, too, it is usually prudent to join the husband as a co-defendant with his wife, for if the wife be sued alone, in the first place a judgment against her will free the husband from any further liability; and, secondly, in such circumstances, execution can only be put in against such separate property of the wife as she is not restrained from anticipating (b). Where, however, it has been ascertained that the wife has separate property which she is not restrained from anticipating, and which will be sufficient to cover any damages which the plaintiff may recover together with the costs of the action, it is unsafe to join the husband as a defendant, for under such circumstances the plaintiff, even if he succeeds in the action, may be ordered to pay the costs of so joining him.

(b) *Bursill* v. *Tanner* (1884), 13 Q. B. D. 691.

Art. 17.—Husband's liability for wife's libel or slander.

A husband is liable for the publication of libel or slander by his wife (1) *during coverture (c); and* (2) *before coverture, to the extent of all property belonging to her which he shall have acquired or become entitled to from or through his wife, after deducting therefrom any payments made by him, and any sums for which judgment may have been bonâ fide recovered against him in any proceeding at law in respect of any debts, contracts, or wrongs, for or in respect of which his wife was liable before her marriage* (d).

Note.—At common law a husband was liable for every tort committed by his wife either before or during coverture; but this liability was restricted as to torts committed before coverture by sect. 14 of the Married Women's Property Act, 1882, the material part of which is set out in the second of the above provisions. As to a wife's torts committed during coverture, it was decided in *Seroka* v. *Kattenburg* (e) that the husband's old common law liability is in no way altered by the Act, so that he may or may not be joined as a co-defendant with her. For the reasons given in the note to the preceding Article it is usually wise to join him.

(c) *Seroka* v. *Kattenburg and wife* (1886), 17 Q. B. D. 177; 55 L. J. Q. B. 375.
(d) Married Women's Property Act, 1882 (45 & 46 Vict. c. 75), s. 14.
(e) (1886), 17 Q. B. D. 177.

ART. 18.—**Aliens—infants—lunatics—bankrupts**.
An alien friend (f), infant (g), lunatic (h), or bankrupt (i), can sue or be sued for libel or slander.

NOTE 1.—*An alien friend.*—An alien friend can sue (k) or be sued (l) for libel or slander where the words complained of have been published in this country. If the plaintiff is not ordinarily resident here he can generally be compelled to give security for costs (m).

Where it is intended to serve the writ out of the jurisdiction, it cannot be issued without the leave of a judge (n). The application for such leave is made by summons in chambers under Ord. II., Rule 4. Leave to serve a writ out of the jurisdiction can be obtained in any of the cases specified in Ord. XI., Rule 1 (o). If the defendant is a British subject residing abroad the writ itself may be served upon him (p), but if neither a British subject nor in British dominions, notice

(f) *Rex* v. *Jean Peltier* (1803), 28 Howell's State Trials, 617; *Pisani* v. *Lawson* (1839), 6 Bing. N. C. 90.
(g) *Defries* v. *Davis* (1835), 7 C. & P. 112; 3 Dowl. 629; *Wild* v. *Tomkinson* (1826), 5 L. J. K. B. 265.
(h) *Mordaunt* v. *Mordaunt* (1870), 39 L. J. P. & M. 59.
(i) *Ex parte Vine, In re Wilson* (1878), 8 Ch. D. 364.
(k) *Pisani* v. *Lawson* (1839), 6 Bing. N. C. 90.
(l) *Rex* v. *Jean Peltier* (1803), 28 Howell's State Trials, 617.
(m) See Article 12, p. 58, *supra*.
(n) Ord. II., r. 4.
(o) See p. 210, *infra*, and the cases there cited.
(p) *Great Australian, &c., Co.* v. *Martin* (1877), 5 Ch. D. 1.

of the writ and not the writ itself must be served upon him (*q*).

Formerly a writ could not be issued without leave against a foreign firm, the members or some of the members of which were resident abroad. This state of the law was altered by Ord. XLVIII. A, which came into operation on July 1, 1891. By Rule 1 of that order, provided that a firm carries on business within the jurisdiction, it may be sued in the firm's name without leave although it be a foreign or colonial firm, the members of which are resident out of the jurisdiction. Under Rule 3 the writ can then be served on any one or more of the partners within the jurisdiction or at the principal place of business of the firm within the jurisdiction upon the manager of such business there (*r*). "But when such a writ has been issued, and has been served in one of the modes pointed out by Rule 3, except as against the property of the partnership as mentioned in Rule 8, the judgment will not affect any partner who was out of the jurisdiction when the writ was issued, and who has not appeared, unless he has been made a party under Ord. XI., or has been served within the jurisdiction after the writ in the action was issued" (*s*).

As to suing a foreign principal for a libel published by an agent in this country, see p. 210, *infra*.

(*q*) Ord. XI., r. 6.
(*r*) *Worcester, &c. Banking Co.* v. *Firbank Pauling & Co.* (1894), 1 Q. B. p. 784.
(*s*) *Ibid., per* Lopes, L. J., at p. 789.

Where the words have been published outside the jurisdiction, the general principle is applicable that in order to maintain an action here in respect of a tort committed outside the jurisdiction, the injury complained of must be wrongful both by the law of England and also by the law of the country where it was committed (*t*). And this principle applies without regard to the nationality of the parties, for " the right of all persons, whether British subjects or aliens, to sue in the English Courts for damages in respect of torts committed in foreign countries has long since been established; and . . . there seems to be no reason why aliens should not sue in England for personal injuries done to them by other aliens abroad, when such injuries are actionable both by the law of England and also by that of the country where they are committed; and the impression which had prevailed to the contrary seems to be erroneous" (*u*). It would thus appear that where a libel, or a slander actionable *per se*, is published outside the jurisdiction, and the publication of such libel or slander is actionable by the law of the country where it is published, an action will lie in this country, provided that if the defendant is out of the jurisdiction the case is either (1) within sub-section (c), (f), or (g) of Order XI., Rule 1, so that the plaintiff can obtain the leave of the Court as mentioned on p. 71, *supra*, or (2) within Order XLVIII. A, as to which see

(*t*) *Per cur.* in *The Halley* (1868), L. R. 2 P. C. at p. 203.
(*u*) *Ibid.* at pp. 202, 203.

p. 72, *supra*. In applying for the leave of the Court under Order XI., Rule 1, the plaintiff must prove that he has a probable cause of action, and the Court in exercising its discretion will consider the facts of the case appearing on the affidavits, so far as may be necessary for that purpose (*x*).

An alien enemy of course cannot sue here, nor is the operation of the Statute of Limitations suspended by the personal disability (*y*).

NOTE 2.—*Infant.*—An infant sues by his next friend (*z*), and defends by a guardian *ad litem* (*a*). The next friend is personally liable for costs (*b*), the guardian *ad litem* only in cases of gross misconduct (*c*).

NOTE 3.—*Lunatic.*—By the Lunacy Act, 1890 (53 Vict. c. 5), which came into operation on May 1st, 1890, the Acts relating to lunatics have been consolidated. Under the Act the jurisdiction of the judge in lunacy is exercised by the Lord Chancellor entrusted by the sign manual with the care and commitment of the custody of the persons and estates of lunatics, acting either alone, or jointly with any one or more of such judges of the Supreme Court as may for the time being

(*x*) *Société Générale de Paris* v. *Dreyfus Brothers* (1887), 37 Ch. D. 215.
(*y*) *De Wahl* v. *Braune* (1856), 1 H. & N. 178; 25 L. J. Ex. 343.
(*z*) Rules of the Supreme Court, 1883, Ord. XVI., r. 16.
(*a*) *Ibid.*
(*b*) *Frank* v. *Mainwaring* (1839), 4 Beav. 37.
(*c*) *Morgan* v. *Morgan* (1865), 11 Jur. N. S. 233.

be entrusted as aforesaid (s. 108). This Act is amended by the Lunacy Act, 1891.

No other judge of the Supreme Court can exercise the special jurisdiction in Lunacy, and when in the Act the term Lord Chancellor merely is used no other person has jurisdiction to act (*d*).

A lunatic, so found, must sue by his committee as co-plaintiff with him; if not so found, or if he has not a committee, or if the committee has some interest adverse to the lunatic, then by his next friend (*e*). The committee must obtain the sanction of the Court of Lunacy before suing. This is done by summons before the master in lunacy, supported by an affidavit showing that the proceedings are necessary. The master will then grant a certificate of approval which must be subsequently approved by the judge (*f*).

A lunatic defends in the same way by his committee, if he has one, who must obtain the above sanction. If he has no committee, or the interest of the committee is adverse, an appearance should be entered for him, and then an application made by motion or by petition of course for the appointment of a guardian *ad litem* (*g*).

NOTE 4.—*Bankrupt.*—The right of action in

(*d*) Pope on Lunacy, 2nd ed. p. 30. See *Re B*——(1892), 1 Ch. p. 462.

(*e*) Rules of the Supreme Court, 1883, Ord. XVI., r. 17; and see the notes thereto in the Annual Practice for 1897, pp. 398, 399.

(*f*) *Ibid.*
(*g*) *Ibid.* See also *Burt* v. *Blackburn* (1887), 3 Times L. R. 356.

respect of a libel or slander upon a person who is subsequently adjudicated bankrupt does not pass to the trustee for his creditors, "although the injury occasioned thereby may have been the sole cause of his bankruptcy" (*h*), and any damages which he may recover do not pass to his trustee under sect. 44 of the Bankruptcy Act, 1882 (*i*). "Assignees of a bankrupt are not to make a profit of a man's wounded feelings; causes of action, therefore, which are, as in this case, purely personal, do not pass to the assignees, but the right to sue remains with the bankrupt" (*k*).

Further, the bankrupt may sue for a libel or slander upon him published during his bankruptcy, and his trustee cannot intercept any damages which he may recover in such an action, or prevent the bankrupt from expending them in the maintenance of himself and his family (*l*). But "if the bankrupt had accumulated the money, and had invested it in some property, that property might be reached by the trustee" (*m*).

The defendant cannot obtain an order for security for costs merely because the plaintiff is

---

(*h*) Per Alderson, B., in *Howard* v. *Crowther* (1841), 8 M. & W. at p. 604.

(*i*) *Drake* v. *Beckham* (1849), 2 H. L. C. 579.

(*k*) Per Lord Abinger, in *Howard* v. *Crowther* (1841), 8 M. & W. at p. 604.

(*l*) *Ex parte Graham, Re Job* (1870), 21 L. T. 802; *Ex parte Vine, Re Wilson* (1878), L. R. 8 Ch. D. 364; 47 L. J. Bank. 116; 38 L. T. 327, 730.

(*m*) Per James, L. J., in *Ex parte Vine, Re Wilson* (1878), 8 Ch. D. at p. 366.

bankrupt (*n*); but the defendant can, upon satisfying the Court that the plaintiff has no visible means of paying the defendant's costs, obtain an order remitting the action to the County Court, unless the plaintiff give security for costs, or satisfy the Court that he has a cause of action more fit to be prosecuted in the High Court than in the County Court (*o*).

ART. 19.—Corporations and incorporated companies.

A corporation or incorporated company can sue for a libel affecting its property (p); it can also sue for slander in relation to its trade or business. It is liable for libel or slander published by its servants o agents, where such publication has been expressl; authorized (q), or in the case of libel where such publication is in pursuance of the general orders given to such servants or agents (r).

NOTE 1.—" The law of libel is one and the same as to all plaintiffs; . . . in every action of

(*n*) *Cook* v. *Whellock* (1890), 24 Q. B. D. 658.
(*o*) County Courts Act, 1888 (51 & 52 Vict. c. 43), s. 66; and see p. 211, *infra*, and the cases there cited.
(*p*) *Mayor, &c. of Manchester* v. *Williams* (1891), 1 Q. B. 94.
(*q*) *Yarborough* v. *Bank of England* (1812), 16 East, 6; *Latimer* v. *Western Morning News* (1871), 25 L. T. 44; *Abrath* v. *North Eastern Rail. Co.* (1886), 11 App. Cas. 253, 254; 55 L. J. Q. B. 466.
(*r*) *Whitfield* v. *S. E. R. Co.* (1858), E. B. & E. 115; 27 L. J. Q. B. 229.

libel, whether the statement is, or is not, a libel, depends on the same question, viz., whether the jury are of opinion that what has been published with regard to the plaintiff would tend, in the minds of people of ordinary sense, to bring the plaintiff into contempt, hatred, or ridicule, or to injure his character. The question is really the same by whomsoever the action is brought, whether by a person, a firm, or a company. There are statements which, with regard to some plaintiffs, would undoubtedly constitute a libel, but which, if published of another kind of plaintiffs, would not have the same effect" (*s*).

And it is clear that not every charge which would be defamatory if made against a private individual, is necessarily so if made against a corporation or company.

"The words complained of in order to entitle a corporation or company to sue for libel or slander, must injuriously affect the corporation or company as distinct from the individuals who compose it. A corporation or company could not sue in respect of a charge of murder or incest or adultery, because it could not commit these crimes. Nor could it sue in respect of a charge of corruption or of an assault, because a corporation cannot be guilty of corruption or of an assault, although the individuals composing it may be. The words complained of must attack the corporation or company in the method of conducting its affairs,

(*s*) *Per* Lord Esher, M. R., in *South Hetton Coal Co.* v. *North-Eastern News Association* (1894), 1 Q. B. at p. 138.

must accuse it of fraud or mismanagement, or must attack its financial position" (*t*). "The limits of a corporation's right of action for libel are those suggested by Pollock, C. B., in *Metropolitan Saloon Omnibus Co.* v. *Hawkins* (*u*). A corporation may sue for a libel affecting property, not for one merely affecting personal reputation" (*x*); and therefore, in *Mayor, &c. of Manchester* v. *Williams* (*y*), where the Statement of Claim in an action for libel brought by a corporation alleged that the defendant had charged the plaintiffs with corrupt practices, but contained no allegation of special damage, it was held that inasmuch as a corporation as distinguished from the individuals composing it cannot be guilty of corrupt practices, the Statement of Claim disclosed no cause of action.

Where, however, a libel on a corporation is in effect a libel on its members, then, provided they can prove that the defamatory statement applies to them, they are entitled to maintain an action in their own names as private individuals (*z*).

NOTE 2.—There is as yet no decision on the difficult question whether a corporation or company

(*t*) *Per* Lopes, L. J., *ibid.* at p. 141.
(*u*) (1859), 4 H. & N. at p. 90.
(*x*) *Per* Day, J., in *Mayor, &c. of Manchester* v. *Williams* (1891), 1 Q. B. at p. 96; cited with approval by Lopes, L. J., in *South Hetton Coal Co.* v. *North-Eastern News Association* (1894), 1 Q. B. at p. 142.
(*y*) (1891), 1 Q. B. 94.
(*z*) See *Booth* v. *Briscoe and others* (1877), 2 Q. B. D. 496 (C. A.), and pp. 6, 7, 57, *supra*.

can be made responsible for a libel where the occasion is privileged, and actual malice must be proved. The question was argued but not decided in *Nevill* v. *Fine Arts, &c. Co.* (*a*). It is submitted, however, that proof of the malice of the agent or servant who published the libel would, under such circumstances, rebut the privilege (*b*).

Art. 20.—Defences to action for libel or slander.

The defences to an action for libel are:—
(1) *Justification* (*c*);
(2) *Fair comment* (*d*);
(3) *Privilege* (*e*); *which may be either—*
   (a) *absolute* (*f*); *or*
   (b) *qualified* (*g*);
(4) *Apology.* This defence is, however, only available when the libel is "contained in a public newspaper or other periodical publication" (*h*);
(5) *Accord and satisfaction* (*i*);
(6) *Release* (*k*);

(*a*) (1895), 2 Q. B. 156; (1897), App. Cas. 68.
(*b*) See particularly the observations of Lopes, L. J., as reported in L. R. (1895), 2 Q. B., at p. 172.
(*c*) Art. 21, p. 81, *infra*.
(*d*) Art. 23, p. 88, *infra*.
(*e*) Art. 24, p. 96, *infra*.
(*f*) Arts. 25, 26, and 27, pp. 101–113, *infra*.
(*g*) Arts. 28–37, pp. 113–149, *infra*.
(*h*) Art. 39, p. 156, *infra*.
(*i*) Art. 40, p. 157, *infra*.
(*k*) Art. 41, p. 158, *infra*.

(7) *Res judicata* (*l*) ;
(8) *Statute of Limitations* (*m*) ;
(9) *Death of plaintiff or defendant before verdict or finding of issues of fact* (*n*) ;
Similar defences, with the exception of (4), *are open to the defendant in an action for slander.*

NOTE.—It may be said that it is also a defence that the words complained of are not defamatory, or do not relate to the plaintiff (*o*), or that there has been no publication (*p*); but in all these cases the onus of proving the contrary is on the plaintiff, and, if he does not do so, he fails to make out even a *primâ facie* case. If, however, the defendant intends to rely upon any of these points at the trial, he should raise them in his Defence.

ART. 21.—**Justification.**

It is a good defence to an action of libel or slander that the words complained of are true in substance and in fact.

NOTE 1.—The reason for this rule is that "the law will not permit a man to recover damages in respect of an injury to a character which he either does not or ought not to possess " (*q*). The plea of

(*l*) Art. 42, p. 158. *infra*.
(*m*) Art. 43, p. 159, *infra*.
(*n*) Art. 44, p. 161, *infra*.
(*o*) pp. 1–5, *supra*.
(*p*) p. 13, *supra*.
(*q*) Per Littledale, J., in *M'Pherson* v. *Daniels* (1829), 10 B. & C. at p. 272.

justification is, however, as has been well said, a dangerous plea to put upon the record, for if the defendant cannot prove it, or withdraws it at the trial, it may, and most probably will, aggravate the damages (*r*). Moreover, in order to succeed, the defendant will have to prove that the *whole* of the defamatory matter is *substantially* true. Thus, where the libel complained of is an article or paragraph preceded by a title, it is not sufficient to prove the truth of the facts stated in the article or paragraph : the title itself must be justified, or the plaintiff will succeed. So that in *Bishop* v. *Latimer* (*s*), where a newspaper published a paragraph, preceded by the title "How Lawyer B. treats his Clients," which contained a report of a case in which *one* client of Lawyer B. had been badly treated, it was held, although the case itself was accurately reported, that the title was not justified by the facts, and that the plaintiff was entitled to damages. And in another case, *Clement* v. *Lewis* (*t*), where a newspaper had published a correct report of certain proceedings in the Insolvent Debtors' Court preceded by the title " Shameful Conduct of an Attorney," the report was held privileged, but damages were recovered for the title.

If there is gross exaggeration, the plea of

(*r*) *Caulfield* v. *Whitworth* (1868), 18 L. T. 527; 16 W. R. 936.
(*s*) (1861), 4 L. T. 775.
(*t*) (1822), 3 Br. & Bing. 297; 7 Moore, 200. See also *Mountney* v. *Watton* (1831), 2 B. & Ad. 673; *Chalmers* v. *Shackell* (1834), 6 C. & P. 475.

justification will fail. Thus, in *Clarkson* v. *Lawson* (*u*), where the libel stated that the plaintiff, a proctor, had been three times suspended for extortion, it was held to be no justification to prove that he had been *once* so suspended. So where the defendant had stated that the plaintiff was a "libellous journalist," it was held that a plea of justification was not supported by proof that the plaintiff had libelled one person, who had obtained judgment against him for 100*l*. (*x*). And to call the editor of a newspaper "a felon editor," is not justified by proof that the person libelled had been convicted of felony, and condemned to a year's imprisonment; inasmuch as a person who has been convicted and suffered his term of imprisonment does not, in law, continue to be a felon (*y*).

Where the libel imputes a crime to the plaintiff, and the defendant pleads justification, there must be "the same strictness of proof as on a trial" for such crime (*z*). "Where a defendant justifies

(*u*) (1829-30), 6 Bing. 266, 587; 4 M. & P. 356. See also *Clarke* v. *Taylor* (1836), 2 Bing. N. C. 654; *Blake* v. *Stevens* (1864), 11 L. T. 543; 4 F. & F. 232.

(*x*) *Wakley* v. *Cooke and Healey* (1849), 19 L. J. Ex. 91; 4 Ex. 511.

(*y*) *Leyman* v. *Latimer* (1877-8), 3 Ex. D. 15, 352; 47 L. J. Ex. 470. Cf. *Alexander* v. *N. E. Rail. Co.* (1865), 34 L. J. Q. B. 152; *Gwynn* v. *S. E. Rail. Co.* (1868), 18 L. T. 738.

(*z*) Per Lord Denman, C. J., in *Willmett* v. *Harmer* (1839), 8 C. & P. at p. 697. See also *Smith* v. *Parker* (1844), 14 L. J. Ex. 52; 13 M. & W. 459; *O'Brien* v. *Bryant* (1846), 16 L. J. Ex. 77; 16 M. & W. 168; *Botterill and another* v. *Whytehead* (1879), 41 L. T. 588.

words which amount to a charge of felony, and proves his justification, the plaintiff may be put upon his trial by that verdict, without the intervention of a grand jury" (*a*). And if the words complained of be that A. B. said that plaintiff did a disgraceful act, proof that A. B. did in fact say so is no defence: the whole of the defamatory words must be justified, and it must be proved that plaintiff did in fact do the act alleged (*b*).

So if an account of a trial be published setting out counsel's speech, and stating that the facts opened were proved, when actually the evidence only bore out part of the facts so stated, it is no defence to plead that the facts were so stated by counsel: the facts so stated must be proved true, or the defendant will fail (*c*).

NOTE 2.—But, on the other hand, it is not necessary to justify every detail of the charge or general terms of abuse, provided that the gist of the libel or slander is proved to be in substance correct, and that the details, &c., which are not justified, produce no different effect on the mind of the reader than the actual truth would do (*d*).

(*a*) *Per* Lord Kenyon, C. J., in *Cook* v. *Field* (1788), 3 Esp. at p. 133.

(*b*) *De Crespigny* v. *Wellesley* (1829), 5 Bing. 392; 2 M. & P. 695; *M'Pherson* v. *Daniels* (1829), 10 B. & C. 263; 5 M. & Rob. 251; *Watkin* v. *Hall* (1868), L. R. 3 Q. B. 396; 37 L. J. Q. B. 125.

(*c*) *Lewis* v. *Walter* (1821), 4 B. & Ald. 605. And see also cases cited on p. 92, *infra*.

(*d*) *Willmett* v. *Harmer and another* (1839), 8 C. & P. 695; *Alexander* v. *N. E. Rail. Co.* (1865), 34 L. J. Q. B. 152. But cf. *Gwynn* v. *S. E. Rail. Co.* (1868), 18 L. T. 738.

Thus, where the libel complained of was that
"L., B., and G. are a gang who live by card-
sharping," it was held to be sufficient justification
to prove that upon two distinct occasions L., B.,
and G. had cheated at cards (e). So, where the
plaintiffs were accused of being "impudent and
ignorant scamps who had the audacity to pretend
to cure all kinds of diseases with one kind of pill,"
and their business was referred to as "homicidal
tricks," and "wholesale poisoning," and it was
stated that several of them "had been convicted
of manslaughter, and fined and imprisoned for
killing people with enormous doses of their
universal vegetable boluses," it was held that
the libel was in substance correct upon proof
"that the plaintiffs' pills when taken in large
doses as recommended by the plaintiffs were
highly dangerous, deadly, and poisonous," and
"that two persons had died in consequence of
taking large quantities of them, and that the
people who had administered these pills were tried,
convicted, and imprisoned for the manslaughter
of these two persons;" and that it was not necessary to further justify the epithets "scamps,"
"rotgut rascals," "wholesale poisoning" (f).

(e) Reg. v. Labouchere (Lambri's case) (1880), 14 Cox, C. C.
419.
(f) Morrison v. Harmer (1837), 3 Bing. N. C. 759; 3 Hodges,
108; 4 Scott, 533. See also Weaver v. Lloyd (1824), 2 B. &
C. 678; 1 C. & P. 295; Edwards v. Bell (1824), 1 Bing. 403;
Warman v. Hine (1837), 1 Jur. 820; Edsall v. Russell (1842),
12 L. J. C. P. 4; 6 Jur. 996; Behrens v. Allen (1862), 3 F. &
F. 135; 8 Jur. N. S. 118.

Where the libel is divisible, the defendant may justify one part and admit liability as to the rest; but the Court will not tolerate a plea leaving in doubt what the defendant justifies and what he does not. He must distinctly sever that which he justifies from that which he does not (*g*).

Art. 22.—Distinction between report and comment.

A report is an account, abbreviated or otherwise, of proceedings which have actually taken place. Comment, on the other hand, is the judgment or opinion of the writer on those proceedings.

Note.—The distinction between report and comment cannot be too strongly emphasised, and the necessity for keeping that distinction clearly in mind cannot be too strongly impressed upon all journalists and writers for the Press. "If any comments are made, they should not be made as part of the report. The report should be confined to what takes place in Court, and the two things, report and comment, should be kept separate" (*h*). And this is equally true, not only of a report of what takes place in Court, but also of all other proceedings, reports of which are *primâ facie* privileged. A report may be absolutely

(*g*) *Fleming* v. *Dollar* (1889), 23 Q. B. D. 388; 58 L. J. Q. B. 548; 61 L. T. 230. See also p. 226, *infra*.

(*h*) Per Lord Campbell, C. J., in *Andrews* v. *Chapman* (1853), 3 C. & K. at p. 288.

privileged (*i*), in which case no action will lie however untrue and malicious the statements which it contains; or it may come under the head of qualified privilege (*k*), when it will be protected unless the plaintiff can prove affirmatively that the defendant has been actuated by malice (*l*). Comment, on the other hand, if fair and *bonâ fide* on a matter of public interest, is no libel (*m*).

It should be noticed that although as stated above a *report* of judicial proceedings is privileged, no comment which is likely to prejudice the case is allowed whilst the proceedings are pending (*n*). Even temperate and judicious comment, which would be perfectly proper after the case is concluded, may be a contempt of Court if published before the end of the case (*o*). " Every libel on a person about to be tried is not necessarily a contempt of Court; but the applicant must show that something has been published, which either is clearly intended, or at least is calculated, to prejudice a trial which is pending (*p*).

(*i*) See Articles 25, 26, 27, pp. 101–113, *infra*.
(*k*) See Articles 28–37, pp. 113–149, *infra*.
(*l*) As to what constitutes malice, see Article 38, pp. 150–155, *infra*.
(*m*) Article 23, p. 88, *infra*.
(*n*) *Reg.* v. *Payne* (1896), 1 Q. B. 577.
(*o*) *Hunt* v. *Clarke*, *Re O'Malley* (1889), 58 L. J. Q. B. 490; 61 L. T. 343; *In re Crown Bank*, *In re O'Malley* (1890), 44 Ch. D. 649; 59 L. J. Ch. 767; *Coats* v. *Chadwick* (1894), 1 Ch. 347; *Reg.* v. *Payne* (1896), 1 Q. B. 577.
(*p*) Per Lord Russell, L. C. J., in *Reg.* v. *Payne* (1896), 1 Q. B. at p. 580. In the case of *In re Bahama Islands* (1893), App. Cas. 138, it was held by the Judicial Committee of the

Art. 23.—**Fair and bonâ fide comment on a matter of public interest.**

No action lies if the defendant can prove that the words complained of are a fair and bonâ fide comment on a matter of public interest.

The Court decides whether the matter commented on is one of public interest; the jury, if the Court is of opinion that there is some evidence that the comment is unfair, finds whether it is so in fact (q).

Note 1.—"It is incorrect to say, as some writers do, that *bonâ fide* comments on matters of public interest come under qualified privilege" (r). The defence in such a case really is, that the words are not defamatory—that fair and proper comment is no libel (s). "It is only when the writer goes beyond the limits of fair criticism that his criticism passes into the region of libel:

Privy Council that a statement, though it might have been made the subject of proceedings for libel, was not in the circumstances calculated to obstruct or interfere with the course of justice or the due administration of the law, and therefore did not constitute a contempt of court.

(q) Since the publication of the first edition of this work, in which the above Article appeared, the law has been laid down in similar language by Lopes, L. J., in *South Hetton Coal Co.* v. *N. E. News Association* (1894), 1 Q. B. at p. 141.

(r) *Per* Blackburn, J., in *Campbell* v. *Spottiswoode* (1863), 3 B. & S. 769. And see the observations of Lord Esher, M. R., and Bowen, L. J., in *Merivale* v. *Carson* (1887), 20 Q. B. D. 275.

(s) *Per* Blackburn, J., 32 L. J. Q. B. at p. 202; and *per* Lopes, L. J., in *South Hetton Coal Co.* v. *N. E. News Association* (1894), 1 Q. B. at p. 143.

at all " (*t*). If such comments *were* privileged, in order to succeed plaintiff would have to prove malice, however false and injurious the words complained of may have been, while defendant would only have to prove that at the time he made the charges he believed that they were true; and this is certainly not the law (*u*); for, though "honest belief may frequently be an element which the jury may take into consideration in considering whether or not an alleged libel was in excess of a fair comment, it cannot in itself prevent the matter being libellous" (*x*).

NOTE 2.—*Fair and bonâ fide comment.* The limits of fair comment on matters of public interest are very wide. "Every latitude must be given to opinion and to prejudice, and then an ordinary set of men with ordinary judgment must say whether any fair man would have made such a comment. Mere exaggeration, or even gross exaggeration, would not make the comment unfair. However wrong the opinion expressed may be in point of truth, or however prejudiced the writer, it may still be within the prescribed limit. The question which the jury must consider is this:—would any fair man, however prejudiced he may be, however exaggerated or obstinate

(*t*) *Per* Bowen, L. J., in *Merivale* v. *Carson* (1887), 20 Q. B. D. at p. 283.
(*u*) See "A Digest of the Law of Libel and Slander," by W. B. Odgers, 2nd ed. p. 33.
(*x*) *Per* Blackburn, J., in *Campbell* v. *Spottiswoode* (1863), 32 L. J. Q. B. p. 202.

his views, have said that which this criticism has said?" (*y*).

"It is only, as was said by Bowen, L. J., in *Merivale* v. *Carson*(*z*), when the writer goes beyond the limits of fair criticism, that his criticism passes into the region of libel at all. It is for the jury to consider what impression would be produced in the mind of an unprejudiced reader who reads the (article complained of) straight through, knowing nothing about the case beforehand. They must not dwell too much on isolated passages, they must consider the (article) as a whole. If there are such deviations from absolute accuracy as to make the comment unfair, they must find for the plaintiff; but, if there are no such deviations, or the deviation is minute and within the latitude of fair discussion, and within the region of that diversity of opinion which may be fairly and reasonably entertained by different persons upon the same subject-matter, they should find for the defendant" (*a*). "It must be assumed that a man is entitled to entertain any opinion he pleases, however wrong, exaggerated, or violent it may be; and it must be left to the jury to say whether the mode of expression exceeds the reasonable limits of fair criticism" (*b*).

(*y*) *Per* Lord Esher, M. R., in *Merivale* v. *Carson* (1887), 20 Q. B. D. at pp. 280, 281.

(*z*) *Ibid.* at p. 283.

(*a*) *Per* Lopes, L. J., in *South Hetton Coal Co.* v. *N. E. News Association* (1894), 1 Q. B. at pp. 143–144.

(*b*) *Per* Bowen, L. J., in *Merivale* v. *Carson* (1887), 20 Q. B. D. at pp. 283–284.

And the question whether the words complained of are or are not fair comment is essentially for the jury. "Nothing is more important than that fair and full latitude of discussion should be allowed to writers upon any public matter, whether it be the conduct of public men or the proceedings in courts of justice or in Parliament, or the publication of a scheme or a literary work. But it is always left to a jury to say whether the publication has gone beyond the limits of a fair comment on the subject-matter discussed. A writer is not allowed to overstep these limits" (c).

All comments must be *bonâ fide*. Criticism must not be made a cloak for malice. There should be no insinuation of improper and dishonourable conduct, unless the critic can prove that such conduct did in fact exist. And in commenting upon conduct which did in fact exist, there must be no imputations of wicked or corrupt motives, unless the critic can prove that such imputations "fairly and properly and legitimately arise out of the conduct itself, and a jury shall be of opinion, not only that the criticism was honest, but also well founded" (d).

The mere fact that the defendant honestly believed the charges to be true is in itself no defence (e).

(c) *Per* Crompton, J., in *Campbell* v. *Spottiswoode* (1863), 3 B. & S. at p. 778.
(d) *Per* Cockburn, C. J., *ibid.*, 32 L. J. at p. 200.
(e) *Cooper* v. *Lawson* (1838), 8 A. & E. 746; *Campbell* v. *Spottiswoode* (1863), 32 L. J. Q. B. 185; 8 L. T. 201; *Harle* v. *Catherall and others* (1866), 14 L. T. 801; *Bryce* v. *Rusden* (1886), 2 Times L. R. 435; *Brenon* v. *Ridgway* (1887), 3 Times L. R. 592.

"If he ... imputes to the person whom he is criticizing base and sordid motives, which are not warranted by facts, I cannot think for a moment that because he *bonâ fide* believes that he is publishing what is true, that is any defence in point of law" (*f*).

The matter commented on must be actual fact. "The very statement" indeed of the rule set out in the above Article, "assumes the matters of fact commented upon to be somehow or other ascertained. It does not mean that a man may invent facts, and comment on the facts so invented in what would be a fair and *bonâ fide* manner on the supposition that the facts were true. ... If the facts as a comment upon which the publication is sought to be excused do not exist, the foundation of the plea fails" (*g*). A newspaper may not set out evidence which might have been, but was not in fact given, and suggest as an inference therefrom that the prisoner though acquitted was really guilty (*h*). It may comment on evidence actually given (*i*), but may not charge a witness with having committed perjury (*k*). The defendant

(*f*) *Per* Cockburn, C. J., in *Campbell* v. *Spottiswoode* (1863), 32 L. J. Q. B. at p. 200.

(*g*) *Per cur.* in *Lefroy* v. *Burnside* (1879), 4 L. R. Ir. at p. 340. See also the judgment of the Court in *Davis and Sons* v. *Shepstone* (1886), 11 App. Cas. at p. 190.

(*h*) *Helsham* v. *Blackwood and another* (1851), 20 L. J. C. P. 187; 11 C. B. 111; 15 Jur. 861; *Hibbins* v. *Lee* (1864), 11 L. T. 541; 4 F. & F. 243.

(*i*) *Hedley* v. *Barlow* (1865), 4 F. & F. 224.

(*k*) *Roberts* v. *Brown* (1834), 10 Bing. 519; 6 C. & P. 757; *Felkin* v. *Herbert* (1863-4), 33 L. J. Ch. 294. See also cases on p. 84, *supra*.

will not, however, be liable for trivial mistakes made accidentally, for "it is not to be expected that a public journalist will always be infallible" (*l*).

NOTE 3.—*Matter of public interest.* Under this description come:—

(1) *All state matters; everything which concerns government, either House of Parliament, or any committee thereof.*—Evidence given before a parliamentary committee (*m*), or a royal commission (*n*); the prevalence of corrupt practices at a parliamentary election (*o*); government appointments (*p*); a petition to parliament (*q*), and a debate in the House thereon (*r*); a report by the Board of Admiralty (*s*).

(2) *The public conduct of every one who takes part in public affairs* (*t*). As Cockburn, C. J., said, in

(*l*) *Per* Cockburn, C. J., in *Woodgate* v. *Ridout* (1865), 4 F. & F. 217.
(*m*) *Hedley* v. *Barlow* (1865), 4 F. & F. 224.
(*n*) *Mulkern* v. *Ward* (1872), L. R. 13 Eq. 622; 41 L. J. Ch. 464.
(*o*) *Wilson* v. *Reed and others* (1860), 2 F. & F. 149.
(*p*) *Turnbull* v. *Bird* (1861), 2 F. & F. 508; *Seymour* v. *Butterworth* (1862), 3 F. & F. 372.
(*q*) *Dunne* v. *Anderson* (1825), 3 Bing. 88; 10 Moore, 407; R. & M. 287; *Wason* v. *Walter* (1868), L. R. 4 Q. B. 73; 38 L. J. Q. B. 34.
(*r*) *Wason* v. *Walter, supra.*
(*s*) *Henwood* v. *Harrison* (1872), L. R. 7 C. P. 606; 41 L. J. C. P. 206; 26 L. T. 938; 20 W. R. 1000. See the observations of Bowen, L. J., on this case in 20 Q. B. D. 282, 283.
(*t*) See the observations of Bramwell, B., in *Kelly* v. *Sherlock* (1866), L. R. 1 Q. B. at p. 689; 35 L. J. Q. B. 209.

Seymour v. *Butterworth* (*u*), "it was not disputed that the public conduct of a public man might be discussed with the fullest freedom, it might be made the subject of hostile criticism and of hostile animadversions, provided the language of the writer was kept within the limits of an honest intention to discharge a public duty, and was not made a means of promulgating slanderous and malicious observations."

Under this head comes the public conduct of statesmen and politicians (*x*), public agitators (*y*), clergymen (*z*), judges and magistrates (*a*), barristers (*b*), candidates for parliament (*c*) and their supporters in public (*d*), vestrymen and waywardens (*e*), petitioners to parliament (*f*); but *not* the private conduct of such persons save in so far as it affects their public relations (*g*).

(3) *Legal* (*h*) *and ecclesiastical* (*i*) *matters.*—The

(*u*) (1862), 3 F. & F. at p. 376.
(*x*) *Parmiter* v. *Coupland and another* (1840), 9 L. J. Ex. 202; 6 M. & W. 105.
(*y*) *Odger* v. *Mortimer* (1873), 28 L. T. 472.
(*z*) *Kelly* v. *Tinling* (1865), L. R. 1 Q. B. 699; 35 L. J. Q. B. 231.
(*a*) *Hibbins* v. *Lee* (1864), 11 L. T. 541; 4 F. & F. 243.
(*b*) *Seymour* v. *Butterworth* (1862), 3 F. & F. 372.
(*c*) *Duncombe* v. *Daniell* (1836), 8 C. & P. 222.
(*d*) *Davis* v. *Duncan* (1874), L. R. 9 C. P. 396; 43 L. J C. P. 185; 30 L. T. 464.
(*e*) *Harle* v. *Catherall* (1866), 14 L. T. 801.
(*f*) *Wason* v. *Walter, supra*.
(*g*) *Pankhurst* v. *Hamilton* (1887), 3 Times L. R. 500.
(*h*) *Per* Cockburn, C. J., in *Cox* v. *Feeney* (1863), 4 F. & F. 13; and in *Purcell* v. *Sowler* (1877), 2 C. P. D. 218 (C. A.).
(*i*) *Kelly* v. *Tinling* (1865), L. R. 1 Q. B. 699; 35 L. J. Q. B. 231.

mode of conducting church services (*i*); but *not* the affairs of a private society established by the incumbent (*k*).

(4) *The administration of public institutions and local affairs.*—Anything done in office by a member of a highways board (*l*); "the management of the poor and the administration of the poor law" (*m*); the report of an inspector of charities under the Charitable Trusts Acts (*n*).

(5) *Places of public amusement or entertainment.*—A flower show (*o*), and a public concert or music hall (*p*).

(6) *Literature.*—The contents of any newspaper (*q*), or book (*r*), or its author as such (*s*); but *not* the private character of an author (*t*), or journalist (*u*).

(*i*) *Kelly* v. *Tinling, supra.*
(*k*) *Gathercole* v. *Miall* (1846), 15 L. J. Ex. 179; 10 J. P. 582; 10 Jur. 337: 15 M. & W. 319.
(*l*) *Harle* v. *Calverall and others* (1866), 14 L. T. 801.
(*m*) Per Cockburn, C. J., in *Purcell* v. *Sowler* (1877), 2 C. P. D. at p. 218.
(*n*) *Cox* v. *Feeney* (1863), 4 F. & F. 13.
(*o*) *Green* v. *Chapman* (1837), 4 Bing. N. C. 92; 5 Scott, 340.
(*p*) *Dibdin* v. *Swan and Bostock* (1793), 1 Esp. 28.
(*q*) *Heriot* v. *Stuart* (1796), 1 Esp. 437; *Stuart* v. *Lovell* (1817), 2 Stark. 93; *Campbell* v. *Spottiswoode, supra.*
(*r*) *Macleod* v. *Wakley* (1828), 3 C. P. 311; *Strauss* v. *Francis* (1866), 15 L. T. 674; 4 F. & F. 939, 1107.
(*s*) *Carr* v. *Hood* (1808), 1 Camp. 355, n.
(*t*) *Fraser* v. *Berkeley* (1836), 7 C. & P. 621.
(*u*) *Russell and another* v. *Webster* (1874), 23 W. R. 59. See also *Strauss* v. *Francis, Heriot* v. *Stuart, Stuart* v. *Lovell, Campbell* v. *Spottiswoode, supra.*

(7) *Art.*—Painting (*x*), and architecture (*y*).

(8) *Anything which invites public attention or criticism* (*z*).—A stage-play (*a*), the contents of a pamphlet (*b*), advertisement (*c*), or handbill issued to the public (*d*). It has also been held that the sanitary condition of a large number of cottages let by the proprietors of a colliery to their workmen is a matter of public interest (*e*).

ART. 24.—Privilege.

In certain cases, even though the matter complained of is defamatory, in the interests of public policy no liability attaches to the publication thereof—in other words, the occasion is privileged.

Privileged occasions are of two kinds:—I. *Occasions of absolute privilege, where no action lies,*

(*x*) *Thompson* v. *Shackell* (1828), 1 Moo. & Mal. 187.
(*y*) *Soane* v. *Knight* (1827), Moo. & Mal. 74.
(*z*) *Morrison* v. *Belcher* (1863), 3 F. & F. 614; *Duplany* v. *Davis* (1887), 3 Times L. R. 184.
(*a*) *Merivale* v. *Carson* (1887), 20 Q. B. D. 275 (C. A.).
(*b*) *Hibbs* v. *Wilkinson* (1859), 1 F. & F. 608; *Kœnig* v. *Ritchie* (1862), 3 F. & F. 413; *Odger* v. *Mortimer* (1873), 28 L. T. 472.
(*c*) *Morrison and another* v. *Harmer and another* (1837), 3 Bing. N. C. 759; *Hunter* v. *Sharpe* (1866), 15 L. T. 421; 4 F. & F. 983.
(*d*) *Eastwood* v. *Holmes* (1858), 1 F. & F. 347; *Paris* v. *Levy* (1860), 30 L. J. C. P. 11; 3 L. T. 324; *Jenner and another* v. *A'Beckett* (1871), L. R. 7 Q. B. 11; 41 L. J. Q. B. 14; 25 L. T. 464.
(*e*) *South Hetton Coal Co.* v. *N. E. News Association* (1894), 1 Q. B. 133 (C. A.).

PRIVILEGE.

however untrue or malicious the statements may have been (*f*). This exists in the following cases :—
(1.) Statements made in parliament or in the course of judicial, naval, military, or state proceedings (*g*).
(2.) Reports, &c., published by order of parliament (*h*).
(3.) Reports in a newspaper (*i*) of proceedings in a court of justice, if published contemporaneously with such proceedings (*k*).

II. *Occasions of qualified privilege.* Upon occasions of this kind, no action lies where the statement is made bonâ fide, and in a manner not exceeding what is reasonably necessary for the occasion. Proof of actual malice will rebut the primâ facie protection afforded by such an occasion, and it is for the plaintiff to prove that the defendant acted in bad faith, not for the defendant to prove that he acted in good faith (*l*).

Qualified privilege exists in the following cases :—
(1.) Reports other than those in a newspaper (*i*) of judicial proceedings; and reports in a newspaper of such proceedings, if not

(*f*) The terms "malicious" and "maliciously" are here and throughout used in the ordinary sense of any corrupt or wrong motive, or as it is technically called "malice in fact," as to which, see Art. 38, p. 150, *infra*.
(*g*) Art. 25, p. 101, *infra*.
(*h*) Art. 26, p. 106, *infra*.
(*i*) As to the meaning of "newspaper," see p. 109, *infra*.
(*k*) Art. 27, p. 107, *infra*.
(*l*) *Clark* v. *Molyneux* (1877), 3 Q. B. D. 237; 47 L. J. Q. B. 230; *Jenoure* v. *Delmege* (1891), App. Cas. 73; 60 L. J. P. C. 11; *Aberdein* v. *Macleay* (1893), 9 Times L. R. 539.

published contemporaneously with such proceedings (m).

(2.) *Extracts from registers kept pursuant to statute* (n).

(3.) *Reports of proceedings in parliament* (o).

(4.) *Reports of proceedings of public meetings* (p).

(5.) *Reports of vestry meetings, &c.* (q).

(6.) *Notices and reports published at request of government office or authority* (r).

(7.) *Statements made to a public servant or other person in authority with the object of preventing or punishing crime, or redressing a public grievance* (s).

(8.) *Statements made with the object of protecting some interest of the writer or speaker, and reasonably necessary for such purpose* (t).

(9.) *Statements made with the object of protecting an interest common to the writer or speaker and the person to whom the statement is made* (u).

(10.) *Statements made in discharge of a legal, moral, or social duty* (x).

NOTE.—" The question whether the occasion is privileged, if the facts are not in dispute, is a question of law only, for the judge, not for the jury. If there are questions of fact in dispute upon which this question depends, they must be

(m) Art. 28, p. 114, *infra.*
(o) Art. 30, p. 120, *infra.*
(q) Art. 32, p. 127, *infra.*
(s) Art. 34, p. 131, *infra.*
(u) Art. 36, p. 136, *infra.*
(n) Art. 29, p. 118, *infra.*
(p) Art. 31, p. 121, *infra.*
(r) Art. 33, p. 130, *infra.*
(t) Art. 35, p. 133, *infra.*
(x) Art. 37, p. 140, *infra.*

left to the jury, but, when the jury have found the facts, it is for the judge to say whether they constitute a privileged occasion" (*y*).

"A confusion is often made between a privileged communication and a privileged occasion. It is for the jury to say whether a communication was privileged; but the question whether an occasion was privileged is for the judge, and that question only arises when there has been publication to a third party" (*z*). In other words, "whether or not the occasion gives that privilege is a question of law for the judge; but whether or not the party has fairly and properly conducted himself in the exercise of it (*i.e.* whether he has acted maliciously), is a question for the jury" (*a*). If the judge rules that the occasion is privileged, "and if there is no evidence of malice to go to the jury, it is his duty to enter judgment for the defendant. On the other hand, if the occasion is not privileged, or if there is any evidence of malice, then the case must be left to the jury" (*b*).

It is, however, frequently a matter of great

(*y*) *Per* Lord Esher, M. R., in *Hebditch* v. *McIlwaine* (1894), 2 Q. B. at p. 58.

(*z*) *Per* Lopes, L. J., in *Pullman* v. *Hill & Co.* (1891), 1 Q. B. at p. 529.

(*a*) *Per* Lord Campbell, C. J., in *Dickson* v. *Earl of Wilton* (1859), 1 F. & F. at p. 419.

(*b*) *Per* Lindley, L. J., in *Stuart* v. *Bell* (1891), 2 Q. B. at p. 345. See also *Aberdein* v. *Macleay* (1893), 9 Times L. R. 539; and as to what constitutes *malice*, see Article 38, p. 150, *infra*.

difficulty to determine whether or not a particular occasion is privileged. As was pointed out by Erle, C. J., in *Whiteley* v. *Adams* (c), in a passage which was lately cited with approval by Lopes, L. J. (d): "Judges who have had from time to time to deal with questions as to whether the occasion justified the speaking or the writing of defamatory matter, have all felt great difficulty in defining what kind of social or moral duty, or what amount of interest, will afford a justification; but all are clear that it is a question for the judge to decide."

Again, in the words of Lindley, L. J., in the case of *Stuart* v. *Bell* (e): "The reason for holding any occasion privileged is common convenience and welfare of society, and it is obvious that no definite line can be drawn so as to mark off with precision those occasions which are privileged, and separate them from those which are not. *Coxhead* v. *Richards* (f), in which four eminent judges were equally divided upon the question whether an occasion was privileged or not, is a striking illustration of the truth of the remark."

(c) (1863), 15 C. B. N. S. at p. 418.
(d) In *Allbutt* v. *General Council of Medical Education and Registration* (1889), 23 Q. B. D. at p. 413. See also the observations of the same learned judge in *Boxsius* v. *Goblet Frères* (1894), 1 Q. B. at p. 846.
(e) (1891), 2 Q. B. at p. 346.
(f) (1846), 2 C. B. 569.

JUDICIAL PROCEEDINGS. 101

ART. 25.—**Statements made in parliament or in the course of judicial, naval, military, or state proceedings.**

Every statement made in parliament or in the course of judicial, naval, military, or state proceedings is absolutely privileged, and no action will lie however false and malicious such statement may have been.

NOTE 1.—*In parliament.* No member is in any way liable for anything said in the House (*g*), but this privilege does not attach to anything said outside the walls of the House, nor to a speech printed and privately circulated outside the House (*h*).

A qualified privilege, *i.e.* a privilege rebuttable by proof of express malice, attaches to a speech printed and circulated by a member amongst his own constituents only (*i*).

A petition to parliament (*j*) or to any committee thereof (*k*) is absolutely privileged. So, too, is anything said by a witness before a Select Committee of either House (*l*).

(*g*) Bill of Rights, 1 Will. M. st. 2, c. 2.
(*h*) *Rex* v. *Abingdon* (1794), 1 Esp. 226; *Rex* v. *Creevey* (1813), 1 M. & S. 273.
(*i*) *Davidson* v. *Duncan* (1857), 7 E. & B. 233; 26 L. J. Q. B. 104; *Wason* v. *Walter* (1868), L. R. 4 Q. B. 95; 38 L. J. Q. B. 42.
(*j*) *Lake* v. *King* (1680), 1 Saund. 131; 1 Lev. 240; 1 Mod. 58.
(*k*) *Kane* v. *Mulvany* (1866), Ir. R. 2 C. L. 402.
(*l*) *Goffin* v. *Donnelly* (1881), 6 Q. B D. 307; 50 L. J. Q. B. 303.

NOTE 2.—*Judicial proceedings.* " The authorities establish beyond all question this : that neither party, witness, counsel, jury, nor judge can be put to answer civilly or criminally for words spoken in office; that no action of libel or slander lies, whether against judges, counsel, witnesses, or parties, for words written or spoken in the course of any proceeding before any court recognized by law, and this though the words written or spoken were written or spoken maliciously, without any justification or excuse, and from personal ill-will and anger against the person defamed " (*m*).

" The ground of that rule is public policy " (*n*). Thus all pleadings (*o*) and affidavits (*p*) are absolutely privileged. So, too, are statements made in an objection to a bill of costs carried in under the provisions of Ord. LXV., Rule 27 (*q*). Similarly, every statement made by an advocate whilst acting in that capacity, whether counsel (*r*), solicitor (*s*), or the party in person (*t*),

(*m*) *Per* Lopes, L. J., in *Royal Aquarium, &c. Soc.* v. *Parkinson* (1892), 1 Q. B. at p. 451.

(*n*) *Per* Lord Esher, M. R., *ibid.* at p. 442.

(*o*) *Lord Beauchamps* v. *Sir R. Croft* (1569), Dyer, 285 a.

(*p*) *Astley* v. *Younge* (1759), 2 Burr. 807 ; *Gompas* v. *White* (1890), 54 J. P. 22; *Lilley* v. *Roney* (1892), 8 Times L. R. 642.

(*q*) *Pedley* v. *May* (1892), 8 Times L. R. 2.

(*r*) *Munster* v. *Lamb* (1883), 11 Q. B. D. 588; 52 L. J. Q. B. 726.

(*s*) *Mackay* v. *Ford* (1860), 5 H. & N. 792; 29 L. J. Ex. 404.

(*t*) *Hodgson* v. *Scarlett* (1818), 1 B. & Ald. 244.

is absolutely privileged, and no action will lie, no matter how false or malicious or irrelevant to the matter in issue the words complained of may have been. Where, however, an advocate is knowingly acting without any sort of authority or retainer, or where his retainer has to his knowledge been withdrawn, it is submitted that his statements would be in no way privileged, even though made in a court of justice.

Further, it is submitted that for reasons of public policy where a professional relation is created between a solicitor and client no action will lie in respect of any communication passing between the solicitor and client with reference to the matter upon which the client is seeking the professional advice of such solicitor, and which is relevant to such matter; and that provided the communication fulfils these conditions the privilege is not destroyed by the fact that the solicitor or client in making such communication is actuated by malice against some third person (*u*). It is also submitted that the same rule would apply to similar communications between counsel and solicitor, and between counsel and client.

With regard to witnesses and jurors, and also with regard to judges of inferior courts, the general rule laid down on the preceding page requires modification. Every statement made by a witness in the box is absolutely privileged,

(*u*) See the observations of Lord Herschell, L. C., in *Browne* v. *Dunn* (1893), 6 R. at pp. 71, 72, and 73; and of Lord Bowen, *ibid.* at p. 80.

provided that it refers to the inquiry before the Court, and this is so even if the statement in question is volunteered (*x*). But no privilege would attach to the statements of a witness wholly unconnected with the matter in issue, and made entirely on his own account, and to serve his own ends, nor to statements made before entering or after leaving the box (*y*). So, too, every observation of a juror made in the jury-box is absolutely privileged if connected with the matter in issue (*z*).

As regards words spoken by a judge, the general rule laid down above is true only of judges of superior courts, *i.e.*, of the House of Lords, the Judicial Committee of the Privy Council, the Court of Appeal, the High Court of Justice, and any Divisional Court thereof (*a*), Courts of Nisi Prius and Assize (*b*). Every statement made in office by a judge of a superior court is absolutely privileged, and under no circumstances will an action lie therefor (*c*). A similar privilege is extended to words spoken in office by the judges of inferior courts of record, provided that the judge has jurisdiction in the matter before him. If he knows, or ought to know, that he has no

(*x*) *Seaman* v. *Netherclift* (1876), 1 C. P. D. 540; 45 L. J. C. P. 798.

(*y*) *Trotman* v. *Dunn* (1815), 4 Camp. 211; *Lynam* v. *Gowing* (1880), 6 L. R. Ir. 259.

(*z*) *Rex* v. *Skinner* (1772), Lofft, 55.

(*a*) Jud. Act, 1873, s. 39.

(*b*) *Ex parte Fernandez* (1861), 30 L. J. C. P. 321.

(*c*) *Anderson* v. *Gorrie* (1895), 1 Q. B. 668.

jurisdiction, he is in no way protected (*d*). No privilege attaches to words spoken out of office (*e*).

'Everything said in office by a justice of the peace is also privileged, and no action lies unless the words complained of are wholly unconnected with the matter in issue, and are spoken maliciously and without reasonable and probable cause (*f*).

It is, however, important to notice that this privilege is confined to statements made in the course of *strictly* judicial proceedings, and is one which will not be extended. "It belongs . . . to courts recognized by law, and to such courts only" (*g*). A meeting of the London County Council for granting music and dancing licences under 25 Geo. 2, c. 36, s. 2, is not such a court; and it was accordingly held by the Court of Appeal in *Royal Aquarium, &c. Soc.* v. *Parkinson* (*h*) that a county councillor, making a defamatory statement at such a meeting with regard to a person applying for a licence, is not entitled to absolute immunity from an action in respect of such statement. He is only entitled to the ordinary qualified privilege which may be rebutted by proof of express malice.

(*d*) *Calder* v. *Halket* (1839), 3 Moo. P. C. C. 28; *Houlden* v. *Smith* (1850), 14 Q. B. 841; 19 L. J. Q. B. 170.
(*e*) *Paris* v. *Levy* (1861), 9 C. B. N. S. 342; 30 L. J. C. P. 11.
(*f*) *Kirby* v. *Simpson* (1854), 10 Exch. 358; *Gelen* v. *Hall* (1857), 2 H. & N. 379.
(*g*) Per Lopes, L. J., in *Royal Aquarium, &c. Soc.* v. *Parkinson* (1892), 1 Q. B. at p. 451.
(*h*) (1892), 1 Q. B. 431.

106 THE LAW OF LIBEL AND SLANDER.

Note 3.—*Naval, military, and state proceedings.* Everything written or said in the course of any naval or military proceeding is absolutely privileged. Thus, any defamatory statement made before a naval or military court-martial, no matter how untrue and malicious, is protected (*i*). Similarly, no action lies in respect of such a statement in a report made in the course of military or naval duty (*k*).

For reasons of public policy the same protection would no doubt be given to anything in the nature of an act of state, for example, to every communication relating to state matters made by one minister to another, or to the Crown.

Art. 26.—**Reports, &c., published by order of Parliament.**

All reports, papers, votes, and proceedings published by order of either House of Parliament, and every verified copy thereof, are absolutely privileged, and all proceedings at law, civil or criminal, will be immediately stayed on production of a certificate that

(*i*) *Dawkins* v. *Lord Rokeby* (1875), L. R. 7 H. L. 744; 45 L. J. Q. B. 8.
(*k*) *Dawkins* v. *Lord Paulet* (1869), L. R. 5 Q. B. 94; 39 L. J. Q. B. 53.
* This passage was cited with approval by Lord Esher, M. R., and Kay, L. J., in *Chatterton* v. *Secretary of State for India in Council* (1895), 2 Q. B. at pp. 191, 194.

such reports, &c., were published by order of either House (l).

Note 1.—This statutory provision terminated the long struggle between the House of Commons and the Courts of Justice, the latter having held, in the famous case of *Stockdale* v. *Hansard* (m), that at common law no privilege attached to the publication of parliamentary reports and papers, even if such publication were by order of the whole House.

Note 2.—The publication of extracts from or abstracts of such reports, &c., is privileged, if, in the opinion of the jury, such publication was *bonâ fide* and without malice (n).

Art. 27.—**Reports in a newspaper of proceedings in a court of justice.**

It is submitted that *a report in any newspaper* (o) *of proceedings publicly heard before any Court exercising judicial authority* (p), *published contemporaneously with such proceedings* (q), *is privileged, provided that it is—*

(l) 3 & 4 Vict. c. 9, ss. 1, 2, pp. 247–249, *infra*.
(m) (1839), 9 A. & E. 1, 243; 7 C. & P. 731.
(n) 3 & 4 Vict. c. 9, s. 3, p. 249, *infra*.
(o) As to the meaning of "newspaper," see p. 109, *infra*.
(p) See pp. 114, 115, *infra*.
(q) See Note 2, p. 110, *infra*.

108   THE LAW OF LIBEL AND SLANDER.

(1.) *Fair and accurate* (*r*).
(2.) *Not prohibited by order of the Court* (*s*) ;
(3.) *Not blasphemous* (*t*), *seditious, or indecent* (*u*).

NOTE 1.—Having regard to sect. 3 of the Law of Libel Amendment Act, 1888 (*v*), it is submitted that the above is an accurate statement of the law as it now stands, and that a report coming within the above Article, and satisfying the provisos contained therein, is absolutely privileged, so that, no matter how malicious may have been the publication of it, no action will lie. For although sect. 3 does not state in express terms that the report shall be *absolutely* privileged, there are no words, as in sect. 4, to the effect that the report shall be privileged "*unless it shall be proved that such report was published or made maliciously.*" Moreover, if this interpretation be incorrect, sect. 3 is merely declaratory of the law as it existed before the passing of the Act. On the other hand, if such reports be in fact absolutely privileged, a remarkable example is afforded of the failure of the legislature to accomplish its intentions, for it is quite clear from the debates in parliament (*w*)

(*r*) See pp. 116–118, *infra*.
(*s*) *Rex* v. *Clement* (1821), 4 B. & Ald. 218 ; 11 Price, 69.
(*t*) *Rex* v. *Mary Carlile* (1819), 3 B. & Ald. 167.
(*u*) *Steele* v. *Brannan* (1872), L. R. 7 C. P. 261 ; 41 L. J. M. C. 85 ; 26 L. T. 509 ; 51 & 52 Vict. c. 64, s. 3.
(*v*) Set out on p. 265, *infra*.
(*w*) Sect. 3 of the Bill as originally submitted to Parliament provided that "a fair and accurate report published in any newspaper of proceedings of and in any Court exercising

evidence of which would, of course, not be admitted to show what those intentions were) that the legislature did not intend that such reports should be privileged if published maliciously.

Newspaper.—By sect. 1 of the Law of Libel Amendment Act, 1888, the meaning of the word " newspaper" for the purposes of such Act is defined to be the same as in the Newspaper Libel and Registration Act, 1881, *i.e.*, "any paper containing public news intelligence or occurrences, or any remarks or observations therein printed for sale, and published in England or Ireland periodically, or in parts or numbers at intervals not exceeding twenty-six days between the publication of any two such papers, parts, or numbers; also any paper printed in order to be dispersed and made public weekly or oftener, or at intervals not exceeding twenty-six days, containing only, or principally, advertisements." Therefore the Act has no application to magazines, or to monthly trade papers, or to any paper or pamphlet, though printed for sale and containing public news, and published periodically, if such publication be at intervals exceeding twenty-six days (x). If any of these contain a report of judicial proceedings,

---

judicial authority, shall be absolutely privileged." In Committee on June 6th, 1888, Sir Algernon Borthwick moved and carried an amendment to the effect that the word ' absolutely" should be omitted, in order, as was then expressly stated, to render such reports unprivileged if it were proved that they had been published maliciously.

(x) *Cf. Att.-Gen.* v. *Bradbury and Evans* (1851), 21 L. J. Ex. 12; 7 Ex. 97.

such report is in no way affected by the Act of 1888—the law still being that it is privileged, provided that it is :—

(1) fair and accurate ;
(2) not prohibited by order of the Court ;
(3) not blasphemous, seditious, or obscene ;

but,—and this is the point to notice,—all privilege which the defendant may have will be effectually rebutted by proving that he published the libel maliciously (*x*). Where the defendant has published the report complained of in the ordinary course of his business as proprietor, editor, or reporter of the newspaper, it will be very difficult, if not impossible, to prove malice ; but where the defendant was a party to the action reported (*y*), or the solicitor for one of the parties (*z*), it will be more easy to satisfy a jury that he published the report maliciously.

NOTE 2.—*If published contemporaneously with such proceedings.* If, as above submitted, sect. 3 of the Act of 1888 extends the privilege hitherto possessed by reports of judicial proceedings published in a newspaper, it is, on the other hand, at least open to question whether by the insertion of these words it does not restrict it. Prior to the passing of this Act every fair and accurate report of judicial proceedings, whether

(*x*) *Salmon* v. *Isaac* (1869), 20 L. T. 885.
(*y*) As in *Dodson* v. *Owen* (1885), 2 Times L, R. 111.
(*z*) As in *Stevens* v. *Sampson* (1879), 5 Ex. D. 53 (C. A.) ; 49 L. J. Ex. 120.

published by a newspaper or not (*a*), and whether published contemporaneously with such proceedings or not, was *primâ facie* privileged, and in order to succeed the plaintiff would have had to prove that the defendant had published the report maliciously. The fact that the report was not published until some time after the proceedings had taken place would be evidence of malice, but that was all; it would not *ipso facto* render the report unprivileged and the jury would have to find malice. Though the matter is not wholly free from doubt, it is submitted that at the present time the law is still the same, except in the case of reports which come within sect. 3 of the Law of Libel Amendment Act, 1888 (*b*). It has been suggested, erroneously in the author's opinion, that the effect of this section is to deprive of all privilege every report in a *newspaper* of proceedings publicly heard before any Court exercising judicial authority, *if it is not published contemporaneously with such proceedings*, even though fair and accurate, and published *bonâ fide* and without malice. It is, however, submitted that if the Court is of opinion that the report is *not* published contemporaneously with the proceedings, the section does not apply, and the privilege is then the qualified privilege given by the common law, which will be rebutted on proof of malice.

(*a*) *Per* Brett, L. J., in *Milissich* v. *Lloyds* (1877), 46 L. J. C. P. 404; 36 L. T. 423.
(*b*) See Art. 27, pp. 107, 108, and Note 1, p. 108, *supra*.

To sum up then, a report of judicial proceedings will fall into one of the following classes :

(1.) Reports in a newspaper as defined by sect. 1 of the Law of Libel Amendment Act, 1888 (*b*), published contemporaneously with such proceedings. These, it is submitted, are absolutely privileged (*c*).

(2.) Reports in a newspaper as so defined not published contemporaneously with such proceedings. These obtain a qualified privilege by the common law; but the fact of their not being published contemporaneously would in the majority of cases be such strong evidence of malice as to render the privilege useless.

(3.) Reports elsewhere than in a newspaper as so defined. These also obtain a qualified privilege by the common law (*d*), which may be rebutted by proof that they were published maliciously by the defendant.

What then is the precise meaning of the words *if published contemporaneously with such proceedings?* Strictly speaking, a report published in an evening paper of a trial which has taken place on the same day is not "published contemporaneously with such proceedings," still less the report in

---

(*b*) For definition, see *supra*, p. 109.
(*c*) See Art. 27, p. 107, and Note 1, p. 108, *supra*.
(*d*) See Art. 28, p. 114, *infra*.

the next morning's paper. It cannot, however, be seriously contended that such reports are not now, as they have been for more than a century, privileged if substantially correct. The difficulty of course arises when we consider what length of time must elapse between the trial and the publication of the report in order to bring the latter within the description "not published contemporaneously with such proceedings." And it is evident that the time in question must vary according to the opportunity and time of publication of the paper. Thus, a report published in a daily paper a fortnight after the proceedings had taken place would be in a very different category from the same report published at the same time by a paper which only appeared once in every fortnight, and which had had no previous opportunity of publishing it.

ART. 28.—Other reports of judicial proceedings.

A report of judicial proceedings other than that dealt with in the preceding Article is privileged, provided that it is (1) *fair and accurate,* (2) *not prohibited by order of the Court, and* (3) *not blasphemous, seditious, or indecent ; but such privilege will be rebutted by proof that defendant published such report maliciously* (e).

(e) As to the meaning of *maliciously*, see p. 150, *infra.*

Note 1.—Prior to 1888 every fair and accurate report of judicial proceedings, whether published in a newspaper or not, obtained at the common law a qualified privilege, which was liable to be rebutted by proof that it was published maliciously. And this is still the law except as to reports coming within Art. 27, p. 107, *supra*, which, as has been submitted, are absolutely privileged, and are protected, no matter how malicious may have been their publication. The qualified privilege at common law is the same "for a private individual as for a newspaper" (*f*); it is not a special privilege accorded to newspapers (*g*).

Note 2.—*Report of judicial proceedings.* Under this description come reports of proceedings before a judge at chambers (*h*), in gaol before a registrar in bankruptcy (*i*), before a County Court judge in his own room to which the public have access (*j*), before examiners duly appointed to inquire into the sufficiency of sureties offered on trial of an election petition (*k*).

(*f*) *Per* Brett, L. J., in *Milissich* v. *Lloyds* (1877), 46 L. J. C. P. 404.
(*g*) See the observations of Day, J., in *Rumney* v. *Walter* (1892), 8 Times L. R. at p. 262.
(*h*) *Smith* v. *Scott* (1847), 2 C. & K. 580.
(*i*) *Ryalls* v. *Leader and others* (1865), L. R. 1 Ex. 296; 35 L. J. Ex. 185; 14 L. T. 563.
(*j*) *Myers* v. *Defries*, Times, July 23, 1877.
(*k*) *Cooper* v. *Lawson* (1888), 8 A. & E. 746.

Having regard to the case of *Usill* v. *Hales* (*l*), it is also now clear law—although it was at one time doubted—that all reports of *ex parte* proceedings are similarly protected, whether such proceedings result in the discharge by the magistrate of the party charged (as in *Curry* v. *Walter* (*m*) and *Lewis* v. *Levy* (*n*)) or not. *Usill* v. *Hales* (*o*) was followed in *Kimber* v. *The Press Association* (*p*), where plaintiff sued the defendants for a libel upon him contained in a fair and accurate report of an *ex parte* application for a summons against him for perjury. It was proved that the only persons present at the hearing were the counsel making the application, the magistrates, their clerk, his assistant, and the defendants' reporter. It was also proved that the defendants had published the report in the ordinary course of their business, and that they had subsequently published a fair and accurate report of the hearing of the summons when the charge against the plaintiff was dismissed as being wholly without foundation. Upon these facts Hawkins, J., non-suited the plaintiff, and this decision was upheld by the Court of Appeal.

(*l*) (1878), 3 C. P. D. 319; 47 L. J. C. P. 323; 38 L. T. 65.
(*m*) (1796), 1 B. & P. 525; 1 Esp. 456.
(*n*) (1858), 27 L. J. Q. B. 282; E. B. & E. 537.
(*o*) (1878), 3 C. P. D. 319; 47 L. J. C. P. 323; 38 L. T. 65.
(*p*) (1892), 8 Times L. R. 671; (1893), 1 Q. B. 65 (C. A.).

NOTE 3.—*Fair and accurate.* It is not necessary that the report should be verbatim, but it must be "substantially a fair account of what took place" in Court (*q*). Thus, "it is sufficient to publish a fair abstract" (*r*). A report is not fair and accurate which contains an epitome of the speeches of counsel, but omits all reference to the evidence (*s*), or only refers to it by stating that the witnesses "proved all that had been stated by the counsel for the prosecution" (*t*); or which states that certain facts appeared from the evidence, when in reality no evidence had been given of such facts (*u*); or which states "from inquiries made by our reporter, &c., &c.," when in fact the reporter had not made inquiries, but had merely copied certain affidavits (*x*). A report which only consists of part of the judgment, material parts of which are omitted, is of course not privileged (*y*). If possible, the summing up of the learned judge should always be given, although this will not protect a report which

(*q*) *Per* Lord Campbell, C. J., in *Andrews* v. *Chapman* (1853), 3 C. & K. 289.
(*r*) *Per* Mellish, L. J., in *Milissich* v. *Lloyds* (1877), 46 L. J. C. P. 404.
(*s*) *Woodgate* v. *Ridout* (1865), 4 F. & F. 202.
(*t*) *Lewis* v. *Walter* (1821), 4 B. & Ald. 605; *Roberts* v. *Brown* (1834), 10 Bing. 519; 6 C. & P. 757.
(*u*) *Pinero* v. *Goodlake* (1866), 15 L. T. 676; *Ashmore* v. *Borthwick* (1885), 49 J. P. 792; 2 Times L. R. 113, 209.
(*x*) *Reg.* v. *Andrew Gray* (1861), 26 J. P. 663.
(*y*) *Hayward & Co.* v. *Hayward & Sons* (1886), 34 Ch. D. 198; 56 L. J. Ch. 287; *Grimwade* v. *Dicks* (1886), 2 Times L. R. 627.

contains in addition such an account of the proceedings at the trial as renders the report taken as a whole unfair and inaccurate (z). As regards the report of a judgment standing by itself, it would appear that "a fair and accurate report of the judgment in an action, published *bonâ fide* and without malice, is privileged, although not accompanied by any report of the evidence given at the trial" (a).

The report must be strictly confined to what actually took place in Court. The reporter must not add any comments of his own; if he does, no privilege will attach thereto (b). "If any comments are made, they should not be made as part of the report. The report should be confined to what takes place in Court, and the two things, report and comment, should be kept separate" (c).

The report of a trial should never be preceded by a title which exaggerates the real facts of the case. If it is, even though the report itself is fair and accurate, damages may be recovered for the libellous title. Thus, damages have been recovered for heading the report of a case

(z) *Milissich* v. *Lloyds* (1877), 46 L. J. C. P. 404; 36 L. T. 423; 13 Cox, C. C. 575.

(a) *Per* Fry, L. J., in *Macdougall* v. *Knight* (1890), L. R. 25 Q. B. D. at p. 11. See, however, the observations of the Lord Chancellor and Lord Bramwell in *Macdougall* v. *Knight* (1889), 14 App. Cas. at pp. 200–203.

(b) *Cooper* v. *Lawson* (1838), 8 A. & E. 746; 2 Jur. 919.

(c) *Per* Lord Campbell, C. J., in *Andrews* v. *Chapman* (1853), 3 C. & K. at p. 288.

118   THE LAW OF LIBEL AND SLANDER.

" Judicial Delinquency " (*d*), " Shameful conduct of an attorney " (*e*), " An honest lawyer " (*f*), " Wilful and corrupt perjury " (*g*) ; the facts in each case not justifying the imputations contained in the heading (*h*).

ART. 29.—Extracts from registers kept pursuant to statute.

The publication of an extract from a register kept pursuant to statute is privileged, provided that it is fair and accurate, but such privilege will be rebutted by proof that defendant published such extract maliciously (*i*).

NOTE.—" Where there is a register kept by virtue of an Act of Parliament for the purpose of giving information to the public, then, if a person makes a copy of it and publishes it, although he

(*d*) *Stiles* v. *Nokes* (1806), 7 East, 493.
(*e*) *Clement* v. *Lewis and others* (1820), 3 Br. & Bing. 297 ; 7 Moore, 200 ; *Bishop* v. *Latimer* (1861), 4 L. T. 775.
(*f*) *Boydell* v. *Jones* (1838), 7 Dowl. 210 ; 1 Horn & H. 408 ; 4 M. & W. 446.
(*g*) *Lewis* v. *Levy* (1858), 27 L. J. Q. B. 282 ; E. B. & E. 537.
(*h*) See also p. 82, *supra*.
(*i*) *Fleming* v. *Newton* (1848), 1 H. L. C. 343 ; *Annaly* v. *Trade Auxiliary Co., Ld.* (1890), 26 L. R. Ir. 394. As to the meaning of " maliciously," see Article 38, p. 150, *infra*.

does so for the purpose of warning the public or tradesmen about to give credit, yet if all that he does is to publish a copy of the register which is intended to be a public document it is a privileged publication" (*k*). "The publication of a mere extract from a record of judgments kept pursuant to statute is on the same footing as a fair report of a judicial proceeding" (*l*), and is therefore privileged, unless the plaintiff can prove that it was published maliciously.

In order to come within the protection of the above rule, the extract must be fair and accurate. Thus it was held by a Divisional Court in the recent case of *Reiss* v. *Perry* (*m*), that there is no privilege for the publication of an inaccurate extract from a register kept, pursuant to the Deeds of Arrangement Act, 1887, even though the extract in question was supplied by a Government official under sect. 12 of the Act, and was thought by the defendant to be a correct copy of the register.

As examples of publications within the protection of the above rule may be mentioned the

(*k*) *Per* Lord Esher, M. R., in *Searles* v. *Scarlett* (1892), L. R. 2 Q. B. at p. 60, confirming *Fleming* v. *Newton* (1848), 1 H. L. C. 363, *q. v.*

(*l*) *Per* Pollock, B., in *Williams* v. *Smith* (1888), L. R. 22 Q. B. D. at p. 139. This case was tried before the Law of Libel Amendment Act 1888 became law, and therefore the learned judge was referring to the qualified privilege which fair reports of judicial proceedings have always obtained at common law. See p. 114, *supra*.

(*m*) (1895), 11 Times L. R. 373.

publication by trade or mercantile journals of receiving orders under the Bankruptcy Act, extracts from registers of bills of sale, County Court judgments, &c.

ART. 30.—**Reports of proceedings in parliament.**

A report of proceedings in either House of Parliament is privileged, provided that it is fair and accurate; but such privilege will be rebutted, if plaintiff prove that defendant published such report maliciously (n).

NOTE.—The above rule was for a long time doubtful, but it is now clearly and satisfactorily settled by *Wason* v. *Walter* (o), in which case the plaintiff sued the proprietor of the *Times* for publishing a report of a debate in the House of Lords commenting severely on plaintiff's conduct in procuring the presentation of a petition to the House of Lords, which charged a high judicial officer with misconduct, and it was held that the report was privileged.

(n) *Wason* v. *Walter* (1868), L. R. 4 Q. B. 73; 38 L. J. Q. B. 34. As to the meaning of *fair and accurate* and *maliciously*, see respectively p. 116, *supra*, and p. 150, *infra*.

(o) (1868), L. R. 4 Q. B. 73; 38 L. J. Q. B. 34.

Art. 31.—Reports of proceedings of public meetings.

A report published in any newspaper of the proceedings of a meeting bonâ fide and lawfully held for a lawful purpose and for the furtherance or discussion of any matter of public concern, whether the admission thereto be general or restricted, is privileged, provided that—(1) the report is fair and accurate; (2) the matter complained of is not blasphemous or indecent; and (3) the matter complained of is of public concern, or the publication thereof is for the public benefit.

This privilege may be rebutted by proof (1) that the report was published maliciously; or (2) that the defendant has after request refused or neglected to insert in his newspaper a reasonable letter or statement by way of contradiction or explanation of such report (p).

Note 1.—The law contained in this article was introduced by s. 4 of the Law of Libel Amendment Act of 1888.

In order to establish privilege for the publication of proceedings at a public meeting, the defendant will have to prove (a) that the report is fair and accurate; (b) that the meeting was *bonâ fide* and lawfully held for a lawful purpose,

---

(p) 51 & 52 Vict. c. 64, s. 4, pp. 265-266, *infra*. As to the meaning of *newspaper*, see p. 109, *supra*; and of the words *fair and accurate* and *maliciously*, p. 116, *supra*, and p. 150, *infra*, respectively.

and for the furtherance or discussion of any matter of public concern; (c) that the matter complained of is of public concern, *or* that the publication of the matter complained of is for the public benefit.

There has been a great deal of discussion as to whether it will be necessary, in order to establish privilege for the publication in a newspaper of any of the proceedings specified in sect. 4 of the Act of 1888, to prove (1) that the matter is of public concern, *and* (2) that the publication thereof is for the public benefit; or whether it will be sufficient to prove either (1) or (2). At first sight the former construction appears to be the correct one, but it is submitted that a careful consideration of the words of the section (*q*) will prove that this is not so. In support of the latter contention, an opinion of counsel has been published to the effect that "it is impossible to give a very confident opinion as to the construction which will finally be put upon the clause; but on the whole it will probably be held that a fair and accurate report in a newspaper of the proceedings of any of the meetings specified is protected, where either the matter is of public concern or the publication is for the public benefit. For the privilege is only taken away where the matter is *not* of public concern, and the publication of it is *not* for the public benefit; and if so, it follows that where either it is of

(*q*) Set out at pp. 265–266, *infra.*

public concern *or* for the public benefit the privilege exists" (*r*).

This opinion is confirmed by a consideration of the clause in the same section which deals with blasphemous or indecent matter. That clause contains two provisos—a proviso that no blasphemous matter shall be protected, and a proviso that no indecent matter shall be protected—consequently the privilege will be taken away if it be proved that the matter is blasphemous, *or* if it be proved that the matter is indecent. On the other hand, the clause dealing with the question under discussion is really only one proviso consisting of two terms, both of which must co-exist in order that the proviso may apply and the privilege be taken away; and should only one of them exist, the proviso fails to apply and the privilege remains. In other words, the Act does not give any new protection where two blemishes occur, the first being that the matter is not of public concern, the second that the publication of it is not for the public benefit.

The effect of the two clauses may be presented in the following tabular form :

I. " Provided that there shall be no privilege where—
(a) the matter is blasphemous, *or*
(b) the matter is indecent."
Therefore if either condition (a) or (b) is satisfied there is no privilege.

(*r*) Times, January 11th, 1889.

II. "Provided that there shall be no privilege where—
   (A) the matter is not of public concern, *and*
   (B) the publication of it is not for the public benefit."

Therefore if condition (A) or (B) is satisfied there is privilege.

One case only has been hitherto reported under this section—*Kelly* v. *O'Malley and others* (*s*)—where the facts were as follows:—A meeting of dock labourers was held for the purpose of discussing the sugar bounties, and the plaintiff had attempted to speak to the meeting, but was unable to do so owing to the noisy and derisive observations of certain persons who had known him some years previously at Bristol, and who were present at the meeting with the express object of preventing him from addressing it. An accurate report of the proceedings appeared in the *Star*, containing, *inter alia*, the substance of the noisy and derisive observations, which had no connection whatever with the sugar bounties, but referred to events which had happened at Bristol some twelve years previously. Mr. Baron Huddleston left it to the jury to say whether such events were matters of public concern, and whether their publication was for the public benefit, and the jury answered both questions in the negative. The point discussed above was not raised by

(*s*) (1889) 6 Times L. R. 62.

counsel on either side, and the learned judge expressed no opinion thereon. In its practical aspect the discussion is perhaps somewhat useless, for it is difficult to imagine any libellous matter of public concern the publication of which would not be for the public benefit, or any libellous matter of private concern which it would be for the public benefit to publish. It is possible that the point may never be judicially decided, for the case of *Pankhurst* v. *Sowler* (t) seems to show that the question is for the jury, not for the judge; and it is most probable that any jury which finds that the matter is of public concern would also find that its publication was for the public benefit.

NOTE 2.—*A meeting bonâ fide and lawfully held for a lawful purpose, and for the furtherance or discussion of any matter of public concern, whether the admission thereto be general or restricted.* The last words of this clause would apparently cover reports of meetings not in the widest sense public, *e.g.*, of meetings to which admission can only be obtained by ticket, provided, of course, that the object of the meeting is lawful and for the furtherance or discussion of any matter of public concern. Probably, also, reports of meetings held at a private house of the same nature at which persons were only present by invitation would be included. The meeting must be "*bonâ fide* . . . *held,*" *i.e.*, it must not be held for the mere purpose of

(t) (1887), 3 Times L. R. 193.

defamation—consequently, the report of any meeting, if the jury were satisfied that it had been held for such purpose, would not be protected. Moreover, the meeting must be "*lawfully held*," *i.e.*, it must not be held in violation of the law, *e.g.*, in contravention of the statutes against tumultuously petitioning Parliament (*u*); and "*for a lawful purpose;*" thus it must not be illegal (*x*), or seditious (*y*), or held under such circumstances as will probably cause a breach of the peace (*z*). It has been held (*a*) that a chapel service is not a "public meeting" within the meaning of the Act, although it had been advertised that the sermon would be preached.

NOTE 3.—*The publication thereof is for the public benefit;* in other words, it is not enough that the report is fair and accurate, and that it is for the public benefit that reports of meetings of the same kind as this particular meeting should be published, *e.g.*, that it is an accurate report of a political meeting—to obtain protection under this head it must be proved that the publication of the very words complained of is for the public benefit. This imposes

(*u*) 13 Car. 2, c. 5; 1 W. & M. sess. 2, c. 2; 57 Geo. 3, c. 19, s. 23.

(*x*) *Rex* v. *Birt and others* (1834), 5 C. & P. 154; *Rex* v. *Fursey* (1835), 6 C. & P. 81.

(*y*) *Redford* v. *Birley and others* (1822), 3 Stark. 103.

(*z*) *Rex* v. *Hunt and others* (1819), 3 B. & Ald. 566; *Reg.* v. *Vincent* (1838), 9 C. & P. 91, 109.

(*a*) *Chaloner* v. *Lansdown & Sons* (1894), 10 Times L. R. 290.

on every editor the duty of editing the whole paper; he must not trust to the proved accuracy of his reporter; he must himself read through the report, and be careful to eliminate all blasphemous, seditious and obscene matter (*b*), every unfair attack on a public man, everything defamatory of a private individual. No doubt this is almost a practical impossibility in the case of a daily paper, where the type has to be set up with the greatest possible speed; but, nevertheless, it seems to be clear law, according to the decision in *Pankhurst* v. *Sowler* (*c*), that unless this is done the proprietors will be liable to an action for libel.

ART. 32.—**Reports of vestry meetings, &c.**

A report published in any newspaper (*d*) *of any meeting of a vestry, town council, school board, board of guardians, board or local authority formed or constituted under the provisions of any Act of Parliament* (*e*), *or of any committee appointed by any of the above-mentioned bodies, or of any meeting of any commissioners authorized to act by letters patent, Act of Parliament, warrant under the Royal Sign Manual,*

(*b*) *Steele* v. *Brannan* (1872), L. R. 7 C. P. 261; 41 L. J. M. C. 85.
(*c*) (1887), 3 Times L. R. 193.
(*d*) As to the meaning of "newspaper," see p. 109, *supra*.
(*e*) This would cover the report of the meeting of a county council.

128   THE LAW OF LIBEL AND SLANDER.

or other lawful warrant or authority, or of select committees of either House of Parliament (f), is privileged, provided that—
  (1.) *Such report is fair and accurate (g);*
  (2.) *The public or a newspaper reporter was admitted, or given an opportunity of admission, to such meeting;*
  (3.) *The matter complained of is not blasphemous or indecent; and*
  (4.) *The matter complained of is of public concern, or the publication thereof is for the public benefit (h).*

This privilege may be rebutted by proof (1) that the report was published maliciously; or (2) that the defendant has after request refused or neglected to insert in his newspaper a reasonable letter or statement by way of contradiction or explanation of such report (i).

NOTE 1.—*The public or a newspaper reporter was admitted,* or given an opportunity of admission, *to such meeting.* It is submitted that the insertion of the words in ordinary type is in accordance with

(*f*) See *Rex* v. *Wright* (1799), 8 T. R. 293. The 4th section of the Law of Libel Amendment Act, 1888 (51 & 52 Vict. c. 64), also protected reports " of any meeting . . . . of justices of the peace in quarter sessions assembled, for administrative or deliberate purposes." These functions of the justices were, however, transferred by the Local Government Act, 1888, to the county councils.
  (*g*) See p. 116, *et seq.*
  (*h*) See Note 3, p. 126, *supra.*
  (*i*) 51 & 52 Vict. c. 64, s. 4, set out on pp. 265–266, *infra.*

and justified by the true construction of the 4th section of the Law of Libel Amendment Act, 1888 (*k*).

NOTE 2.—It must be remembered that the report of any such meeting as the above, if published elsewhere than in a newspaper, as defined by the Newspaper Libel and Registration Act, 1881, *e.g.*, in a magazine or a monthly trade paper, is in no way privileged (*l*). Moreover, no report of any meeting other than those dealt with in Articles 30, 31, and 32 (*m*), is privileged, whether published in a newspaper or elsewhere. Thus, if a newspaper or periodical publishes a fair and accurate report of the proceedings at a meeting of the creditors of a bankrupt or the shareholders of a company, such report is in no way privileged, and anyone defamed thereby can maintain an action for libel. In such a case the defendant has only two courses open to him—to justify the words complained of (*n*), or to apologise and pay money into Court (*o*). The fact that the report is a fair and accurate account of what actually took place is no defence (*p*), though it may operate to mitigate the damages (*q*).

(*k*) See pp. 265, 266, *infra*.
(*l*) See p. 109, *supra*.
(*m*) pp. 120–128, *supra*.
(*n*) See p. 81, *supra*.
(*o*) See p. 156, *infra*.
(*p*) *Davidson* v. *Duncan* (1857), 26 L. J. Q. B. 104; 28 L. T. O. S. 265; 7 E. & B. 229.
(*q*) *Duncombe* v. *Daniell* (1837), 8 C. & P. 222; *per* Wightman, J., in *Davis* v. *Cutbush* (1859), 1 F. & F. 487; and see pp. 169, 170, *infra*.

Art. 33.—**Notices and reports published at request of Government office or authority.**

The publication at the request of (1) *any government office or department*, (2) *officer of state*, (3) *commissioner of police, or* (4) *chief constable, of any notice or report issued by them for the information of the public, is privileged, provided that* (i.) *the matter complained of is not blasphemous or indecent; and* (ii.) *the matter complained of is of public concern, or the publication thereof is for the public benefit. But this privilege may be rebutted by proof* (1) *that such publication was published or made maliciously; or* (2) *that the defendant has, after request, refused or neglected to insert in his newspaper a reasonable letter or statement by way of contradiction or explanation of such publication* (r).

Note.—It will be observed that this Article only deals with notices or reports published *at the request of any Government office or authority.*

Two points should be noticed—

(1.) That the publication of a notice or report issued by any other body, *e.g.*, a vestry, is not privileged until officially published; and it would seem that this is so, even where official publication is authorized by Act of Parliament (s).

(2.) That the publication of all reports, papers,

(r) 51 & 52 Vict. c. 64, s. 4, set out on pp. 265, 266, *infra.*
(s) *Popham* v. *Pickburn* (1862), 31 L. J. Ex. 133; 5 L. T. 846.

votes, and proceedings by order of either House of Parliament is absolutely privileged (*t*).

Art. 34.—Statements made in order to redress public grievances or punish crime.

Every statement made to a public servant or to other person in authority with the object of redressing a public grievance or preventing or punishing crime is privileged, but such privilege will be rebutted if plaintiff prove that defendant made such statement maliciously.

Note.—Thus every communication affecting a Government official is privileged, provided it is addressed to the proper person, *e.g.*, a letter written to the Postmaster-General concerning the conduct of a postmaster (*u*); or to a bishop concerning the conduct of a parson in his diocese (*x*); or a memorial to the Lord Chancellor concerning the conduct of a magistrate, and praying for his removal (*y*); or a petition to the House of Commons concerning the conduct of the Vicar-General (*z*), or to the Privy Council concerning

(*t*) 3 & 4 Vict. c. 9; *supra*, p. 106.
(*u*) *Blake* v. *Pilfold* (1832), 1 Moo. & Rob. 198; *Woodward* v. *Lander* (1834), 6 C. & P. 548.
(*x*) *James* v. *Boston* (1845), 2 C. & K. 4.
(*y*) *Harrison* v. *Bush* (1855), 5 E. & B. 344; 25 L. J. Q. B. 25, 99.
(*z*) *Lake* v. *King* (1669), 1 Lev. 240; 1 Saund. 131; Sid. 414.

a sanitary inspector removable by them (*a*), or to the Secretary of War, with the object of compelling a military officer to pay a debt (*b*).

So, too, everything *bonâ fide* said or written to the proper person with the object of preventing or punishing crime is, in the interests of society, privileged. Thus, it has been held that anything honestly communicated for that purpose to the master (*c*) or father (*d*) of the plaintiff, or to a constable (*e*), is privileged.

But if the statement is not honestly made with this object (*f*), or is made recklessly (*g*), or to more persons than necessary (*h*), or by (*i*) or to (*k*) some one unconnected with the matter, there will be no privilege (*l*).

Moreover, if such a communication is made to a person who has no interest or duty in regard to the subject-matter of the communication, the occasion will not be privileged, even though the

---

(*a*) *Proctor* v. *Webster* (1885), 16 Q. B. D. 112; 55 L. J. Q. B. 150; 53 L. T. 765.

(*b*) *Fairman* v. *Ives* (1822), 5 B. & Ald. 642.

(*c*) *Kine* v. *Sewell* (1838), 3 M. & W. 297; *Amann* v. *Damm* (1860), 8 C. B. N. S. 597; 8 W. R. 470.

(*d*) *Fowler et ux.* v. *Homer* (1812), 3 Camp. 294.

(*e*) *Johnson* v. *Evans* (1800), 3 Esp. 32.

(*f*) *Hooper* v. *Trustcott* (1836), 2 Bing. N. S. 457; 2 Scott, 672.

(*g*) *Smith* v. *Hodgeskins* (1633), Cro. Car. 276.

(*h*) *Jones* v. *Williams* (1885), 1 Times L. R. 572.

(*i*) *Harrison* v. *Fraser* (1881), 29 W. R. 662.

(*k*) *Hebditch* v. *McIlwaine* (1894), 2 Q. B. 54.

(*l*) *Padmore* v. *Lawrence* (1840), 11 A. & E. 380; *Jones* v. *Thomas* (1885), 34 W. R. 104; 53 L. T. 678; 2 Times L. R. 95.

defendant *bonâ fide* and reasonably believed that such person had such an interest or duty (*m*).

ART. 35.—Statements made in order to protect interest of writer or speaker.

Every statement made with the object of protecting some interest of the writer (n), or speaker (o), and reasonably necessary for such purpose, is privileged, but such privilege will be rebutted if plaintiff prove that defendant published such statement maliciously.

NOTE.—Thus, if the plaintiff has previously attacked the defendant, any statement made by the latter which is necessary in order to protect himself, and which is in any way relevant to the accusations made against him by the plaintiff, is privileged.

"If a man *bonâ fide* writes a letter in his own defence, and for the defence and protection of his interests and rights, and is not actuated by any malice, that letter is privileged, although it may impute dishonesty to another, but in such cases malice may either be proved by the letter itself

---

(*m*) *Hebditch* v. *McIlwane* (1894), 2 Q. B. 54.
(*n*) *Blackam* v. *Pugh* (1846), 2 C. B. 611; 15 L. J. C. P. 90.
(*o*) *Somerville* v. *Hawkins* (1851), 10 C. B. 583; 20 L. J. C. P. 131; 16 L. T. O. S. 283; *Manby* v. *Witt*, and *Eastmead* v. *Witt* (1856), 18 C. B. 544; 25 L. J. C. P. 294.

or by other evidence" (*p*); *e.g.*, where the policy holder of an insurance company published a pamphlet charging the directors with fraud, and the directors published a pamphlet in reply defending themselves, and accusing the plaintiff of making false and calumnious accusations, and further stating that he had upon a certain occasion made statements on oath in direct contradiction of statements which he had previously made in writing, it was left to the jury to say whether the counter-charges made by the defendants were made *bonâ fide*, and whether they went beyond the occasion, and the jury found for the defendants (*q*). So, too, where the plaintiff has previously attacked the defendant in the newspapers (*r*), or in public (*s*), and the defendant retaliates by publishing in the papers in self-defence a statement of the case from his point of view, and in so doing makes defamatory statements concerning the plaintiff, such statement is privileged if made *bonâ fide*.

Again, if the plaintiff has enticed the defendant into making the defamatory statement in the presence of a third party (*t*), or if a friend

(*p*) *Per* Littledale, J., in *Coward* v. *Wellington* (1836), 7 C. & P. at p. 586.

(*q*) *Kœnig* v. *Ritchie* (1862), 3 F. & F. 413; *Reg.* v. *Veley* (1867), 4 F. & F. 1117.

(*r*) *Coward* v. *Wellington* (1836), 7 C. & P. 531.

(*s*) *Laughton* v. *Bishop of Sodor and Man* (1872), L. R. 4 P. C. 495; 42 L. J. P. C. 11.

(*t*) *Kine* v. *Sewell* (1838), 3 M. & W. 297; *Griffiths* v. *Lewis* (1846), 7 Q. B. 67; 14 L. J. Q. B. 249; *Palmer* v. *Hummerston* (1883), 1 Cab. & E. 36.

or agent of the plaintiff at his request (*u*), or with his knowledge or consent (*x*), has induced the defendant to make the statement complained of, such statement is privileged. If, however, the defendant first made unprivileged statements concerning the plaintiff which led the latter to seek for an explanation from the defendant, such explanation will not be privileged (*y*).

The privilege noticed above has also been held to apply to any statement which is necessary to protect the interests of a principal (*z*) or client (*a*), and the fact that such statement is unauthorized will not destroy the privilege (*b*).

All privilege will, however, be lost if the statement is too widely published (*c*), or is unnecessarily strong (*d*); if, for example, the defendant has been attacked by the plaintiff in an obscure local paper and retaliates in a leading London paper, or the retaliation goes beyond what is actually necessary in order to protect the plaintiff's

---

(*u*) *Weatherston* v. *Hawkins* (1786), 1 T. R. 110.

(*x*) *Smith* v. *Wood* (1813), 3 Camp. 323; *Hopwood* v. *Thorn* (1850), 8 C. B. 293; 19 L. J. C. P. 94; *Whiteley* v. *Adams* (1863), 15 C. B. N. S. 392; 33 L. J. C. P. 89.

(*y*) *Smith* v. *Matthews* (1831), 1 Moo. & Rob. 151.

(*z*) *Hargrave* v. *Le Breton* (1769), 4 Burr. 2422.

(*a*) *Steward* v. *Young* (1870), L. R. 5 C. P. 122; 39 L. J. C. P. 85.

(*b*) *Watson* v. *Reynolds* (1826), Moo. & Mal. 1.

(*c*) *Jones* v. *Williams* (1885), 1 Times L. R. 572.

(*d*) *Cooke* v. *Wildes* (1855), 5 E. & B. 328; 24 L. J. Q. B. 367; *Huntley* v. *Ward* (1859), 1 F. & F. 552; 6 C. B. N. S. 514.

interests (*e*). And the honest belief of the defendant that the statement complained of is necessary for his own protection or that of his principal or client will not in itself render the occasion privileged. It must be in fact reasonably necessary that the statement in question should be made (*f*).

ART. 36.—**Statements made in order to protect a common interest.**

Every statement made with the object of protecting an interest common to the writer or speaker, and the person to whom such statement is made, and reasonably necessary for such purpose, is privileged, but such privilege will be rebutted if plaintiff prove that defendant made such statement maliciously.

NOTE.—" If the communication was of such a nature that it could be fairly said that those who made it had an interest in making such a communication, and those to whom it was made had a corresponding interest in having it made to them,—when those two things co-exist, the occasion is a privileged one " (*g*).

(*e*) *Robertson* v. *M'Dougall* (1828), 4 Bing. 670 ; 3 C. & P. 259; *Tuson* v. *Evans* (1840), 12 A. & E. 733; *Hancock* v. *Case* (1862), 2 F. & F. 711.

(*f*) *Hebditch* v. *McIlwaine* (1894), 2 Q. B. 54.

(*g*) Per Lord Esher, M. R., in *Hunt* v. *G. N. Rail. Co.* (1891), 2 Q. B. at p. 191.

STATEMENTS TO PROTECT COMMON INTEREST. 137

This common interest may be in respect of very varied and different matters, indeed, the only limitation appears to be that it should be something legitimate and proper, something which the Courts will take cognizance of, and not merely an interest which is due to idle curiosity or a desire for gossip (*h*). Thus, it was held that the occasion was privileged in the following cases :— A letter written by a ratepayer affecting the character of the parish constable, to be read at a parish meeting at which the accounts of the parish were to be considered (*i*); an accusation made by a parishioner, before justices sitting in special sessions, objecting to the plaintiff who was about to be sworn in as parish constable (*k*); charges made at a parish meeting for the nomination of officers as to the previous conduct in office of a parish officer seeking re-election (*l*); anything said by a life governor of a school, to its steward, concerning one of the tradesmen employed to supply the school (*m*); correspondence between a curate of one parish and incumbent of another, as to the character of a parishioner of the latter who had formerly lived in the parish in which such curate worked (*n*); a bishop's charge to his

(*h*) Per Coltman, J., in *Rumsey* v. *Webb et ux.* (1842), Car. & M. at p. 105; *Botterill and another* v. *Whytehead* (1879), 41 L. T. 588.
(*i*) *Spencer* v. *Amerton* (1835), 1 Moo. & Rob. 470.
(*k*) *Kershaw* v. *Bailey* (1848), 1 Ex. 743; 17 L. J. Ex. 129.
(*l*) *George* v. *Goddard* (1861), 2 F. & F. 689.
(*m*) *Humphreys* v. *Stilwell* (1861), 2 F. & F. 590.
(*n*) *Whiteley* v. *Adams* (1864), 15 C. B. N. S. 392; 33 L. J. C. P. 89.

clergy (*o*); communications between vicar and curate as to ecclesiastical matters (*p*); statements made by a member of a Trade Protection Society in pursuance of the rules of such society to the secretary concerning the conduct of another member (*q*); a letter written by one creditor who had been appointed the trustee in liquidation of a debtor's estate to another creditor (*r*), or by a solicitor acting for certain shareholders of a company to other shareholders (*s*); communications made to a lady by a relation or connection as to the character of her intended husband (*t*).

But in all these cases the privilege will be lost if the statement is made to an unnecessarily large number of persons (*u*); thus, where the defendant published an advertisement in a public paper, reflecting strongly on the character of the plaintiff, who had been adjudicated bankrupt, it was

---

(*o*) *Laughton* v. *Bishop of Sodor and Man* (1872), L. R. 4 P. C. 495; 42 L. J. C. P. 11.

(*p*) *Clark* v. *Molyneux* (1877), 3 Q. B. D. 237; 47 L. J. Q. B. 230; 14 Cox, C. C. 10.

(*q*) *White and others* v. *Batey and Co. Ld. and another* (1892), 8 Times L. R. 698.

(*r*) *Spill* v. *Maule* (1869), L. R. 4 Ex. 232; 38 L. J. Ex. 138.

(*s*) *Quartz Hill Gold Mining Co.* v. *Beall* (1882), 20 Ch. D. 501; 51 L. J. Ch. 874.

(*t*) *Todd* v. *Hawkins* (1837), 8 C. & P. 88; 2 M. & Rob. 20.

(*u*) *Toogood* v. *Spyring* (1834), 1 C. M. & R. 181; *Duncombe* v. *Daniell* (1836), 8 C. & P. 222; *Martin* v. *Strong* (1836), 5 Ad. & E. 535; *Hoare* v. *Silverlock* (1848), 12 Q. B. 624; 17 L. J. Q. B. 306; *Parsons* v. *Surgey* (1864), 4 F. & F. 247.

held that such a publication was in no way privileged, although published with the avowed intention of convening a meeting of the creditors for the purpose of consulting upon the measures proper to be adopted for their own security (*x*). " A communication sufficient for the purpose," said Lord Ellenborough (*y*), " might have been made in measured language. The want of proper caution had rendered the publication actionable, as being published to the world at large."

In such a case the fact that the defendant believed in the truth of the defamatory statement which he was making will afford him no defence. "I am clearly of opinion," said Kelly, C. B., in *Botterill* v. *Whytehead* (*z*), " that if a man should receive information which is injurious if true to the character of another, he is not justified in publishing that information to the prejudice of him to whom it relates, merely because he believes it to be true." Nor is it any defence that the defendant *bonâ fide* believed that the occasion was privileged when in fact it was not (*a*).

So, too, there will be no privilege if the statement contains exaggerated and unwarrantable expressions (*b*).

And where part of the communication extends

(*x*) *Brown* v. *Croome* (1817), 2 Stark. 297.
(*y*) *Ibid.* at p. 301.
(*z*) (1879), 41 L. T. at p. 590.
(*a*) *Hebditch* v. *McIlwaine* (1894), 2 Q. B. 54.
(*b*) *Bromage* v. *Prosser* (1825), 4 B. & C. 247; *Fryer* v. *Kinnersley* (1863), 15 C. B. N. S. 422; 33 L. J. C. P. 96.

to matters outside those matters in which the plaintiff and defendant have a common interest, such part will not be protected. Thus, where the plaintiff and defendant were jointly interested in property in Scotland of which C. was manager, and the defendant wrote to C. a letter principally about the property and the conduct of the plaintiff with reference thereto, but containing a charge against the plaintiff with reference to his conduct to his mother and aunt; it was held that though the part of the letter about the plaintiff's conduct as to the property might be confidential and privileged, such privilege could not extend to the part of the letter about the plaintiff's conduct to his mother and aunt (c).

The privilege will not, however, be lost by the publication to printer's men who set up the type, provided that printing is necessary (d).

ART. 37.—**Statements made in discharge of a duty.**

Every statement made in discharge of a legal, moral, or social duty, and reasonably necessary for the due discharge of such duty, is privileged, but such privilege will be rebutted if plaintiff prove that defendant made such statement maliciously.

(c) *Warren* v. *Warren* (1834), 1 C. M. & R. 250.
(d) *Davis* v. *Cutbush and others* (1859), 1 F. & F. 487; *Lawless* v. *Anglo-Egyptian Cotton Co.* (1869), L. R. 4 Q. B. 262; 10 B. & S. 226; 38 L. J. Q. B. 129.

STATEMENTS IN DISCHARGE OF DUTY. 141

NOTE.—" The rule is this, that when the circumstances are such as to cast on the defendant the duty of making the communication to a third party, the occasion is privileged" (*e*).

"The duty may be legal, social, or moral" (*f*).

"Where," says Blackburn, J. (*g*), "the person is so situated that it becomes right in the interests of society that he should tell to a third person certain facts, then if he *bonâ fide* and without malice does tell them, it is a privileged communication." Thus, where a person answers an inquiry *bonâ fide* and without malice, the answer is a privileged communication. And this is true of every answer to a confidential inquiry, for " every one owes it as a duty to his fellow-men to state what he knows about a person when inquiry is made" (*h*). Further, "when once a confidential relation is established between two persons with regard to an inquiry of a private nature, whatever takes place between them relevant to the same subject, though at a time and place different from those at which the confidential relation began, may be entitled to protection as well as what

(*e*) *Per* Lopes, L. J., in *Pullman* v. *Hill & Co.* (1891), 1 Q. B. at p. 530.

(*f*) *Per* Lopes, L. J., in *Stuart* v. *Bell* (1891), 2 Q. B. at p. 353. See also *per* Williams, J., in *Fryer* v. *Kinnersley* (1863), 33 L. J. C. P. at p. 98.

(*g*) *Davies* v. *Snead* (1870), L. R. 5 Q. B. 611; 39 L. J. Q. B. 202, cited with approval by Jessel, M. R., and Brett, L. J., in *Waller* v. *Loch* (1881), 7 Q. B. D. 621, 622; 51 L. J. Q. B. 274.

(*h*) *Per* Grove, J., in *Robshaw* v. *Smith* (1878), 38 L. T. at p. 423.

passed at the original interview, and it is a question for the jury whether any further conversation on the same subject, though apparently casual and voluntary, does not take place under the influence of the confidential relation already established between them, and is, therefore, entitled to the same protection " (*i*).

Even if volunteered, the communication may fall within the protection of the general rule laid down above, for "it is not necessary in all cases that the information should be given in answer to an inquiry" (*k*). "Even in this case, the jury is to consider whether the words were dictated by a sense of duty" (*l*). Under such circumstances it will, of course, be more difficult for the defendant to satisfy a jury that in making the communication he was not actuated by malice (*m*).

Under this head of privilege come communications as to the characters of clerks and servants. "There is no law to compel the master to give the servant a character; it might be a duty which his feelings might prompt him to perform, but there is no law to enforce the doing of it" (*n*). If, however, he does it, he must do it honestly,

(*i*) *Per* Pollock, C. B., in *Beatson* v. *Skene* (1860), 29 L. J. Ex. at p. 438.

(*k*) *Per* Jessel, M. R., in *Waller* v. *Loch* (1881), 7 Q. B. D. 621; 51 L. J. Q. B. 274.

(*l*) *Per* Coltman, J., in *Rumsey* v. *Webb et ux.* (1842), Car. & M. at p. 105.

(*m*) *Pattison* v. *Jones* (1828), 8 B. & C. 586; 3 C. & P. 387.

(*n*) *Per* Lord Kenyon, C. J., in *Carrol* v. *Bird* (1800), 3 Esp. at p. 202.

and then, even if the character be in fact untrue, the master will be protected (*o*).

" No action lies for giving the *true* character of a servant upon application made to his former master to inquire into his character with a view of hiring him, unless there should be extraordinary circumstances of express malice " (*p*).

Moreover, "if I have given a servant a good character, and I afterwards find that I have been deceived, I am bound to make the same communication then as I should have made before if the fact had been known to me" (*q*), and any such communication made *bonâ fide* will be privileged (*r*).

Again, if a master discharges one of his servants, and tells the others why he has done so, such communication will also be privileged (*s*).

Thus, where the plaintiff was a guard in the service of the defendants a railway company, and the defendants dismissed him on the ground that he had been guilty of gross neglect of duty, and published his name in a printed monthly circular addressed to their servants, stating in it that he

---

(*o*) *Rogers* v. *Clifton* (1803), 3 B. & P. 587; *Murdoch* v. *Funduklian* (1885), 2 Times L. R. 215, 614.

(*p*) *Per* Lord Mansfield in *Hargrave* v. *Le Breton* (1769), 4 Burr. at p. 2425.

(*q*) *Per* Coleridge, J., in *Gardner* v. *Slade and wife* (1849), 18 L. J. Q. B. at p. 336.

(*r*) *Ibid.*, and see *Child* v. *Affleck and wife* (1829), 9 B. & C. 403.

(*s*) *Somerville* v. *Hawkins* (1851), 10 C. B. 590; 20 L. J. C. P. 131.

had been dismissed and the ground of his dismissal, it was held that such circular was privileged if published *bonâ fide* and without malice towards the plaintiff (*t*).

A similar protection is extended to all communications made honestly, and on reasonable grounds, to a father or master as to the doings of his child (*u*) or servant (*x*); by one friend to another as to a doctor (*y*), or tradesman (*z*), or an intending suitor (*a*); by a servant to his master (*b*); by an under-master to the head master (*c*); by an official in the army or navy or any government office to his superior (*d*); by a master concerning his servant or a child entrusted to his charge to the parent or guardian of such servant or child (*e*); by a parishioner to the bishop of his diocese as to the conduct of the vicar (*f*) or curate, or *locum tenens*; by a parishioner to his vicar as to the conduct of his *locum*

(*t*) *Hunt* v. *G. N. Rail. Co.* (1891), 2 Q. B. 189.
(*u*) Per Erle, C. J., in *Whiteley* v. *Adams* (1863), 33 L. J. C. P. at p. 95.
(*x*) *Masters* v. *Burgess* (1886), 3 Times L. R. 96.
(*y*) *Dixon* v. *Smith* (1860), 29 L. J. Ex. 125; 5 H. & N. 450.
(*z*) *Storey* v. *Challands* (1837), 8 C. & P. ?34.
(*a*) 15 C. B. N. S. 410, 411.
(*b*) *Scarll* v. *Dixon* (1864), 4 F. & F. 250; *Mead* v. *Hughes and wife* (1891), 7 Times L. R. 291.
(*c*) *Hume* v. *Marshall* (1878), 42 J. P. 136.
(*d*) *Sutton* v. *Plumridge* (1867), 16 L. T. 741; *Stace* v. *Griffith* (1869), L. R. 2 P. C. 420; 20 L. T. 197; *Henwood* v. *Harrison* (1872), L. R. 7 C. P. 606; 41 L. J. C. P. 206.
(*e*) *Fowler and wife* v. *Homer* (1812), 3 Camp. 294.
(*f*) *James* v. *Boston* (1845), 2 C. & K. 4.

tenens or curate (*g*); by a ratepayer to a member of the Watch Committee as to the conduct of a superintendent of police (*h*); by the secretary of a charity organization society to a stranger as to the deserts of an applicant to such stranger for charity (*i*); by a member of a trade protection society to the secretary of the society (*k*); and by the director of a company to the members thereof concerning the character of an official of such company (*l*).

On the same ground " if a communication made by a solicitor to a third party is reasonably necessary and usual in the discharge of his duty to his client, and in the interests of his client, the occasion is privileged " (*m*).

It has also been held that the publication of the minutes of the General Council of Medical Education, containing a statement that the name of a specified medical practitioner has been removed from the register on the ground that, in the opinion of the Council, he has been guilty of

(*g*) *Clark* v. *Molyneux* (1877), 3 Q. B. D. 237; 47 L. J. Q. B. 230.
(*h*) *Bannister* v. *Kelly* (1895), 59 J. P. 793.
(*i*) *Waller* v. *Loch* (1881), 7 Q. B. D. 619; 51 L. J. Q. B. 274.
(*k*) *White and others* v. *Batey & Co., Ltd.* (1892), 8 Times L. R. 698.
(*l*) *Harris* v. *Thompson* (1853), 13 C. B. 333.
(*m*) Per Lopes, L. J., in *Boxsius* v. *Goblet Frères* (1894), 1 Q. B. at p. 846. See also *Wright* v. *Woodgate* (1835), 2 C. M. & R. 573, and *Baker* v. *Carrick* (1894), 1 Q. B. 838. As to communications made by a solicitor to his client, see p. 103, *supra*.

infamous conduct in a professional capacity, is, if the report be accurate, and published *bonâ fide* and without malice, privileged, and the medical practitioner cannot maintain an action of libel against the Council in respect of the publication (*n*).

Nor, as was held by the Court of Appeal in the recent case of *Andrews* v. *Nott Bower* (*o*), will an action lie in respect of statements contained in a report published *bonâ fide* and without malice by the head-constable of a borough in obedience to an order lawfully given to him by the magistrates of such borough. In delivering judgment in this case, Lord Esher, M. R., said (*p*): "I think the head-constable was obeying an order which the magistrates had power to give him, and which he was bound to obey. It was an order of a Court given to one of its officers with regard to the mode in which its business should be carried on. I am of opinion that the publication of the report was, under these circumstances, upon a privileged occasion."

But statements made by a clergyman as to the knowledge of an architect employed for church work are *not* privileged, such clergyman being in no way connected with the church in question, either as a subscriber towards the work or otherwise (*q*).

(*n*) *Allbutt* v. *General Council of Medical Education and Registration* (1889), 23 Q. B. D. 400.
(*o*) (1895), 1 Q. B. 888.
(*p*) *Ibid.*, at p. 894.
(*q*) *Botterill* v. *Whytehead* (1879), 41 L. T. 588.

As has been already pointed out, it is sometimes a matter of the greatest difficulty to determine whether an occasion is privileged or not. It was remarked by Lindley, L. J., in the Court of Appeal (r) : " *Coxhead* v. *Richards* (s), in which four eminent judges were equally divided upon the question whether an occasion was privileged or not, is a striking illustration of the truth of the remark. In that case the mate of a ship wrote to the defendant, a friend of his, a letter reflecting on the character of the captain. The defendant, who was a stranger to the owner of the ship, showed the letter to the owner; the owner dismissed the captain, who sued the defendant for libel. Tindal, C. J., and Erle, J., held the occasion privileged. Coltman and Cresswell, JJ., held that it was not. In *Amann* v. *Damm* (t) the late Willes, J., said he was fully prepared to go the whole length of the doctrine laid down by Tindal, C. J., and Erle, J., in *Coxhead* v. *Richards* (s). Lord Blackburn also approved of it in *Davies* v. *Snead* (u). Having carefully considered all the four judgments in that celebrated case *Coxhead* v. *Richards* (s), I have no hesitation in saying that the judgment of Tindal, C. J., is the one which carries conviction to my own mind, and is the one which I consider the most accurate and safe to take as a guide, nor am I aware of

(r) In *Stuart* v. *Bell* (1891), 2 Q. B. at p. 346.
(s) (1846), 2 C. B. 569.
(t) 8 C. B. (N. S.) 597.
(u) (1870), L. R. 5 Q. B. 608–611.

any subsequent case in which that judgment has been disapproved."

In all the above cases it must be remembered that "the belief of the defendant that there was a duty to make the communication is irrelevant to the question whether the occasion is privileged" (*x*), and further that the privilege does not extend to expressions wholly unwarranted by the circumstances of the case (*y*), nor to unnecessary publication (*z*). On the other hand, "the simple fact that there has been some casual bystander cannot alter the nature of the transaction" (*a*). That there were other persons present than those to whom the defendant was under a duty to make the statement in question will not necessarily destroy the privilege; if their presence was accidental, or could not be prevented by the defendant, the privilege will not be lost. Thus, in *Pittard* v. *Oliver* (*b*) it was held that the privilege which would have attached to defamatory statements made at a meeting of a board of guardians of which the defendant was a member was not destroyed by the presence of reporters.

(*x*) *Per* Lord Esher, M. R., in *Hebditch* v. *McIlwaine* (1894), 2 Q. B. at p. 61.

(*y*) *Per* Parke, B., in *Warren* v. *Warren* (1834), 1 C. M. & R. at p. 252; *Gilpin* v. *Fowler* (1854), 9 Ex. 615; 23 L. J. Ex. 152; *Fryer* v. *Kinnersley* (1863), 33 L. J. C. P. 96.

(*z*) *Brown* v. *Croome* (1817), 2 Stark. 297; *Lay* v. *Lawson* (1836), 4 A. & E. 795; *Botterill and another* v. *Whytehead* (1879), 41 L. T. 588.

(*a*) *Per cur.* in *Toogood* v. *Spyring* (1834), 1 C. M. & R. at pp. 193–194.

(*b*) (1891), 1 Q. B. 474.

"Was the defendant's duty to the guardians and to the ratepayers generally taken away by the presence of these other persons, who were not called in by him, and over whose presence he could exercise no control? The question answers itself; the presence of these persons left his duty to discuss the matter untouched; the occasion was privileged for the performance of that duty, and the privilege was not taken away by the presence of such people under such circumstances" (c).

"Where, indeed, an opportunity is *sought* for making such a charge before third persons, which might have been made in private, it would afford strong evidence of malicious intention, and thus deprive it of that immunity which the law allows to such a statement when made with honesty of purpose; but the mere fact of a third person being present does not render the communication absolutely unauthorized, though it may be a circumstance to be left with others, including the style and character of the language used, to the consideration of the jury, who are to determine whether the defendant has acted *bonâ fide* in making the charge, or been influenced by malicious motive" (d).

(c) *Per* Lord Esher, M. R. (1891), 1 Q. B. at p. 478.
(d) *Per cur.* in *Toogood* v. *Spyring* (1834), 1 C. M. & R. at p. 194.

Art. 38.—Malice.

Malice is any corrupt or wrong motive, or personal spite or ill-will (e).

NOTE.—" If the occasion is privileged, the plaintiff must prove malice in fact; the burden of proving this is on him, as was settled in *Clark* v. *Molyneux* (f). Malice in fact is not confined to personal spite and ill-will, but includes every unjustifiable intention to inflict injury on the person defamed, or, in the words of Brett, L. J. (g), every wrong feeling in a man's mind " (h).

" It lies on the party who would deprive the other party of his privilege to show what the law calls *malice*. But by that term is meant, not only spite, for any indirect motive other than a sense of duty is what the law calls *malice* " (i).

And in the recent case of *Royal Aquarium, &c. Soc.* v. *Parkinson* (j) Lord Esher thus explained the meaning of the word malice in relation to a privileged occasion. " The question is, whether the defendant is using the occasion honestly or abusing it. If a person on such an occasion states

---

(e) *Stuart* v. *Bell* (1891), 2 Q. B. 351; *Royal Aquarium, &c. Society* v. *Parkinson* (1892), 1 Q. B. 434.

(f) (1877), 3 Q. B. D. 237. See also *Jenoure* v. *Delmege* (1891), App. Cas. 73.

(g) In *Clark* v. *Molyneux* (1877), 3 Q. B. D. at p. 247.

(h) *Per* Lindley, L. J., in *Stuart* v. *Bell* (1891), 2 Q. B. at p. 351.

(i) *Per* Lord Campbell, C. J., in *Dickson* v. *The Earl of Wilton* (1859), 1 F. & F. at p. 419.

(j) (1892), 1 Q. B. at pp. 443, 444.

what he knows to be untrue, no one ever doubted that he would be abusing the occasion. . . . But there is a state of mind, short of deliberate falsehood, by reason of which a person may properly be held by a jury to have abused the occasion, and in that sense to have spoken maliciously. If a person from anger or some other wrong motive has allowed his mind to get into such a state as to make him cast aspersions on other people, reckless whether they are true or false, it has been held, and I think rightly held, that a jury is justified in finding that he has abused the occasion. Therefore, the question seems to me to be whether there is evidence of such a state of mind on the part of the defendant. It has been said that anger would be such a state of mind; but I think that gross and unreasoning prejudice, not only with regard to particular people, but with regard to a subject-matter in question, would have the same effect. If a person charged with the duty of dealing with other people's rights and interests has allowed his mind to fall into such a state of unreasoning prejudice in regard to the subject-matter that he was reckless whether what he stated was true or false, there would be evidence upon which a jury might say that he abused the occasion."

In the same case Lopes, L. J., said (*k*), "Not only must the occasion create the privilege, but the occasion must be made use of *bonâ fide* and without malice. The defendant is only

(*k*) (1892), 1 Q. B. at p. 454.

entitled to the protection of the privilege if he uses the occasion in accordance with the purpose for which the occasion arose. He is not entitled to the protection of the privilege if he uses the occasion for some indirect or wrong motives. This casts upon the plaintiff the burden of proving express malice or malice in fact. If it be proved that out of anger or for some other wrong motive the defendant has stated as true that which he does not know to be true, and he has stated it not stopping or taking the trouble to ascertain whether it is true or not—stated it recklessly by reason of his anger or other indirect motive—the jury may infer that he used the occasion not for the reason that justifies it, but for the gratification of his anger or other indirect motive."

Thus, malice may be proved by showing that the defendant knew the words were untrue when he wrote or spoke them (*l*), or that they were uttered with the intention of injuring the plaintiff (*m*), or that the plaintiff and defendant were rivals or had previously quarrelled (*n*), or that the defendant was actuated by personal resentment (*o*) or any other wrong motive (*p*).

(*l*) *Gerard* v. *Dickenson* (1590), 4 Rep. 18; Cro. Eliz. 197; *Smith* v. *Hodgeskins* (1633), Cro. Car. 276.
(*m*) *Peacock* v. *Reynal* (1612), 2 B. & G. 151.
(*n*) *Hooper* v. *Truscott* (1836), 2 Bing. N. C. 457; 2 Scott, 672.
(*o*) *Gilpin* v. *Fowler* (1854), 9 Ex. 615; 23 L. J. Ex. 152; 18 Jur. 293; *Dickson* v. *Earl of Wilton* (1859), 1 F. & F. 419.
(*p*) *Rogers* v. *Clifton* (1803), 3 B. & P. 587; *Jackson* v. *Hopperton* (1864), 16 C. B. N. S. 829; 12 W. R. 913; 10 L. T. 529.

Sometimes, also, malice may be proved by the unnecessarily extensive publication of the words (*q*), or by their unnecessary violence (*r*). " No doubt a customer may complain to a tradesman with whom he deals of what he deems irregular or dishonest; but if he does so outside the door of the tradesman's shop—so as to be heard by the public—or even inside the shop, he speaks slanderous words unnecessarily in the presence of third parties, or to third parties, and uses language which is extreme and beyond the occasion; all this, with the tone and manner in which the words were spoken, will be evidence for the jury to consider whether, in law, the words were spoken maliciously and without excuse" (*s*). "It may be that the language used in a libel, though under other circumstances justifiable, may be so much too violent for the occasion and circumstances to which it is applied as to form strong evidence of malice upon the issue of whether the communication is covered by the privilege, and that an inference of actual malice may be drawn from its use" (*t*).

On the other hand, as Lord Esher, M. R., pointed out in the very recent case of *Nevill* v. *Fine Arts*

(*q*) *Gilpin* v. *Fowler* (1854), 9 Ex. 615; 23 L. J. Ex. 152.
(*r*) Per Parke, B., in *Wright* v. *Woodgate* (1835), 2 C. M. & R. at p. 578; *Fryer* v. *Kinnersley* (1863), 15 C. B. N. S. 422; 33 L. J. C. P. 96.
(*s*) Per Lush, J., in *Oddy* v. *Lord George Paulet* (1865), 4 F. & F. at p. 1010.
(*t*) Per Cockburn, C. J., in *Spill* v. *Maule* (1869), L. R. 4 Ex. at pp. 235, 236.

and General Insurance Co. (*u*), " a man may use excessive language and yet have no malice in his mind." In the words of Lopes, L. J. (*x*), in the same case, " where the excess merely is that the statement made with reference to the privileged occasion is too strong, the authorities show that such excess may be evidence of actual malice ; but it is not in every case in which the words used are somewhat too strong that there is evidence to be left to the jury of actual malice. They must be too strong to a substantial extent in order to afford evidence upon which a jury can find actual malice."

All evidence showing the state of defendant's mind at the time he uttered the words complained of is admissible in order to rebut the plea of privilege by showing malice, and upon this principle proof is allowed that the defendant has previously (*y*) or subsequently (*z*) published other libels or slanders of the plaintiff.

But it is no evidence of malice to prove that the defendant, under a sense of duty, volunteered to write or speak the words complained of (*a*), or

---

(*u*) (1895), 2 Q. B. at p. 170.

(*x*) *Ibid.* at p. 172.

(*y*) *Stuart* v. *Lovell* (1817), 2 Stark. 93; *Barrett* v. *Long* (1851), 3 H. L. C. 395.

(*z*) *Mead* v. *Daubigny* (1792), Peake, 168; *Pearson* v. *Lemaitre* (1843), 5 M. & Gr. 700; 12 L. J. Q. B. 253; 7 Jur. 748; 6 Scott, N. R. 607.

(*a*) *Gardner* v. *Slade et ux.* (1849), 13 Q. B. 798; 18 L. J. Q. B. 336.

published them by mistake (b), or that the words used were not in fact true (c).

And though it is no doubt some evidence, and generally speaking strong evidence, of malice, it is not necessarily conclusive proof of malice to show that the defendant did not believe his statement to be true, for as Kelly, C. B., observed in *Botterill* v. *Whytehead* (d), " he may believe it to be untrue, and yet may be perfectly justified in publishing it to persons with whom he is in communication, and with whom it may be his duty to communicate freely on the subject of the information he has received." So, too, " it is not enough to show a want of reasoning power or stupidity, for those things of themselves do not constitute malice. A man may be wanting in reasoning power, or he may be very stupid, still he may be acting *bonâ fide*, honestly intending to discharge his duty. The question is not whether the defendant has done that which other men, as men of the world, would not have done, or whether the defendant acted in the belief that the statements he made were true, but whether he acted as he did from a desire to discharge his duty " (e).

(b) *Scarll* v. *Dixon* (1864), 4 F. & F. 250; *Brett* v. *Watson* (1872), 20 W. R. 723; *Tompson* v. *Dashwood* (1883), 11 Q. B. D. 43; 52 L. J. Q. B. 425; 48 L. T. 943.
(c) *Caulfield* v. *Whitworth* (1868), 16 W. R. 936; 18 L. T. 527.
(d) (1879), 41 L. T. at p. 590.
(e) *Per* Cotton, L. J., in *Clark* v. *Molyneux* (1877), 3 Q. B. D. at p. 249, cited with approval in *Murdoch* v. *Funduklian* (1885), 2 Times L. R. at p. 217.

Art. 39.—**Defence of apology under sect. 2 of Lord Campbell's Act, 6 & 7 Vict. c. 96.**

In an action for libel contained in any public newspaper or other periodical publication, *it is a good defence to prove that such libel was inserted in such newspaper or other periodical publication without actual malice, and without gross negligence, and that before the commencement of the action, or at the earliest opportunity afterwards, the defendant inserted in such newspaper or other periodical publication a full apology for the said libel; or if the newspaper or periodical publication in which the said libel appeared should be ordinarily published at intervals exceeding one week, that he had offered to publish the said apology in any newspaper or periodical publication to be selected by the plaintiff in such action* (*f*).

There must, however, be a payment of money into Court by way of amends at the time the plea is filed (8 & 9 Vict. c. 75, s. 2); and therefore, having regard to Order XXII. rule 1, *no other defence denying liability can be pleaded together with such plea.*

Note.—It should be noticed that this defence is only available in an action for a libel contained in any *public newspaper or other periodical publication*, words which would apparently cover almost every kind of journalistic publication. It is not enough for the defendant to plead that he inserted the apology "at the earliest opportunity after" the commencement of the action, if he had

(*f*) 6 & 7 Vict. c. 96 (Lord Campbell's Act), s. 2.

an opportunity before action (*g*). Any defendant relying upon this defence must offer some evidence to prove positively that there was no gross negligence on his part (*h*).

The apology should be full and free, and published in a conspicuous part of the paper. It should be given at least as prominent a position as the words complained of.

Art. 40.—Accord and satisfaction.

Accord and satisfaction is an agreement that the plaintiff will forego his right of action on the execution of a valuable consideration. Such agreement may be made by the defendant himself (*i*), *or by one jointly liable with him* (*k*), *or by a third party* (*l*), *and is a good defence to an action for libel or slander.*

Note.—Thus the defendant will escape liability by proving that the plaintiff agreed to accept from him certain apologies in full discharge of

(*g*) Per Keating, J., in *Ravenhill* v. *Upcott* (1869), 33 J. P. 299.

(*h*) Per Wills, J., in *Peters and another* v. *Edwards and another* (1887), 3 Times L. R. 423.

(*i*) *Boosey* v. *Wood* (1865), 34 L. J. Ex. 65; 3 H. & C. 484; *Marks* v. *Conservative Newspaper Co.* (1886), 3 Times L. R. 244.

(*k*) *Thurman* v. *Wild and another* (1840), 11 A. & E. 453; *Bainbridge* v. *Lax and others* (1846), 9 Q. B. 819.

(*l*) *Jones and another* v. *Broadhurst* (1850), 9 C. B. 173.

the plaintiff's cause of action, and that in pursuance
thereof he published such apologies in the manner
agreed upon (*m*).

ART. 41.—Release.

*The plaintiff may release his cause of action by
executing a deed to that effect.*

ART. 42.—Res Judicata.

*It is a good defence that the plaintiff has already
brought an action in respect of the same words
against the defendant or a third person with whom
the defendant was jointly concerned in the publication
of such words.*

NOTE.—This is so whether the plaintiff has
failed or succeeded in the previous action.

The defendant must be *jointly* not *severally* concerned with the third party. Thus, where the
third person against whom the previous action has
been brought is a partner of the defendant in a
firm of printers or publishers, the liability being
joint, the fact that there has been a previous
action against one of the partners is an answer to

(*m*) *Boosey* v. *Wood* (1865), 34 L. J. Ex. 65; 3 H. & C. 484;
Marks v. *Conservative Newspaper Co.* (1886), 3 Times L. R. 244.

an action in respect of the same libel against the other partner (*n*). Similarly where an action for libel has been brought against the editor of a newspaper and judgment recovered against him, the plaintiff cannot subsequently maintain an action against the proprietor in respect of the same libel, for the cause of action is in both cases the same, there being a joint publication.

But where the liability is *several*, as, *e.g.*, in the case of the author of a libel and the proprietor of the newspaper in which it has appeared (*o*), a previous action against one of them is no answer to an action against the other (*p*).

ART. 43.—**Statute of Limitations.**

An action of libel, and of slander for words actionable only by reason of special damage, must be brought within six years from the time of publication and the time when such special damage was sustained respectively (*q*), *and an action of slander for words actionable* per se *within two years from the time of publication, but if the plaintiff was at such time an*

(*n*) *Brinsmead* v. *Harrison* (1872), L. R. 7 C. P. 547.
(*o*) See pp. 59, 61, *supra*.
(*p*) *Creevy* v. *Carr* (1835), 7 C. & P. 64; *Frescoe* v. *May* (1860), 2 F. & F. 123.
(*q*) *Lord Saye and Sele* v. *Stephens* (1628), cited Cro. Car. 535; Litt. 342.

infant or a lunatic (*r*), *or the defendant was beyond the seas, the action must be brought within six years, or two years respectively from the time at which such disability is removed* (*s*).

Note.—*Beyond the seas.* This expression does not include any part of the United Kingdom or the Channel Islands. Formerly, by 21 Jac. 1, c. 19, if at the date of publication of the libel the plaintiff were imprisoned or beyond the seas, he could bring his action at any time within six years from his freedom or return, but this right was abolished by the Mercantile Law Amendment Act, 1856 (19 & 20 Vict. c. 97), sect. 10.

It should be noticed that if once the disability cease—in which case the time begins to run—no subsequent disability can affect the operation of the statute or prevent the time from continuing to run against the plaintiff.

A publication contrived by the plaintiff, *e.g.*, a sale of the libellous newspaper by the defendant to the plaintiff's agent, brought about for the express purpose of maintaining the action,

---

(*r*) Formerly this was also true in regard to married women. Since the Married Women's Property Act, 1882, however, a married woman is no longer under disability, but can sue as if she were a feme sole, see *Lowe* v. *Fox* (1885), 15 Q. B. D. 667.

(*s*) 21 Jac. 1, c. 19, s. 7; 4 & 5 Anne, c. 3 [al. c. 16], s. 19; 3 & 4 Will. 4, c. 42, s. 7; 19 & 20 Vict. c. 97, s. 12. See, however, in the case of slander for words actionable only by reason of special damage, *Littleboy* v. *Wright* (1674), 1 Lev. 69; 1 Sid. 95.

is a fresh publication from the date of which the time will begin to run again, even though the real grievance be a publication many years before that date. Thus, in the case of *The Duke of Brunswick* v. *Harmer* (*t*), a sale to the plaintiff's agent of a copy of the newspaper containing the libel seventeen years after its original publication, was held to constitute a fresh publication, from the date of which the Statute of Limitations would begin to run anew.

Art. 44.—Death of plaintiff or defendant.

The maxim actio personalis moritur cum personâ applies to every action for libel or slander, and, therefore, where a libel or slander has been published by or in respect of any person, and such person dies, no right of action survives either for or against his executor or administrator.

Note 1.—Even though the action has been commenced before the death of plaintiff or defendant, the death of either party before verdict puts an end to it. On the other hand, it is specially provided, by Ord. XVII., Rule 1, that "there shall be no abatement by reason of the death of either party between the verdict or finding of the issues of fact and the judgment, but judgment may in

(*t*) (1849), 19 L. J. Q. B. 20; 3 C. & K. 10; 14 Jur. 110; 14 Q. B. 185.

such case be entered, notwithstanding the death." The effect of this rule would appear to be that *Ireland* v. *Champneys* (*u*) is no longer law. In that case, the plaintiff in an action for libel died after interlocutory judgment had been signed, a writ of inquiry issued, and damages assessed, and it was held that final judgment could not be entered for the plaintiff for the damages assessed, the suit having abated by his death.

Where the plaintiff dies after final judgment has been entered in his favour, the executors and administrators are entitled to appear as respondents on appeal from such judgment (*x*).

NOTE 2.—It may be noticed here that where the Court in an action for administration appoints receivers for the purpose of conducting a newspaper, and the receivers publish a libel in such newspaper, they may be sued therefor. The estate alone will be liable for any damages recovered against them, but they will be personally liable for the costs of the action (*y*).

A libel on the business carried on by a receiver and manager appointed by the Court is a contempt of Court, and may be punished by committal of the offender (*z*).

(*u*) (1813), 4 Taunt. 884.
(*x*) *Twycross* v. *Grant and others* (1878), 4 C. P. D. 40; 47 L. J. Q. B. 676; 39 L. T. 618.
(*y*) *Stubbs* v. *Marsh* (1866), 15 L. T. 312.
(*z*) *Helmore* v. *Smith* (1886), 35 Ch. D. 449; 56 L. J. Ch. 145; 56 L. T. 72.

ART. 45.—**Evidence in aggravation of damages.**

At the trial of an action for libel or slander the plaintiff may prove in aggravation of damages the circumstances under which the words were published (a), *and, if it has been pleaded, the special damage if any which such words have caused.*

NOTE 1.—*The circumstances under which the words were published.* Thus, the plaintiff may show that the libel was scattered broadcast when the defendant was under no duty and had no right to publish it except to a limited number of persons (b). He may show that the defendant was culpably negligent (c); that he could without any difficulty have discovered that his charges were unfounded, or that he persisted in maintaining their truth even at the trial itself (d). So, too, where the action is for the publication of a libel in a newspaper, evidence is admissible in aggravation of damages to show that the defendant knew that the words published would be, and that the same in fact were, repeated and

(a) *Vines* v. *Serell* (1835), 7 C. & P. 163; *Darby* v. *Ouseley* (1856), 25 L. J. Ex. 233; *Blake* v. *Stevens and others* (1864), 11 L. T. 543; 4 F. & F. 232; *Risk Allah Bey* v. *Whitehurst* (1868), 18 L. T. N. S. 615.

(b) *De Crespigny* v. *Wellesley* (1829), 5 Bing. 402; *Stockdale* v. *Hansard* (1839), 9 A. & E. 149; *Gathercole* v. *Miall* (1846), 15 L. J. Ex. 179; 10 Jur. 337; 15 M. & W. 319.

(c) *Smith* v. *Harrison* (1856), 1 F. & F. 565.

(d) *Simpson* v. *Robinson* (1848), 12 Q. B. 511; 18 L. J. Q. B. 73.

published in other editions of the same newspaper; and therefore where the Statement of Claim contained an allegation to that effect, the Court refused an application by the defendant to strike it out (e).

"In actions for libel . . . the jury, in assessing damages, are entitled to look at the whole conduct of the defendant from the time the libel was published down to the time they gave their verdict. They may consider what his conduct has been before action, after action, and in court during the trial" (f). But the plaintiff is not allowed, in order to aggravate the damages, to give evidence of his good character unless the defendant has previously suggested on the pleadings or in cross-examination that it is bad (g). Neither is he allowed, with the same object in view, to prove that the defendant has published other libels of him (h). Where, however, there is a plea of qualified privilege, and therefore a question of malice, evidence of other libels is, as has been already stated, admissible (i).

NOTE 2.—*Special damage.* Special damage, if properly pleaded, may also be proved in aggravation of damages. The plaintiff is always required

(e) *Whitney and others* v. *Moignard* (1890), L. R. 24 Q. B. D. 630.
(f) Per Lord Esher, M. R., in *Praed* v. *Graham* (1889), 24 Q. B. D. at p. 55.
(g) *Guy* v. *Gregory* (1840), 9 C. & P. 587; *Brine* v. *Bazalgette* (1849), 18 L. J. Ex. 348; 3 Ex. 692.
(h) *Pearson* v. *Lemaitre* (1843), 12 L. J. Q. B. 253.
(i) See p. 154, *supra.*

to prove strictly that the special damage is immediately caused by the defendant's words (*k*). It is not sufficient that such words conduced to the damage; they must have been the main factor in producing it.

If the damage is mainly attributable to the caprice or unreasonable conduct of a third party, or conduct which under the circumstances could not be reasonably anticipated, the defendant is not liable (*l*). Thus where the defendant, who was a married woman, accused another married woman of having committed adultery, and the latter told her husband of the accusation, and he thereupon insisted upon a separation, it was held that the defendant was not liable (*m*).

In *Speight* v. *Gosnay* (*n*), the defendant uttered a slander consisting of a false imputation upon the chastity of the plaintiff, an unmarried woman, in the presence of plaintiff's mother. The mother repeated it to the plaintiff, who repeated it to the man to whom she was engaged to be married, and he broke off the engagement. There being no evidence that the defendant authorized or intended the repetition of the slander, or that he knew of the plaintiff's engagement, it was held by the Court of Appeal that an action of slander could

(*k*) See p. 23, *supra*.
(*l*) *Ashley* v. *Harrison* (1793), 1 Esp. 48; Peake, 256.
(*m*) *Parkins et ux.* v. *Scott et ux.* (1862), 1 H. & C. 153; 31 L. J. Ex. 331.
(*n*) (1891), 60 L. J. Q. B. 231; 55 J. P. 501; but now an action would lie for such an imputation without proof of special damage; see pp. 36, 37, *supra*.

not be maintained against him, on the ground that the special damage was too remote.

So where the plaintiff was a veterinary surgeon, and in order to prove special damage a person was called to say he had ceased to employ the plaintiff since the words complained of were spoken; but it appeared that he was not present when the defendant uttered them, and therefore must have heard them from some third person, it was held by Martin, B., that such evidence of damage was inadmissible (*o*).

Where, however, the words are actionable *per se*, the rules as to the admissibility of evidence do not always appear to be so rigidly applied as in other cases; *e.g.*, in the former case the jury, in estimating the damages, have been allowed to consider mental pain and anxiety (*p*), which, as has been already stated (*q*), does not constitute special damage so as to sustain an action where the words are not actionable *per se*.

ART. 46.—**Evidence in mitigation of damages.**

At the trial of an action for libel or slander, the defendant may prove in mitigation of damages (1) (*after notice in writing of his intention so to do duly*

(*o*) *Hirst* v. *Goodwin* (1862), 3 F. & F. 257.
(*p*) *Per* Lord Wensleydale in *Lynch* v. *Knight and Wife* (1861), 9 H. L. C. at p. 598.
(*q*) See p. 21, *supra*.

given to the plaintiff at the time of filing or delivering the plea in such action) that he made or offered an apology to the plaintiff for such defamation before the commencement of the action, or as soon afterwards as he had an opportunity of doing so, in case the action shall have been commenced before there was an opportunity of making or offering such apology (r); and (2) the circumstances under which the libel or slander was published, or the character of the plaintiff, provided that he has furnished the particulars thereof to the plaintiff seven days at least before the trial, or has pleaded the truth of the words complained of, otherwise he cannot give such evidence except by leave of the judge (s). At the trial of an action for a libel in any newspaper the defendant may also prove in mitigation of damages (3) that the plaintiff has already recovered (or brought actions for) damages, or has received, or agreed to receive, compensation in respect of a libel or libels, to the same purport or effect as the libel for which such action has been brought (t).

NOTE 1.— The first and second of the above provisions may be taken advantage of by any defendant to an action for libel or slander. Wherever the defendant can make use of the latter provision he should be careful to give the

(r) Lord Campbell's Act (6 & 7 Vict. c. 96), s. 1, see Note 1.
(s) Rules of Supreme Court, 1883, Ord. XXXVI., r. 37, see also pp. 168, 169, *infra*.
(t) Law of Libel Amendment Act, 1888 (51 & 52 Vict. c. 64), s. 6, see Note 2, p. 171, *infra*.

seven days' notice required by it, as otherwise
he will not be entitled, without the special leave
of the judge who tries the case, to give evidence
which in many cases will prevent the plaintiff
from obtaining other than nominal damages. The
effect of Ord. XXXVI., Rule 37, which provides
for the above notice being given, is not to enable
the defendant to give in evidence what, before
that rule came into force, he could not give, but
merely to prevent him from giving the evidence
therein specified, unless he does give such notice.
He may not, of course, go into irrelevant
matters (*u*). Thus he cannot be permitted to
show that the plaintiff has not contradicted or
complained of previous publications by some other
persons of the same libel (*v*). And where no justification has been pleaded, he may not give
evidence which tends to prove that the libel is in
fact true (*x*). Thus, in *Penny* v. *Stubbs* (*y*), where
the plaintiff brought an action for slander, alleging
that the defendant had accused him of having
committed perjury, and the defendant paid 40*s.*
into Court and apologised, and then proposed to
give evidence under Ord. XXXVI., Rule 37, to
prove that the plaintiff had made statements in
the witness-box in another action which were not

(*u*) *Darby* v. *Ouseley* (1856), 25 L. J. Ex. 227; 1 H. & N. 1.
(*v*) *Per* Maule, J., in *Ingram* v. *Lawson* (1840), 9 C. & P.
333; and *Pankhurst* v. *Hamilton* (1886), 2 Times L. R. 682.
(*x*) *Smith* v. *Richardson* (1737), Willes, 20; *Underwood* v.
Parks (1744), 2 Strange, 1200; *Speck* v. *Phillips* (1839), 5 M.
& W. 279 : 8 L. J. Ex. 277.
(*y*) Unreported, tried in the Q. B. D., Feb. 19th, 1892.

in fact true, Vaughan Williams, J., held that such evidence was inadmissible.

The defendant may, however, always give evidence to prove that he was not acting maliciously but in good faith. Thus, in *Harle* v. *Catherall and others* (z), where the defendant, an editor, declined to discover the name of the writer of the libel, but threw open his columns to the plaintiff, who wrote a number of letters in explanation and contradiction of the charge which the defendant inserted, it was held that the defendant was entitled to prove these facts in mitigation of damages. So, too, in *Smith* v. *Scott* (a), where the libel was contained in an inaccurate report of proceedings in a court of justice, evidence was admitted to show that the inaccuracy was caused by accident, and was not intentional on the part of the defendant.

That some other newspaper or individual has previously published the same charges against the plaintiff and has not been sued is no defence, nor is it even admissible as evidence in mitigation of damages (b). If, however, the defamatory statement appears on the face of it to be copied from a certain newspaper or communicated by a particular individual, the defendant may prove in

(z) (1866), 14 L. T. 801.
(a) (1847), 2 C. & K. 580. See also *Charlton* v. *Watton* (1834), 6 C. & P. 385; *Pearson* v. *Lemaitre* (1843), 12 L. J. Q. B. 253; 7 J. P. 336.
(b) *Saunders* v. *Mills* (1829), 6 Bing. 213; 3 M. & P. 520; *Talbutt* v. *Clark and another* (1840), 2 M. & Rob. 312; *Tucker* v. *Lawson* (1886), 2 Times L. R. 593.

mitigation of damages that a paragraph to the same effect did appear in that newspaper, or that the statement complained of was in fact communicated to him by such person (c). And it would seem that general evidence of bad reputation is admissible in mitigation of damages (d), although evidence of rumours to the same effect as the libel complained of is inadmissible (e). If however the defendant can prove that in copying the libel from another newspaper, or (semble) in repeating the slander, he omitted certain parts which referred in very adverse terms to the plaintiff, the fact that he did so is admissible as evidence to prove absence of malice, and this necessitates the admission in evidence of the original libel (f). And defendant can prove in mitigation of damages that plaintiff had, prior to the publication of the libel complained of, libelled or slandered the defendant, provided that he can also prove that this provoked him to retaliate by publishing the libel sued for (g), but not otherwise (h).

(c) *Duncombe* v. *Daniell* (1837), 8 C. & P. 222; 2 Jur. 32; 1 W. W. & H. 101; *per* Wightman, J., in *Davis* v. *Cutbush* (1859), 1 F. & F. 487.

(d) *Scott* v. *Sampson* (1882), 8 Q. B. D. 491; 51 L. J. Q. B. 380; 46 L. T. 412; *Wood* v. *Durham* (1888), 21 Q. B. D. 501; 57 L. J. Q. B. 547; 57 L. T. 770. See also *Wood* v. *Cox* (1888), 4 Times L. R. 550; and the observations of Lord Coleridge, L. C. J., in summing up the case to the jury at the trial of the last-mentioned case as reported in 4 Times L. R. at p. 655.

(e) *Scott* v. *Sampson, supra.*

(f) *Creevey* v. *Carr* (1835), 7 C. & P. 64.

(g) *Wakley* v. *Johnson* (1826), Ry. & M. 422; *Tarpley* v. *Blabey* (1835–36), 2 Bing. N. C. 437; 7 C. & P. 395; *Watts* v. *Fraser and another* (1837), 7 A. & E. 223; 7 C. & P. 369.

(h) *May* v. *Brown* (1824), 3 B. & C. 113; 4 D. & R. 670.

NOTE 2.—The third of the above provisions, which was introduced by s. 6 of the Law of Libel Amendment Act, 1888, is very valuable to newspaper proprietors. For example, if prior to that Act a country newspaper had copied a libellous article from a London newspaper, evidence could not be given that the plaintiff had already recovered damages against the London paper for the same article (*i*). It will be observed that the provision is confined to libels appearing in a newspaper as defined by the Act, so that it has no application to any libel which appears elsewhere, *e.g.*, in a monthly periodical or book (*k*).

ART. 47.—**Consolidation of actions.**

It shall be competent for a judge or the Court, upon an application by or on behalf of two or more defendants in actions in respect to the same, or substantially the same, libel, brought by one and the same person, to make an order for the consolidation of such actions, so that they shall be tried together; and after such order has been made, and before the trial of the said actions, the defendants in any new actions instituted in respect to the same, or substantially the same, libel, shall also be entitled to be joined in a common action upon a joint application being made by such new defendants

(*i*) *Hunt* v. *Algar and others* (1833), 6 C. & P. 245.
(*k*) See p. 109, *supra*.

and the defendants in the actions already consolidated (*l*).

NOTE.—This is a most valuable provision to newspaper proprietors, and is aimed at preventing the repetition of such cases as *Tucker* v. *Lawson* (*m*) and *Colledge* v. *Pike* (*n*), where a series of actions were brought against different newspapers for the same libel which they had all copied, and heavy damages recovered against each. Prior to the Law of Libel Amendment Act, 1888, it was held in the last-mentioned case that in such circumstances, inasmuch as there were distinct and separate publications, and consequently the liabilities of the various defendants were different, there could be no consolidation of the actions, and the only relief which the defendants could obtain was in regard to costs, and this was effected by obtaining a stay of all the actions except one. Each defendant was then liable for whatever damages the plaintiff recovered in that action, and by this means a plaintiff could recover enormous damages for what was really the same libel. By this Act, however, such a course is rendered impossible, as the actions may be consolidated; and, as will be seen by the next Article, the jury can now apportion the amount of damages between the defendants. The Court will make an order

---

(*l*) 51 & 52 Vict. c. 64, s. 5.
(*m*) (1886), 2 Times L. R. 593.
(*n*) (1886), 56 L. T. 124.

for consolidation where the application appears to be reasonable, even though the defences raised are different (*o*).

Art. 48.—Assessment of damages in a consolidated action.

In a consolidated action, the jury shall assess the whole amount of damages (if any) in one sum, but a separate verdict shall be taken for or against each defendant in the same way as if the actions consolidated had been tried separately ; and if the jury shall have found a verdict against the defendant or defendants in more than one of the actions so consolidated, they shall proceed to apportion the amount of damages which they shall have so found between and against the said last-mentioned defendants ; and the judge at the trial, if he awards to the plaintiff the costs of the action, shall thereupon make such order as he shall deem just (*p*) *for the apportionment of such costs between and against such defendants* (*q*).

Note.—This enables a jury, after assessing the damages suffered by the plaintiff in a consolidated action (see preceding Article), *i.e.*, the amount recoverable in all the actions, to go further, and

(*o*) *Eddison* v. *Dalziel* (1893), 9 Times L. R. 334.
(*p*) See *Hopley* v. *Williams* (1889), 6 Times L. R. 3 ; 53 J. P. 822.
(*q*) 51 & 52 Vict. c. 64, s. 5.

apportion the amount of damages recoverable against each defendant. Without this provision, each defendant would of course be liable for all the damage, as indeed he still is in any action not coming within the meaning of a consolidated action under sect. 5 of the Law of Libel Amendment Act, 1888.

ART. 49.—Injunctions.

The Court has jurisdiction in an action of libel or slander to restrain by injunction either before or at the trial any further publication of such libel or slander (s), *but before the trial such jurisdiction will be exercised with great caution* (t).

NOTE.—In order to obtain an interim injunction, the plaintiff must prove that the words complained of are untrue (u), and that therefore any subsequent publication by the defendant would be *malâ fide* (x); and there must be " such

---

(s) *Saxby* v. *Easterbrook* (1878), 3 C. P. D. 339; 27 W. R. 188; *Thorley's Cattle Food Co.* v. *Massam* (1880), 14 Ch. D. 781 (C. A.); 42 L. T. 851; *Kerr* v. *Gandy* (1886), 3 Times L. R. 75; *Hayward* v. *Hayward and Sons* (1886), 34 Ch. D. 198.

(t) *Quartz Hill Gold Mining Co.* v. *Beall* (1882), 20 Ch. D. 501 (C. A.); *Bonnard* v. *Perryman* (1891), 2 Ch. 269 (C. A.).

(u) *Burnett* v. *Tak* (1882), 45 L. T. 743.

(x) *Halsey* v. *Brotherhood* (1881), 19 Ch. D. 386 (C. A.); 51 L. J. Ch. 233; 45 L. T. 640; *Anderson* v. *Liebig's Extract of Meat Co., Limited* (1882), 45 L. T. 757; *Hill* v. *Hart-Davies* (1882), 21 Ch. D. 798; 51 L. J. Ch. 845; 47 L. T. 82; *Société Anonyme des Manufactures de Glaces* v. *Tilghman's Patent*

immediate and pressing injury to person or property threatened by the defendant's proceedings as to make it desirable . . . that (the Court) should interfere" (*y*). Where, however, the words complained of affect the plaintiff in the way of his business, it seems that such injury will be presumed (*z*).

The jurisdiction of the Court to issue injunctions in cases of libel is not, as has been supposed, confined to cases of libels affecting trade or property (*a*). It is also applicable to libels affecting character only; "in all cases where the Court shall think it just and convenient, the remedy exists" (*b*).

There have lately been several important cases on this branch of the law, and the Court of Appeal has stated that such an injunction will only be granted "in the clearest cases where any jury would say that the matter complained of was libellous, and where, if the jury did not so find, the Court would set aside the verdict as unreasonable" (*c*).

Sand Blast Co. (1883), 25 Cb. D. 1; 53 L. J. Ch. 1; 49 L. T. 451 (C. A.).

(*y*) Per North, J., in *Salomons* v. *Knight* (1891), 2 Ch. at p. 297, cited with approval by the Court of Appeal, *ibid.* at p. 298.

(*z*) *Thomas* v. *Williams* (1880), 14 Ch. D. 864; 49 L. J. Ch. 605; 43 L. T. 91.

(*a*) Per Lord Halsbury in *Monson* v. *Tussauds, Limited; Monson* v. *Louis Tussaud* (1894), 1 Q. B. at p. 690. See also the observations of Davey, L. J., *ibid.* at p. 698.

(*b*) Per Lord Halsbury, *ibid.* at p. 690.

(*c*) Per Lord Esher, M. R., in *Coulson* v. *Coulson* (1887), 3 Times L. R. 846, approved and adopted by the Court in

Thus, in *Collard* v. *Marshall* (*d*), an interlocutory injunction was granted to restrain the defendant, who was the secretary of a trade union, from publishing a placard stating that there was a strike now on at the plaintiff's works, that the sweating system was practised, and the polishing badly done there; these statements being held to be untrue, and the defendant not suggesting that he could produce further evidence in support of them (*e*). No such injunction will be granted when the defendant swears that he will be able to justify the libel, and the Court is not satisfied that he may not be able to do so (*f*), or where the words complained of are *primâ facie* privileged (*g*), or may be fair and *bonâ fide* comment on a matter of public interest (*h*).

The Court has also a general jurisdiction to restrain by injunction the publication of any

Bonnard v. *Perryman* (1891), 2 Ch. at p. 284. See also *Liverpool Household Stores Association* v. *Smith* (1887), 37 Ch. D. 170; and the observations of Lord Herschell, L. C., in *White* v. *Mellin* (1895), App. Cas. at pp. 162, 163.

(*d*) (1892), 1 Ch. 571.

(*e*) See also *Pink* v. *Federation of Trades and Labour Unions*, (1892), 67 L. T. 258; *Trollope* v. *London Building Trades Federation* (1895), 11 Times L. R. 228 and 280.

(*f*) *Bonnard* v. *Perryman* (1891), 2 Ch. 269; *Collard* v. *Marshall* (1892), 1 Ch. 571.

(*g*) *Quartz Hill Gold Mining Co.* v. *Beall* (1882), 20 Ch. D. 501 (C. A.); 51 L. J. Ch. 874; 46 L. T. 746; *Allinson* v. *General Council of Medical Education, etc.* (1892), 8 Times L. R. 784 (C. A.); *Champion and Co., Limited* v. *Birmingham Vinegar Brewery Co., Limited* (1893), 10 Times L. R. 164.

(*h*) *Armstrong and others* v. *Armit and others* (1886), 2 Times L. R. 887.

matter which tends to prejudice the administration of justice, provided that application for such relief is made without delay. Thus the publication of any comments which are calculated to prejudice the fair trial of an action which is pending will be restrained (*i*).

Further, by the Corrupt and Illegal Practices Prevention Act, 1895 (*j*), the Court has power to restrain by injunction any false statement of fact made before or during any parliamentary election concerning the personal character or conduct of any candidate at such election, and made for the purpose of affecting the return of such candidate thereat.

ART. 50.—Costs.

If the action is tried without a jury the costs are in the discretion of the judge, and if he makes no order each party must pay his own costs. If the action is tried with a jury, the costs follow the event, unless for good cause shown the judge otherwise orders (*k*).

NOTE.—In actions for libel or slander either party is entitled as of right to have the case tried with a jury (*k*), and this is almost the invariable

---

(*i*) *Reg.* v. *Payne* (1896), 1 Q. B. 577 ; and see p. 87, *supra,* and cases there cited in foot-notes (*a*) and (*b*).

(*j*) 58 and 59, Vict. c. 40, ss. 1, 3.

(*k*) Rules of the Supreme Court, 1883, Ord. LXV., r. 1.

practice. Generally speaking, therefore, if the plaintiff recovers any damages at all he gets his costs, unless the judge for good cause deprive him of them. "No general rule can be laid down" as to what constitutes *good cause*, "but the conduct of the parties in each case and the facts of each case must be looked at" (*l*). "The facts must show the existence of something, having regard either to the conduct of the parties or to the facts of the case, which makes it more just that an exceptional order should be made than that the case should be left to the ordinary course of taxation" (*m*). "The smallness of the damages awarded does not of itself constitute 'good cause,' although it is always a matter to be considered in deciding whether or not good cause exists" (*n*).

Art. 51.—New trial.

The Court will grant a new trial (1) *on the ground of misdirection or improper admission or rejection of evidence, provided that some substantial wrong or miscarriage of justice has been occasioned thereby* (*o*),

(*l*) Per Lord Esher, M. R., in *Wood* v. *Cox* (1889), 5 Times L. R. at p. 274.

(*m*) *Ibid.* in *Jones* v. *Curling* (1884), 13 Q. B. D. at p. 268. See also *Hughes* v. *Merrett* (1886), 17 Q. B. D. 373.

(*n*) *Ibid.* in *O'Connor* v. *The Star Newspaper Co.* (1893), 9 Times L. R. at p. 234. See also *per* A. L. Smith, L. J., *ibid.* at p. 235.

(*o*) *Phillips* v. *L. & S. W. Rail. Co.* (1879), 5 Q. B. D. 78; 49 L. J. Q. B. 833.

or (2) *if it be proved that the jury have not exercised a reasonable discretion* (p).

Note.—By Ord. XXXIX., Rule 6, of the Rules of the Supreme Court, 1883, " a new trial shall not be granted on the ground of misdirection, or of the improper admission or rejection of evidence, or because the verdict of the jury was not taken upon a question which the judge at the trial was not asked to leave to them, unless in the opinion of the Court to which the application is made some substantial wrong or miscarriage has been thereby occasioned in the trial, and if it appear to such Court that such wrong or miscarriage affects parts only of the matter in controversy or some or one only of the parties, the Court may give final judgment as to part thereof, or some or one only of the parties, and direct a new trial as to the other part only or as to the other party or parties."

In the very recent action of *Bray* v. *Ford* (q), where the judge misdirected the jury in favour of the plaintiff, upon a material part of the alleged libel, and the jury returned a verdict for the plaintiff for £600 damages, it was held by the House of Lords that, since the assessment of damages is peculiarly within the province of the jury in an action for libel, and since the jury had returned their verdict on what they were erroneously led to think was the case, and not on the real case

(p) Rules of the Supreme Court, 1883, Ord. XXXIX., r. 6; and see *Bray* v. *Ford* (1896), App. Cas. 44.

(q) (1896), App. Cas. 44.

which the defendant was entitled to have submitted to them, and might, in assessing the damages, have been influenced by the misdirection, there had been a substantial wrong or miscarriage within Order XXXIX., Rule 6, and that there must be a new trial. And this ruling would be in no way affected by the fact that the Court might think that the jury would have given the same damages if the law had been correctly expounded (*r*).

A new trial has been granted in an action for libel on the ground that at the trial, although the libel was admitted on the pleadings, the judge directed the jury that it was for them to say whether the words complained of were a libel or not, and also that he was wrong in admitting evidence for the defendants of facts not referred to in their particulars in mitigation of damages and in rejecting rebutting evidence tendered on the plaintiffs' behalf (*s*). And in another case, where privilege was pleaded, it was held to be a misdirection by the learned judge to tell the jury that the question of privilege depended upon their finding whether the defendant did or did not believe his statement to be true, inasmuch as the onus is on the plaintiff to show malice, not upon the defendant to negative its existence (*t*).

It will be found that the different grounds on

(*r*) (1896), App. Cas. 44.

(*s*) *Maclaren and Sons* v. *Davis and another* (1890), 6 Times L. R. 372.

(*t*) *Clark* v. *Molyneux* (1877), 3 Q. B. D. 237; 47 L. J. Q. B. 230; *Jenoure* v. *Delmege* (1891), App. Cas. 73.

which the Court has set aside the verdict of a jury fall within the principle set out in the last part of the above Article. In order to obtain a new trial it must be conclusively proved that the jury have not exercised any reasonable discretion at all (*u*). Thus, in *Praed* v. *Graham* (*v*), where the Court was asked to set aside the verdict on the ground that the damages given by the jury were excessive, Lord Esher said, " If . . . . the Court thinks that, having regard to all the circumstances of the case, the damages are so excessive that no twelve men could reasonably have given them, then they ought to interfere in the verdict." It is not sufficient that the Court itself would have come to a different conclusion, for estimates and opinions may differ widely. "Judges have no right to overrule the verdict of a jury as to the amount of damages merely because they take a different view and think that if they had been the jury they would have given more or would have given less" (*w*).

The Court has power to refuse an application for a new trial where such application is made merely on the ground that the damages are excessive, upon the plaintiff then and there consenting

---

(*u*) *Metropolitan Rail. Co.* v. *Wright* (1886), 11 App. Cas. 152; *Commissioner for Railways* v. *Brown* (1887), 13 App. Cas. 133. See also *Australian Newspaper Co.* v. *Bennett* (1894), App. Cas. at p. 287.

(*v*) (1889), 24 Q. B. D. at p. 55.

(*w*) Per James, L. J., in *Phillips* v. *L. & S. W. Rail. Co.* (1879), 5 Q. B. D. at p. 85.

to the damages being reduced to such an amount as the Court would consider not excessive had they been given by the jury. Under these circumstances the defendant has no voice in the matter (*x*).

The Court of Appeal has jurisdiction on a motion for a new trial under the Supreme Court of Judicature Act, 1890 (*y*) to direct judgment to be entered for either of the parties, instead of ordering a new trial (*z*).

(*x*) *Belt* v. *Lawes* (1884), 12 Q. B. D. 356.
(*y*) 53 & 54 Vict. c. 44.
(*z*) *Allcock* v. *Hall* (1891), 1 Q. B. 444.

Part II.—OF CRIMINAL PROCEEDINGS.

Art. 1.—Libel a crime.

The publication of a libel is a misdemeanor punishable by fine and imprisonment (a), for which proceedings may (subject to Art. 4, infra) be taken by way of indictment or information.

Note 1.—Libel as the subject of criminal proceedings is either (1) defamatory, or (2) blasphemous, seditious, or obscene (b). Whatever amounts to a libel in a civil action (see p. 1, *supra*) will be held a defamatory libel on a criminal trial, and criminal proceedings will sometimes lie where an action will not. Thus, it is a defamatory libel and a crime, though not actionable (c), to write and publish words injurious to the reputation of any deceased person (d), or of any collection of

(a) See 6 & 7 Vict. c. 96, ss. 4, 5, p. 250, *infra*.
(b) As to blasphemous, seditious, and obscene libels, see p. 194, *infra*.
(c) Owing to there being no proper plaintiff. *Rex* v. *Darby* (1687), 3 Mod. 139.
(d) *Rex* v. *Topham* (1791), 4 T. R. 126; *per contra Reg.* v. *Ensor* (1887), 3 Times L. R. 366. The dicta in *Reg.* v. *Labouchere* (*Vallombrosa's case*) (1884), 12 Q. B. D. 320, only affect the remedy by way of information.

individuals, without referring to any individual in particular (*d*), provided that in each case such words tend to provoke a breach of the peace. Thus, it has been held a libel in criminal law to write and publish of "certain Jews lately arrived from Portugal and living near Broad Street," that they had murdered a Jewish woman and her child because the child was begotten by a Christian, in consequence of which publication, as sworn to on the affidavits, many Jews in various parts of the city had been threatened with death, and had been maltreated (*e*). Similarly, it was held that criminal proceedings would lie for imputing that a certain nunnery was a brothel of prostitution, although no reference was made to any special individual (*f*), and in another case a criminal information was granted against the proprietor and publisher of a newspaper for publishing observations defamatory of the clergy of a particular diocese, though no mention was made of any particular clergyman (*g*).

So, too, in some cases there may be a good defence to an *action*, on the ground that the words complained of are true, but this in itself is no answer to criminal proceedings: there the defendant must be prepared to go further and prove not

(*d*) *Rex* v. *Osborn* (1732), W. Kelynge, 230; 2 Barnard. 138, 166; *Rex* v. *Williams* (1822), 2 B. & Ald. 595; *Rex* v. *Gathercole* (1838), 2 Lewin, C. C. 237.

(*e*) *Rex* v. *Gathercole, supra*.

(*f*) *Rex* v. *Osborn, supra*.

(*g*) *Rex* v. *Williams, supra*.

only that the words complained of are true, but also that their publication is for the public benefit. Moreover, no action will lie where the words complained of have been communicated only to the plaintiff himself, it being necessary, as has already been pointed out (*h*), to prove that the defendant has communicated the words to some third person. But in criminal proceedings it is sufficient that the libel has been published to the plaintiff himself, the foundation of such proceedings being the natural tendency of such words to provoke a breach of the peace. And this is, of course, the foundation of the old maxim, " The greater the truth the greater the libel," which only applies to criminal proceedings. In a civil action the truth of the words complained of is a complete defence (*i*).

On the other hand, slander, as such, is never a crime, though the words complained of may come within the criminal law as being blasphemous, seditious, or obscene (*k*), or as being a solicitation to commit a crime (*l*), or a contempt of Court (*m*).

Further, by sect. 1 of the Corrupt and Illegal Practices Prevention Act, 1895 (*n*), "any person who, or the directors of any body or association

(*h*) See p. 13, *supra*.
(*i*) See p. 81, *supra*.
(*k*) See p. 194, *infra*.
(*l*) *Rex* v. *Higgins* (1801), 2 East, 5.
(*m*) *Rex* v. *Pocock* (1741), 2 Strange, 1157.
(*n*) 58 and 59 Vict. c. 40.

corporate which, before or during any Parliamentary election, shall, for the purpose of affecting the return of any candidate at such election, make or publish any false statement of fact in relation to the personal character or conduct of such candidate shall be guilty of an illegal practice within the meaning of the provisions of the Corrupt and Illegal Practices Prevention Act, 1883, and shall be subject to all the penalties for and consequences of committing an illegal practice in the said Act mentioned." By sect. 2, however, "no person shall be deemed to be guilty of such illegal practice if he can show that he had reasonable grounds for believing, and did believe, the statements made by him to be true."

Sect. 3 provides for the granting of an injunction (*o*) to prevent the repetition of any such statement, and sect. 4 exonerates a candidate in certain cases from liability for the publication of such statements by his agents.

It will be noticed that in order to amount to an illegal practice within the meaning of the Act it is immaterial in what form the statement is made.

NOTE 2.—The following is a brief outline of the different steps to be taken in a prosecution for libel, according as the proceedings are by way of indictment or information.

(*o*) As an instance of a case in which such an injunction was granted, see *Bayley* v. *Edmunds and others* (1895), 11 Times L. R. 537.

I. *Where the proceedings are by way of indictment.* Generally speaking the first step taken by the prosecutor is to charge the defendant before a stipendiary magistrate or two justices of the peace, but whenever the libel has been published in a newspaper, and it is desired to prosecute the proprietor, publisher, editor, or other person responsible for such publication, the prosecutor must first obtain the leave of a judge at chambers under sect. 8 of the Law of Libel Amendment Act (*p*)

On a charge of libel before justices, the defendant usually appears in answer to a summons; but if he does not do so the Court may, if satisfied that the summons has been duly served upon him, proceed to hear the case although he is not present, or—the course generally adopted in practice—issue a warrant for his apprehension, under 11 & 12 Vict. c. 42, s. 1. At common law, upon the hearing there are only two questions for the consideration of the Court—" first, whether the matter complained of was libellous, and secondly, whether the publication of it was brought home to the accused " (*q*). After hearing the complainant's case the Court will inquire of the accused whether he wishes to call any witnesses (*r*), and evidence on his behalf will then be admissible to prove that the words complained

---

(*p*) See Art. 4, p. 198, *infra*, and note thereto.
(*q*) *Per* Cockburn, C. J., in *Reg.* v. *Carden* (1879), 5 Q. B. I 6, 7; 49 L. J. M. C. 1; 41 L. T. 504.
(*r*) 30 & 31 Vict. c. 35, s. 3.

of are no libel (*s*); that they do not relate to the complainant (*t*); that they were not published by the accused (*u*); that their publication is absolutely privileged (*x*); or that they are a fair and *bonâ fide* comment on a matter of public interest (*y*). The Court will then either dismiss the case, or, if satisfied that there are reasonable grounds for doing so, will commit the accused for trial.

So much, then, for the jurisdiction at common law. Next, as to the alterations which have been introduced by statute. In the first place, by sect. 4 of the Newspaper Libel and Registration Act, 1881 (44 & 45 Vict. c. 60), "a Court of summary jurisdiction, upon the hearing of a charge against a proprietor, publisher, or editor or any person responsible for the publication of a newspaper, for a libel published therein, may receive evidence as to the publication being for the public benefit, and as to the matters charged in the libel being true, and as to the report being fair and accurate and published without malice, and as to any matter which under this or any other Act or otherwise might be given in evidence by way of defence by the person charged on his trial on indictment, and the Court, if of opinion after hearing such evidence that there is a strong

(*s*) See pp. 183, 184, *supra*.
(*t*) See pp. 3–5, *supra*.
(*u*) See pp. 197, 198, *infra*.
(*x*) See pp. 97, 101–113, *supra*.
(*y*) See pp. 88–96, *supra*.

or probable presumption that the jury on the trial would acquit the person charged, may dismiss the case."

This section effected a great change in the law so far as the press were concerned. Its object is to enable a magistrate, upon the hearing of a charge of libel against any of the persons mentioned, to receive and hear such evidence as would be admissible on the trial of an indictment for libel, and, if he should be of opinion that at the trial the defendant would be acquitted, to dismiss the case. "Independently of statute the magistrate could not receive evidence of the truth of the libel" (*z*), because that was no defence to criminal proceedings. "The question then arises," said Cockburn, L. C. J. (*z*), "whether [sect. 6 of] Lord Campbell's Act (*a*) enables him to do so. In my opinion it does not, because the defence founded upon the truth of the libel does not arise at that stage and cannot be put forward before the magistrate. Suppose the defendant had succeeded fully and entirely in showing the truth of the libel; what, then, would have been the duty of the magistrate? He would nevertheless have been bound to send the case for trial, because by the statute the truth of the libel does not constitute a defence until the statutory conditions are complied with, and they cannot be complied with at that stage of the inquiry."

It is clear, then, that the only cases in which

(*z*) *Reg.* v. *Carden* (1879), 5 Q. B. D. at pp. 6, 7.
(*a*) See pp. 251, 252, *infra.*

a magistrate can receive evidence of the truth of the libel are: (1) where the defendant is charged under sect. 4 of Lord Campbell's Act with maliciously publishing a defamatory libel, *knowing the same to be false* (*b*); and (2) by virtue of sect. 4 of the Newspaper Libel and Registration Act, 1881, upon the hearing of a charge against a proprietor, publisher, editor, or any person responsible for the publication of a newspaper, for a libel published therein. It must be remembered that the latter section is, however, limited in its application, owing to the special meaning to be attached to the term "newspaper" (*c*).

If there be a committal, the accused will be released on reasonable bail. If, on the other hand, the case be dismissed, then, inasmuch as by sect. 6 of the Newspaper Libel and Registration Act, 1881, every libel is to be deemed an offence within the Vexatious Indictments Act, 1859 (22 & 23 Vict. c. 17), the Court may be "required to take the recognizance of the prosecutor to prosecute the charge .... and to transmit such recognizance .... and depositions to the Court in which such indictment ought to be preferred."

Lastly, it may be noticed that by sect. 5 of the Newspaper Libel and Registration Act, 1881 (*d*), where the party charged is the proprietor,

---

(*b*) *Ex parte Ellisen*, not reported, approved by Lush, J., in *Reg.* v. *Carden* (1879). 5 Q. B. D. 11, 13.

(*c*) See p. 109, *supra*.

(*d*) 44 & 45 Vict. c. 60.

publisher, editor, or any person responsible for the publication of the newspaper in which the libel has appeared, he may, after he is shown to have been guilty and if the Court thinks the libel trivial, elect to be summarily dealt with—in which case the Court may summarily convict him, and adjudge him to pay a fine not exceeding £50. It is difficult, however, to see the practical utility of the above provision, for it is only applicable when the Court of summary jurisdiction "is of opinion .... that the libel was of a trivial character," and it is surely most improbable that in such a case the judge in chambers would make the preliminary order for a criminal prosecution, which must be "first had and obtained" under sect. 8 of the Law of Libel Amendment Act, 1888 (*e*).

If the defendant is committed for trial, the prosecutor will prefer an indictment before the grand jury at the Central Criminal Court or the assizes, as the case may be, and will then proceed to trial before judge and jury. The prosecution must satisfy the jury that the words complained of are libellous, that they referred to the prosecutor, and would be so understood by those to whom they were published (*f*), that they were published by the defendant (*g*), and in the county in which the venue has been laid. As to the defences which may then be set up, see pp. 200, 201, *infra*.

(*e*) See p. 198, *infra*.
(*f*) See p. 9. *supra*.
(*g*) See pp. 197, 198, *infra*.

II. *Where the proceedings are by way of information.* A criminal information may be (1) *ex officio*, *i.e.*, filed by the Attorney-General,—a course which is however only adopted in very serious and pressing cases of a public nature, and of which the latest example was in 1830 ; or (2) filed by the Queen's coroner and attorney by express order of the Queen's Bench Division in open Court (*h*). In the latter case, also, "there must be some pressing circumstances to entitle the applicant to that extraordinary remedy" (*i*), and it would appear from the judgment of the Court in the important case of *The Queen* v. *Labouchere* (*Vallombrosa's case*) (*k*) that as a general rule the remedy is reserved for cases of libel upon persons in an official or judicial position, and filling some office or post which makes it for the public interest necessary that such jurisdiction should be exercised for the refutation of the libellous charges made. The Court in this case quoted (*l*) with approval, as illustrating the principle upon which such information should be granted to a private person the following passage from Blackstone (*m*) : "The objects of the other species of information filed by the Master of the

(*h*) Will. & Mary, c. 18, s. 1 ; Crown Office Rules, 1886, r. 46.
(*i*) *Per* Manisty, J., in *ex parte Littleton* (1888), 52 J. P. at p. 264.
(*k*) (1884), 12 Q. B. D. 320.
(*l*) *Ibid.* at p. 330.
(*m*) Book IV. c. 23, p. 309.

Crown Office upon the complaint or relation of a private subject, are, any gross and notorious misdemeanors, riots, batteries, libels, and other immoralities of an atrocious kind not peculiarly tending to disturb the government (for those are left to the care of the Attorney-General) but which on account of their magnitude or pernicious example deserve the most public animadversion."

In the case of a criminal information coming within the second of the classes mentioned above, counsel for the prosecution must within a reasonable time after the offence complained of move the Divisional Court upon affidavits for an order *nisi*, calling upon the defendant to show cause why an information should not be filed (*n*). The rule *nisi*, if granted, is then drawn up and served on the defendant, who shows cause. If the rule is then made absolute, the prosecutor enters into a recognizance of £50 effectually to prosecute such information, and to abide by and observe such orders as the Court shall direct, and then proceeds to trial as directed by the Crown Office Rules, 1886. The trial itself is similar to the trial of an indictment.

(*n*) Crown Office Rules, 1886, r. 48.

ART. 2.—**Blasphemous, seditious, and obscene words, &c.**

The publication (o) of blasphemous (p), seditious (q), or obscene (r) matter, whether in writing, printing, or by word of mouth, is a misdemeanour, punishable by fine and imprisonment, for which proceedings may be taken either by way of information or indictment.

NOTE 1.—It is difficult to precisely define the meaning of the word *blasphemous*, but it would seem that to come within that meaning the matter must relate to the Deity, any Person of the Trinity, the Bible, the Book of Common Prayer, or Christianity in general (*p*), and the publication must be made with intent to wound the feelings of believers, or to lead astray the uneducated. This particular intent is the gist of the offence, and is usually inferred from the intemperate and scurrilous tone adopted by the defendant. In the absence of such an intent there is no blasphemy. In the words of Best, C. J., "every man may fearlessly advance any

(*o*) As to what constitutes *publication*, see pp. 197, 198, *infra*.
(*p*) *Rex* v. *Williams* (1797), 26 How. St. Tr. 656 ; *Rex* v. *Carlile* (1819), 3 B. & Ald. 167 ; 1 Edw. 6, c. 1, s. 1 ; 2 & 3 Edw. 6, c. 1, ss. 2, 3 ; 1 Eliz. c. 2, ss. 2, 3 ; 13 Eliz. c. 12, s. 2 ; 14 Car. 2, c. 4, s. 1 ; 9 Will. 3, c. 35 ; 53 Geo. 3, c. 160.
(*q*) 60 Geo. 3 & 1 Geo. 4, c. 8, s. 1.
(*r*) *Rex* v. *John Wilkes* (1770), 4 Burr. 2527 ; 2 Wils. 151 ; *Reg.* v. *Carlile* (1845), 1 Cox, C. C. 229 ; *Reg.* v. *Hicklin* (1868), L. R. 3 Q. B. 360 ; 37 L. J. M. C. 89 ; 18 L. T. 398.

new doctrines, provided he does so with proper respect to the religion and government of the country" (s); or, as Erskine, J., put it in a later case, "by the law of this country, every man has a right to express his sentiments in decent language" (t); and finally, to quote the latest expression of judicial opinion on the subject, that of the late Lord Chief Justice in *Reg.* v. *Ramsay and Foote* (u), "if the decencies of controversy are observed, even the fundamentals of religion may be attacked without a person being guilty of blasphemous libel."

NOTE 2.—For words to be *seditious* they must be published with intent "to bring into hatred or contempt or to excite disaffection against the person of her Majesty, her heirs or successors, or the government and constitution of the United Kingdom as by law established, or either House of Parliament, or the administration of justice, or to excite her Majesty's subjects to attempt, otherwise than by lawful means, the alteration of any matter in Church or State by law established, or to raise discontent or disaffection amongst her Majesty's subjects, or to promote feelings of ill-will and hostility between different classes of such subjects" (v).

(s) *Rex* v. *Burdett* (1821), 4 B. & Ald. 314.
(t) *Reg.* v. *Adams* (1842), Trial of Holyoake, London, 1842.
(u) (1883), 48 L. T. 739; 1 C. & E. 146; 15 Cox, C. C. 231.
(v) Stephen's Digest of the Criminal Law, 5th ed. Art. 98, pp. 70-71. See 60 Geo. 3 & 1 Geo. 4, c. 8, s. 1, at pp. 244, 245, *infra*.

NOTE 3.—As to what constitutes "*obscene*" matter, according to Cockburn, L. C. J., in *Reg.* v. *Hicklin* (x), "the test of obscenity is this, whether the tendency of the matter charged as obscenity is to deprave and corrupt those whose minds are open to such immoral influences and into whose hands a publication of this sort may fall." The question what circumstances will be sufficient to justify the publication of obscene matter is a difficult one. Sir James Stephen, in his Digest of the Criminal Law (y), has dealt with it at length, and comes to the conclusion that "a person is justified in publishing obscene books, papers, writings, prints, pictures, drawings, or other representations, if their publication is for the public good, as being necessary or advantageous to religion or morality, to the administration of justice, the pursuit of science, literature or art, or other objects of general interest; but the justification ceases if the publication is made in such a manner, to such an extent, or under such circumstances, as to exceed what the public good requires in regard to the particular matter published."

As to the power of a stipendiary magistrate or two justices of the peace to suppress and destroy obscene publications, see 20 & 21 Vict. c. 83 (z).

As to summary conviction for affixing to

(x) (1868), L. R. 3 Q. B. 360; 37 L. J. M. C. 89; 18 L. T. 398.
(y) 5th ed. Art. 191, pp. 133–134.
(z) Set out in Appendix B, p. 256, *infra*.

any wall, fence, hoarding, &c., or publishing, any picture, or printed or written matter, which is of an indecent or obscene nature, see the Indecent Advertisements Act, 1889 (*a*).

NOTE 4.—It should be noticed that a defendant is not allowed to set up as a defence upon the trial of an indictment or information for the publication of a blasphemous, seditious, or obscene libel that such words are true, and that it is for the public benefit that they should be published (*b*).

ART. 3.—Publication.

In criminal cases it is not necessary as in the case of a civil action, that there should be publication in the sense of a communication by the defendant of the words complained of to some third party—it is sufficient if the words complained of be communicated by the defendant to the prosecutor himself, provided that their natural tendency is to provoke the prosecutor and excite him to commit a breach of the peace (*c*).

(*a*) 52 & 53 Vict. c. 18, set out in Appendix B., p. 268, *infra*.
(*b*) *Cooke* v. *Hughes* (1824), Ry. & M. 115; *Reg.* v. *Duffy* (1870), 9 Ir. L. R. 329; 2 Cox, C. C. 45; *Ex parte O'Brien* (1883), 12 L. R. Ir. 29; 15 Cox, C. C. 180.
(*c*) *Rex* v. *Garret, Hicks' case* (1618), Hob. 215; Poph. 139; *Rex* v. *Wegener* (1817), 2 Stark. 245; *Reg.* v. *Brooke* (1856), 7 Cox, C. C. 251.

NOTE.—It must also be remembered that in criminal cases the question of publication is entirely a question for the jury (*b*); not, as in civil cases (*c*), partly for the judge and partly for the jury. With the exception of this difference, and that pointed out above, the law of publication in criminal libel is the same as that in civil cases (*b*). Not only the person who originally composed the libel, but every one who prints, sells, gives away, or exposes a copy of it is guilty of publication at law, and is liable to be prosecuted (*d*).

ART. 4.—**No prosecution for newspaper libel except by leave of judge.**

No criminal prosecution by way of indictment shall be commenced against any proprietor, publisher, editor, or any person responsible for the publication of a newspaper (*e*), *for any libel published therein without the preliminary order of a judge at chambers. Such application shall be made on notice to the person accused, who shall have an opportunity of being heard against it* (*f*).

(*b*). See p. 205, *infra*.
(*c*) See p. 17, *supra*.
(*d*) See the observations of Lord Mansfield, in *Rex* v. *Almon* (1770), 20 How. St. Tr., at p. 851; Bayley, J., in *Rex* v. *Carlile* (1819), 3 B. & Ald., at p. 169; and Best, J., in *Rex* v. *Burdett* (1820), 4 B. & Ald., at p. 126.
(*e*) As to meaning of "newspaper," see p. 109, *supra*.
(*f*) See 51 & 52 Vict. c. 64, s. 8, the provisions of which would appear to have no application to any criminal *informa-*

Note.—This article is based upon sect. 8 of the Law of Libel Amendment Act, 1888, which replaced sect. 3 of the Newspaper Libel and Registration Act, 1881, which required the fiat of the Director of Public Prosecutions before any such criminal prosecution could be commenced. The repealed section really afforded little protection to the proprietor or editor of a newspaper, for, as the late Lord Chief Justice pointed out in the House of Lords, the Director of Public Prosecutions frequently issued his fiat for the institution of criminal proceedings for libels in newspapers when he ought to have refused it. The judge in chambers will make no order under this section unless he is satisfied that the case is one which will not be met by a civil action, and there is no appeal from his decision whether he grant or refuse the order (*g*).

Moreover, the advantages of the above provision are limited to "the proprietor, publisher, editor, or any person responsible for the publication of a newspaper," as to which several points are noticeable. In the first place it affords no protection to the actual composer, or author of the libel, to the reporter, or the writer of any article, even though attached to the staff of the newspaper, or to the compositor, or the office boy,

tion, having regard to the construction placed by the Court of Appeal in *Yates* v. *The Queen* (1885), 14 Q. B. D. 848 upon s. 3 (now repealed), of the Newspaper Libel and Registration Act, 1881.

(*g*) *Ex parte Pulbrook* (1892), 1 Q. B. 86.

all of whom are liable to be prosecuted at common law. It is doubtful whether it includes the printer under the phrase "person responsible for the publication." The Act of 1888, unlike that of 1881, contains no definition of proprietor, so that it is difficult to say precisely what construction the Court will put upon the term. It would seem unlikely, in the absence of any express clause to that effect, that the wide meaning given to it in the Act of 1881 will be held applicable. Further, it will be noticed that the section is confined to *newspapers* as defined by the Act of 1881 (*h*). Therefore it has no application to books or periodicals not coming within that definition.

Art. 5.—Defences.

The defences to criminal proceedings for a defamatory libel are—

1. That the words complained of are true, and that it was for the public benefit that they should be published (*i*).

2. That the publication of the words complained of is privileged (*k*).

(*h*) 51 & 52 Vict. c. 64, s. 1, set out on p. 265, *infra*.
(*i*) 6 & 7 Vict. c. 96, s. 6. Art. 6, p. 202, *infra*.
(*k*) See Note, and pp. 96–98, *supra*.

DEFENCES TO CRIMINAL PROCEEDINGS.

3. *That the words complained of are a fair and bonâ fide comment on a matter of public interest* (*l*).

4. *That the publication was made without the authority or knowledge of the defendant, and did not arise from want of due care or caution on his part* (*m*).

The last-mentioned defence is also available upon the trial of an indictment or information for the publication of blasphemous, seditious, or obscene words (*m*).

NOTE.—Of the above defences those numbered 2 and 3 have already been fully dealt with in treating of the defences to an action (*n*). Whether the defence be that the words complained of were published on a privileged occasion (*o*), or were a fair and *bonâ fide* comment on a matter of public interest (*p*), the law is precisely the same in civil and criminal proceedings. And here again, as was observed in treating of the defences to an action, it may be said that it is also a defence that the words complained of are not libellous (*q*), or do not relate to the prosecutor (*r*), or that there has been no publication (*s*); but in all these cases the onus of proving the contrary is on the prosecutor,

(*l*) See Note, and pp. 88–96, *supra*.
(*m*) 6 & 7 Vict. c. 96, s. 7; and see Art. 7, pp. 203, 204, *infra*.
(*n*) See pp. 88–98, *supra*.
(*o*) See pp. 96–98, *supra*.
(*p*) See pp. 88–96, *supra*.
(*q*) See pp. 1–9, *supra*.
(*r*) See pp. 3–5, *supra*.
(*s*) See pp. 197, 198, *supra*.

and if he does not do so, he fails to make out even a *primâ facie* case.

Art. 6.—Defence under sect. 6 of Lord Campbell's Act (6 & 7 Vict. c. 96).

On the trial of any indictment or information for a defamatory libel, it is a good defence to prove that the words complained of are true, and that it was for the public benefit that they should be published (t).

NOTE.—It has already been pointed out that the truth of the words complained of affords a good defence to an *action* for libel (u), but this is not so in the case of criminal proceedings; the defendant must be prepared to go further and prove not only that the words complained of are true, but also that it was for the public benefit that they should be published. If he can satisfy a jury on both these points, he will be entitled to a verdict of not guilty by virtue of sect. 6 of Lord Campbell's Act (x). The defendant must prove the truth of the words complained of with the same exactness as is required of him in a civil action (u). It is provided by the section cited that this defence will not be available unless it be specially pleaded. Moreover, it has no application to blasphemous, seditious, or obscene words (y).

(t) 6 & 7 Vict. c. 96, s. 6, pp. 251, 252, *infra*.
(u) See p. 81, *supra*.
(x) 6 & 7 Vict. c. 96.
(y) *Ex parte O'Brien* (1883), 12 L. R. Ir. 29; 15 Cox, C. C. 180.

ART. 7.—**Employer's criminal liability for libels published by his servants.**

Upon the trial of any indictment or information for the publication of a libel, it is a good defence to prove that such publication was made without the authority, consent, or knowledge of the defendant, and that the said publication did not arise from want of due care or caution on his part (z).

NOTE.—This defence owes its existence to sect. 7 of Lord Campbell's Act, and is peculiar to the criminal law. The general rule of law, as we have seen (a), is that a principal or master is liable for any libel published by his agent or servant, with his authority or consent; and this is true not only as regards liability to an action, but also as regards criminal liability. Moreover, as has been pointed out, provided that the agent or servant, in publishing such libel, was acting in pursuance of general orders, the master is equally liable to *an action*, though he was totally ignorant of the fact of publication; and, prior to Lord Campbell's Act, he would have been *criminally* liable also (b).

Now, however, in accordance with the above

(z) 6 & 7 Vict. c. 96, s. 7, p. 252, *infra*.
(a) p. 62, *supra*.
(b) *Nutt's case* (1727), 1 Barnard. K. B. 306; Fitz. 47; *Rex* v. *Dodd* (1736), 2 Sess. Cas. 33; *Rex* v. *Cuthell* (1799), 27 How. St. Tr. 642; *Rex* v. *Walter* (1799), 3 Esp. 21; *Rex* v. *Gutch and others* (1829), Moo. & Mal. 433.

provision, the proprietor of a newspaper is not criminally liable for a libel which has been inserted in it without his knowledge or consent merely because he has given the editor a general authority to publish what he thinks proper therein (*c*). So, too, the directors of a printing company are not criminally liable for a libel contained in a paper printed by the servants of the company unless they knew of or saw the libel before its publication, or gave express instructions for its appearance (*d*). In all such cases, it will be a question for the jury whether the publication arose from any want of due care or caution on the defendant's part; and the fact that the defendant has employed an editor for the management of a particular department of the newspaper, and has entrusted to him the business of deciding what articles should be inserted in the paper, is not necessarily proof of the defendant's having consented to the publication of the libel by him (*e*). This defence is available upon the trial of any indictment or information for the publication of a defamatory libel, or of blasphemous, seditious, or obscene words (*f*).

(*c*) *Reg.* v. *Holbrook and others* (1877), 3 Q. B. D. 35; 37 L. T. 530; (1878), 4 Q. B. D. 42; 48 L. J. Q. B. 113; 39 L. T. 536.

(*d*) *Reg.* v. *Allison and others* (1888), 59 L. T. 933; 53 J. P. 215.

(*e*) *Per* Cockburn, C. J., and Lush, J.; Mellor, J., *diss.*, in *Reg.* v. *Holbrook, supra.*

(*f*) *Reg.* v. *Bradlaugh and others* (1883), 15 Cox, C. C. 217; *Reg.* v. *Ramsay and Foote* (1883), 48 L. T. 734; 1 C. & E. 132; 15 Cox, C. C. 231.

Art. 8.—Libel or no libel a question for the jury.

On the trial of every indictment or information the jury sworn to try the issue may give a general verdict of guilty or not guilty upon the whole matter put in issue upon such indictment or information (g).

NOTE.—This well-known provision was passed in the reign of George III., mainly through the instrumentality of Mr. Fox, and is contained in the statute known as Fox's Libel Act (32 Geo. 3, c. 60). Prior to this provision becoming law it had come to be the practice for the judge, and not the jury, to decide whether the words complained of were or were not a libel, inasmuch as, on proof of publication by the defendant of the words complained of and of the sense ascribed to them in the indictment or information, the judge would, as in the famous trial of the Dean of St. Asaph (*h*), direct the jury to find the defendant guilty. The judge is, of course, still at liberty to explain to the jury any point of law, and, if he thinks it proper to do so, he may state his own opinion (*i*), but the jury "are the sole judges of the guilt or innocence of the defendant . . . . (they) are the judges of law and fact, and

---

(*g*) 32 Geo. 3, c. 60 (Fox's Act), s. 1.
(*h*) *Rex* v. *Shipley* (1784), 4 Dougl. 73; 21 St. Tr. 1043; 3 T. R. 428, n.
(*i*) 32 Geo. 3, c. 60, s. 2.

on them rests the whole responsibility. In this sense the jury are the true guardians of the liberty of the press" (k). It may be mentioned that sect. 3 of the Act expressly reserves the right of the jury to find " a special verdict in their discretion, as in other criminal cases."

(k) Per Fitzgerald, J., in *Reg.* v. *Sullivan* (1868), 11 Cox, C. C. 52.

APPENDIX A.

On the Conduct of a Civil Action, with Forms and Precedents.

It is always wise not to issue a writ for libel or slander in a hurry. In no class of cases perhaps is a judicious handling of the case in its preliminary stages more essential for a client's success. Indiscretion and want of tact are, far more than is generally supposed, the cause of ultimate failure in an action of this kind. The plaintiff himself, in nine cases out of ten, is highly indignant, often unreasonably so, seeing only his own view of the case, and is anxious to issue a writ with all speed in order that he may at the earliest possible moment properly punish his opponent and set himself right with his friends and the public. The plaintiff's solicitor will not, however, if he is wise, allow himself to be carried away by his client's wishes on this point, but will insist upon carefully considering his client's legal position before moving in the matter. It is always prudent before commencing proceedings to write a judiciously worded letter to the defendant, giving him an opportunity to withdraw and apologise. Such a course will frequently secure for the plaintiff a verdict in a doubtful case, and, where his case is a strong one, will materially increase his chance of obtaining heavy damages. Whatever be the circumstances, such a letter can do no harm, and at the trial it will always find favour both with the judge and jury.

In cases where the libel is contained in a paper or book, there is sometimes difficulty in proving publication at law, and in discovering the names and addresses of the persons responsible for such publication. To meet this difficulty the legislature has passed several statutes. By 2 & 3 Vict. c. 12, s. 2, every paper or book which is meant to be published or dispersed must bear on it the name and address of the printer; and by 39 Geo. 3, c. 79, s. 29, the printer must for six calendar months carefully preserve at least one copy of each paper printed by him, and write thereon the name and address of the person who employed and paid him to print it, and show the same to any justice of the peace who, within such six calendar months, shall require to see the same.

As a rule, rather than be made the defendant in an action for libel, the printer will readily disclose the name of his employer. If, however, he declines to do so, the plaintiff can usually secure the services of a justice of the peace for the purpose of making the necessary demand. If such demand is not complied with, the penalty can be recovered in a summary manner, in accordance with the provisions of 39 Geo. 3, c. 79, ss. 34, 36, and 9 & 10 Vict. c. 33, s. 1 (a).

Where the libel has been published in a newspaper, difficulty is often met with in attempting to ascertain the author of the libel, for an editor will not, as a rule, give this information, nor is he bound to do so. To quote the words of Baron Martin, in *Harle* v. *Catherall and others* (b): "When a man went to an editor to ask for the name of an anonymous correspondent, no blame attached to the editor for refusing to give the name. Indeed, an editor would be almost mad to do so. I should blame no editor for so refusing."

The plaintiff, therefore, generally has to satisfy himself with suing the proprietor and editor, who usually procure an indemnity from the author. The proprietor's name

(a) Set out in Appendix B., pp. 243, 254–255, *infra*.
(b) (1866), 14 L. T. at p. 802.

and address can generally be ascertained without any difficulty by virtue of the provisions of the Newspaper Libel and Registration Act, 1881 (c). Under this Act a register of newspaper proprietors was established at Somerset House (d), which is open to the inspection of any person on payment of one shilling (e). Such register is at present to be found in Room No. 7. It is the duty of the printers and publishers of every newspaper to make a return to the registry office each July, containing the title of the newspaper and the names, occupations, and addresses (business and residential) of all the proprietors of the paper (f); and a certified copy of an entry in this register is sufficient *primâ facie* evidence of all matters and things thereby appearing (g).

If the newspaper is published by a limited company, the Act has no application (h). Even when the defendant is not a limited company, the plaintiff cannot be sure that the defendant was proprietor of the newspaper at the time the libel was published merely because his name appears on the register, for since the return was made he may have ceased to be proprietor; and though the transfer of interest *may* have been registered by either party thereto (i), there is no provision which renders it illegal not to do so.

The plaintiff may of course succeed in fixing the defendant with proprietorship at the time of publication by administering interrogatories, or by proving that the newspaper was bought from the defendant or on the defendant's premises.

If the publisher has in the first instance been sued, the proprietor can, upon the hearing of a summons

(c) 44 & 45 Vict. c. 60.
(d) Ibid. s. 8.
(e) Ibid. ss. 13, 14.
(f) Ibid. s. 9.
(g) Ibid. s. 15.
(h) Ibid. s. 18.
(i) Under s. 11.

P

before a master in chambers, be made a co-defendant (*k*).

A difficulty sometimes met with in practice is to decide how to sue a person, who is out of the jurisdiction and not ordinarily resident within it, for a libel published by an agent in this country. This difficulty may sometimes be overcome by adding to the claim for libel a claim for an injunction to restrain the further publication of the words complained of, and then applying for leave to serve the writ out of the jurisdiction under sub-section (f) of Ord. XI., Rule 1 (*l*). But this course will not succeed if the Court thinks it improbable that the libel will be repeated and is satisfied that the claim for an injunction is not made *bonâ fide*, but merely in order to bring the case within the rule (*m*). So, too, leave will be refused if the injunction could not, if granted, be rendered effectual against the defendant, even though it might be against his agent (*n*). Another course which may sometimes succeed is to first sue the agent, and then to apply for leave to join the principal as a necessary and proper party under Ord. XI., Rule 1, sub-section (g) (*o*).

Where the document containing the libel is in the possession of a third person, it is always well for the plaintiff's solicitor to give such person formal notice to preserve it.

In actions for slander, where so much depends upon the exact words spoken, it is prudent to obtain signed proofs from the witnesses as early as possible.

Trial without pleadings, which is now permitted, subject to certain conditions (*p*), is not generally advisable in the interests of a plaintiff in an action for libel or slander;

(*k*) *Edward* v. *Lowther* (1876), 45 L. J. C. P. 417; 34 L. T. 255; 24 W. R. 434.
(*l*) *Tozier* v. *Hawkins* (1885), 15 Q. B. D. 680.
(*m*) *De Bernales* v. *New York Herald* (1893), 2 Q. B. 97, n.
(*n*) *Ibid.* See also *Marshall* v. *Marshall* (1888), 38 Ch. D. 330.
(*o*) *Croft* v. *King* (1893), 1 Q. B. 419; *Williams* v. *Cartwright* (1895), 1 Q. B 142 (C. A.); *Chance* v. *Beveridge and Freeman's Journal* (1895), 11 Times L. R. 528.
(*p*) Order XVIII., A.

for under such circumstances he will not know until he gets to trial what defence will be raised against him.

The writ should be indorsed:

"The plaintiff's claim is for damages for libel" [*or* "for slander"].

Proceedings having commenced, it is imperative that the defendant should carefully consider his position, if indeed he has not already done so. This is especially necessary where the libel has been published in a newspaper, for if the defence of apology under Lord Campbell's Act is to be raised, such apology must be inserted in the paper "either before the commencement of the action or at the earliest opportunity afterwards" (*q*). And let the defendant remember that if he offers the plaintiff an apology it must be full and free, not half-hearted or niggardly. If he has a bad case the sooner he recognizes that fact the better, for by so doing he will save much expense and anxiety. Generally speaking, if the plaintiff is ordinarily resident out of the jurisdiction, the defendant can compel him to give security for costs (*r*). And provided that the defendant can prove that the plaintiff has no visible means of paying the defendant's costs, an order will be made that the action be remitted to the County Court, unless the plaintiff shall, within a certain time, give full security for the defendant's costs, or satisfy the Court that he has a cause of action fit to be prosecuted in the High Court (*s*). The application for such order is made by summons before a master, and must be supported by affidavit. In order to defeat it, the plaintiff must show that he has a cause of action more fit to be tried in the High Court than in the County Court (*t*), and in *Critchley* v. *Brown* (*u*) a Divisional Court held that, where the alleged slander was an imputation

(*q*) See p. 156, *supra*.
(*r*) See p. 58, *supra*.
(*s*) County Courts Act, 1888 (51 & 52 Vict. c. 43), s. 66.
(*t*) *Farrer* v. *Lowe & Co. & Medley* (1889), 5 Times L. R. 234; *Banks* v. *Hollingsworth* (1893), 1 Q. B. 442 (C. A.); *Williams* v. *Morris* (1894), 10 Times L. R. 603.
(*u*) (1886), 2 Times L. R. 238.

upon the chastity of a married woman, the imputation was sufficiently grave to make the action fit to be tried in the High Court.

The Statement of Claim must be carefully drafted. It is the invariable practice to allege that the defendant published the words "falsely and maliciously." It is, however, unnecessary to aver that the defendant published the words maliciously (*x*). Further, as the plaintiff need not in his Statement of Claim "allege any matter of fact which the law presumes in his favour, or as to which the burden of proof lies upon the other side" (*y*), and as the law presumes in his favour that the words complained of are false (*z*), it is submitted that the omission of the word "falsely" would not invalidate the Statement of Claim. The Statement of Claim should contain the *precise words* complained of, for they are "material facts" within the meaning of Ord. XIX., Rule 4 (*a*). This is sometimes impossible, for example, where the action is for libel, and the document containing the libel is in the possession of the defendant or some third party who declines to allow the plaintiff to copy or even to inspect it.

If the libel is in the possession of the defendant, the plaintiff should find out as nearly as he can the exact words of the libel from those persons to whom the defendant has shown it, and should insert these words in his Statement of Claim. He should then apply for discovery of documents, when, unless the defendant successfully claims that the document in question is privileged from discovery, the plaintiff will be able to obtain inspection of it, and can then deliver an amended Statement of Claim setting out the precise words used.

If the libel is in the possession of some third person who

(*x*) Per Bayley, J., in *Bromage* v. *Prosser* (1825), 4 B. & C. at p. 255. See also the observations of Lord Russell, L. C. J., in *Reg.* v. *Munslow* (1895), 1 Q. B. at p. 763.
(*y*) Order XIX., r. 25.
(*z*) Per Field, J., and Huddleston, B., in *Belt* v. *Lawes* (1882), 51 L. J. Q. B. at p. 361.
(*a*) *Harris* v. *Warre* (1879), 4 C. P. D. 125.

will not allow the plaintiff to inspect it, the only course open to the plaintiff is to set out the supposed contents of the libel in his Statement of Claim, give such third person a formal notice to preserve the document in question, serve him with a *subpœna duces tecum* to produce it at the trial, and trust to the judge allowing the Statement of Claim to be amended if necessary when the case comes on for hearing. Such a course is necessarily unsatisfactory, for even if the libel is not contained in a document which is absolutely privileged from production, the plaintiff is obliged, until he gets to trial, to rely upon the statements of those to whom the alleged libel has been shown, and there is always a possibility of his discovering at the eleventh hour that the words complained of do not amount to a libel. Unless therefore he can rely implicitly upon the recollection of those who have seen the alleged libel, he will be very unwise to bring an action.

Moreover, official documents, such as communications made by one officer to another in the course of his duty (*b*), or official communications between persons employed by the State (*c*), are absolutely privileged from production on the ground of public policy, and if the alleged libel be contained in such a document, and the objection to produce it at the trial be taken by the proper person, the plaintiff must fail, as no secondary evidence is allowed of the contents of such a document (*d*). So, too, in the case of a professional communication passing between a solicitor and client, the original document is similarly privileged from production. In this case, however, if privilege from production of the document is claimed at the trial, the plaintiff will be entitled to give secondary evidence of its contents (*e*).

(*b*) *Ford* v. *Blest* (1890), 6 Times L. R. 295.
(*c*) *Beatson* v. *Skene* (1860), 5 H. & N. 838; 29 L. J. Ex. 430; H.M.S. *Bellerophon* (1874), 44 L. J. Ad. 5; *Hughes* v. *Vargas* (1893), 9 Times L. R. 551 (C. A.).
(*d*) *Anderson* v. *Hamilton* (1816), 2 B. & B. 156, n.; *Stace* v. *Griffith* (1869), L. R. 2 P. C. at p. 428.
(*e*) *Marston* v. *Downes* (1834), 1 A. & E. 31, 6 C. & P. 381; *Mills* v. *Oddy* (1834), 6 C. & P. 728; *Newton* v. *Chaplin* (1850), 10 C. B. 356; and see pp. 233, 234, *infra*.

In drafting the Statement of Claim, in addition to setting out the *precise words* complained of, the pleader should also be careful to insert an *innuendo* where the meaning of the words or their application to the plaintiff is not clear, otherwise his client may be non-suited. Thus in an action for slander (*f*), where the words complained of were, "Did he have a fire twice? He is a funny fellow," it was held that, as neither the words themselves nor the innuendo accused the plaintiff of a crime, the pleading was defective, and the plaintiff was non-suited.

It is sufficient for the innuendo to allege a criminal offence; it is not necessary to specifically state what is the precise offence which the plaintiff alleges the words mean (*g*).

Strictly speaking, it would seem that allegations which merely go to aggravate the damages ought not to be inserted in the Statement of Claim, as they are not "material facts" within the meaning of Ord. XIX., Rule 4 (*h*). It is, however, the recognized practice in chambers to allow such matters to be pleaded, and an application to strike them out of the Statement of Claim would probably be refused (*i*). Thus in *Whitney* v. *Moignard* (*k*), an allegation that defendant knew that the libel would be, and that in fact it was repeated in other journals, was allowed.

Moreover, if the plaintiff interrogates as to matters of this kind, he will find it useful, on the hearing of a summons for further and better answers to such interrogatories, to have these matters in issue on the record.

It is very often convenient not to set out in the Statement of Claim the names of the persons to whom and the places where the words complained of have been

---

(*f*) *Jacobs* v. *Schmaltz* (1890), 62 L. T. 121; 6 Times L. R. 155.
(*g*) *Webb* v. *Beavan* (1883), 11 Q. B. D. 609.
(*h*) *Harris* v. *Warre* (1879), 4 C. P. D. 125.
(*i*) See *Millington* v. *Loring* (1880), 6 Q. B. D. 190 (C. A.).
(*k*) (1890), 24 Q. B. D. 630.

published, but to leave it to the defendant to take out a summons for particulars of such names and places. This course gives the plaintiff's solicitor time in which to collect additional information on the subject, and in some cases it is both inconvenient and impossible to give all the necessary particulars in the Statement of Claim.

Where the words affect the plaintiff in the way of his office, profession, or trade, the pleader should be careful to insert an averment to that effect; and where the words are spoken, he should also allege that at the time the words were spoken the plaintiff held such office or carried on such profession or trade (*l*).

If the words are not actionable *per se*, the pleader must specifically allege in his Statement of Claim the special damage sustained by the plaintiff.

PRECEDENTS.

No. 1.—*Libel on Surgeon contained in a Letter.*

In the High Court of Justice.   1897. B. No. 111.
   Queen's Bench Division.

Writ issued the 20th day of March, 1897.

Between A. B.....................Plaintiff,
               and
      C. D.....................Defendant.

Statement of Claim.

1. The plaintiff is and at the time hereinafter mentioned was a surgeon practising in the city of E. and the neighbourhood thereof. The defendant is also a surgeon practising in the said city.

2. On or about February 14th, 1897, the defendant falsely and maliciously wrote and published of the plaintiff, and of him in the way of his profession of a surgeon, in a letter sent to one B. C., the words following, that is to say [*set out the precise words complained of*].

3. The defendant meant and was understood to mean thereby that the plaintiff was ignorant, unskilful, and negligent in his said profession and in the discharge of his professional duties.

(*l*) See pp. 9, 27, *supra*.

4. The plaintiff has been thereby greatly injured in his credit and reputation, and in the way of his said profession, and has been brought into public scandal, odium, and contempt.

And the plaintiff claims 1000*l.* damages.

No. 2.—*Libel in Newspaper published by Company reflecting on Solicitor and Clerk to Borough Magistrates.*

Statement of Claim.

1. The plaintiff is a solicitor of the Supreme Court of Judicature, and is clerk to the justices of the borough of W., in the county of B. He has practised the profession of a solicitor in the said borough of W., and has held the said office of clerk to the borough justices for the last seven years.

2. The defendant E. F. is the editor of "The ———," a paper which is widely read in W., and throughout South Bedfordshire, and which has a larger circulation than any other local weekly paper. The defendant company is the proprietor, printer, and publisher of the said paper.

3. On or about January 23rd, 1897, the defendants falsely and maliciously printed and published in their said newspaper of the plaintiff, and of him in the way of his said profession and office, the words following, that is to say :—

[*Here set out in full the libel.*]

4. The defendants meant, and were understood to mean thereby, that the plaintiff had been guilty of dishonourable and unprofessional conduct; that he had acted corruptly in, and was wholly unfit for, his said office; and that he ought at once to be discharged therefrom, and struck off the rolls.

5. The plaintiff has been thereby greatly prejudiced and injured in his credit and reputation, and in his said office, and brought into public scandal, odium, and contempt.

And the plaintiff claims 3000*l.* damages.

No. 3.—*Libel on Firm of Printers published in Newspaper, and in Newspaper Posters.*

Statement of Claim.

1. The plaintiffs are a firm of printers, who for upwards of fifty years have carried on, and are now carrying on, business at A. Street, in the city of London, and for several years past also at C., in the county of S. The defendant X. Y. is the managing editor and proprietor of a weekly journal, called "The D. J." The defendants E. F. & Co., are the printers,

and the defendant G. H. is the publisher, of the said journal. The said journal has a large and extensive circulation in London, Leeds, Newcastle, and elsewhere.

2. In the issue of the said journal for March 6th, 1897, the defendant X. Y. falsely and maliciously wrote and caused to be printed and published, and the defendants E. F. & Co. falsely and maliciously printed and published, and the defendant G. H. falsely and maliciously published of the plaintiffs, and of them in the way of their said business, the words following, that is to say :—

[*Set out the exact words complained of.*]

3. On or about the said date the defendants falsely and maliciously caused to be printed and published, in the form of a certain libellous poster, of the plaintiffs, and of them in the way of their said business, the words following, that is to say :—

[*Set out words in full.*]

4. The defendants caused several of such posters to be posted up in the neighbourhood of the plaintiffs' printing establishments.

5. The defendants meant, and were understood to mean thereby, that the plaintiffs were unfit to be trusted by, or to employ decent or respectable persons, and that they had been guilty of shameful, dishonest, and dishonourable dealings with, and were in the habit of cheating and defrauding, those who dealt with or were employed by them, and that they would not employ, and would discharge from their employment, any one whom they believed to be a tradeunionist, and that they had in fact discharged persons from their employment for that reason, and that they treated their employés with cruelty and inhumanity, and that they oppressed and ground them down, and deliberately overworked them and drove them like slaves, and that an illustration and type of such cruelty and inhumanity was the plaintiffs' treatment of the persons employed to print " The R. N.," who were employed on the express condition that they should work continuously through the night for eleven hours without any break for rest or refreshment, and that after only one hour's rest they should resume their regular day work.

6. The plaintiffs have been thereby greatly injured in their character, credit, and reputation, and in the way of their said business, and have been brought into public ridicule, odium, and contempt.

And the plaintiffs claim 1000*l*. damages.

No. 4.—*Libel on Pickle Manufacturers in Journal—Injunction.*

Statement of Claim.

1. The plaintiffs carry on business as pickle manufacturers at A. During the last ten years the sales of the plaintiffs' pickles have been largely increased. The amount of such sales is mainly dependent upon the high reputation for purity of the plaintiffs' pickles among grocers and others in the retail trade from whom the plaintiffs obtain orders through their travellers.

2. The defendant is proprietor, editor, and publisher of a weekly journal called "The F—— Journal." The said journal has a large and extensive circulation throughout A., and particularly amongst grocers and others in the retail trade.

3. In the issue of the said journal for February 13th, 1897, the defendant contriving and intending to injure the plaintiffs in the way of their business of pickle manufacturers, and with the object of inducing the plaintiffs' customers and others to believe that the pickles manufactured by the plaintiffs were adulterated and unfit for use, falsely and maliciously wrote and printed and published of the plaintiffs and of them in the way of their said business and in relation to the pickles manufactured by them, the following words:—

[*Set out words.*]

4. The defendant meant and was understood to mean by the words set out above that the pickles manufactured by the plaintiffs were adulterated and unfit for use and ought not to be purchased by the public, and could not be bought by grocers with confidence, and that the plaintiffs knew them to be such and could not prove to the contrary, that they had acted in a most unjustifiable and discreditable manner, and had most unfairly and dishonourably attacked the G. Co., and had represented the pickles manufactured by the said company to be adulterated when they knew such was not the fact, and that the plaintiffs had been guilty of shameful and dishonest dealings, and were in the habit of cheating and defrauding those who dealt with them, and that they were unfit to be trusted by honest tradesmen, and that the defendant could prove such to be the fact.

5. The defendant continues and threatens, and intends to continue, the publications hereinbefore complained of.

6. By reason of the facts hereinbefore stated the plaintiffs

have been and will be prejudiced in their said business, and the reputation of the pickles manufactured by them has been impaired, and the plaintiffs have been greatly injured in their credit and reputation, and have been brought into public hatred, ridicule, and contempt.

And the plaintiffs claim—

1. Damages.
2. An injunction to restrain the defendant, his agents and servants from further writing, circulating, distributing, or otherwise publishing the said libels, or any further or other libels affecting the plaintiffs in their said business or otherwise.

No. 5.—*Slander on Grocer—Special damage.*

Statement of Claim.

1. The plaintiff is a grocer carrying on his trade at P., in the county of Cambridge.
2. On or about January 2nd, 1897, the defendant falsely and maliciously spoke and published of the plaintiff, in the way of his trade and in relation to his conduct therein, the words following, that is to say [*here set out the actual words spoken*], meaning thereby that the plaintiff cheated, and was guilty of fraudulent, corrupt, and dishonest practices in his said trade.
3. In consequence of the said words the plaintiff was injured in his credit and reputation as a grocer, and in his trade, and A., B., and C., who had hitherto dealt with the plaintiff in his said trade, ceased to deal with him, and the D. E. & F. Co., who had previously supplied the plaintiff with goods on credit, thereupon refused to sell any more goods to the plaintiff on credit as the said company otherwise would have done.

And the plaintiff claims 300*l.* damages.

No. 6.—*Form of Declaration used in the Lord Mayor's Court in the City of London.*

In the Mayor's Court, London.

The 22nd March, 1897.

Between A. B. ....Plaintiff,
and
The C. D. Publishing Co...Defendants.

Declaration.

A. B., by Messrs. E. F., his solicitors, sues the C. D. Publishing Co. for that the defendants on or about March 6th,

1897, falsely and maliciously printed and published of the plaintiff, and of him in the way of his business of a ———, in a newspaper called "———," the words following, that is to say [*set out exact words complained of*]. And the plaintiff also sues the defendants for that the defendants in the issue of their said newspaper for March 7th, 1897, falsely and maliciously printed and published of the plaintiff, and of him in the way of his said business, the words following, that is to say [*set out exact words used*]. And the defendants meant and were understood to mean thereby, &c. And by reason of the publication of the said words the plaintiff has been injured in his credit and reputation and in his said business, &c.

And the plaintiff claims ———*l.*

No. 7.—*Statement of Claim in action for Libel removed by Writ of Certiorari from the Lord Mayor's Court, London, into the Queen's Bench Division of the High Court of Justice.*

In the High Court of Justice.
  Queen's Bench Division.
  Removed from the Lord Mayor's Court in the City of London by her Majesty's writ of *certiorari*, issued on the ——— day of ———, 1897, out of the Queen's Bench Division of the High Court of Justice.

Between A. B..................Plaintiff,
           and
       C. D..................Defendant.

Statement of Claim.

1. The plaintiff is a stock and share broker and dealer, carrying on business at ——— in the City of London. The defendants are a company incorporated under the Companies Acts, 1862 to 1890, and are the proprietors and publishers of a daily paper called "The F. P.," which has an extensive circulation in London and the provinces.

2. On or about March 10th, 1897, in the Lord Mayor's Court in the City of London, an action was tried in which the plaintiff sued the Rev. A. B. for 150*l.*, money due and owing to him in respect of certain dealings in stocks and shares. The said action was settled in Court, and a juror was withdrawn upon terms.

3. Thereupon, in their issue of the said paper for March 11th, 1897, the defendants published a report of the trial of the said action, and falsely and maliciously caused to be written and printed and published of the plaintiff, and of

him in the way of his said business, the words following, that is to say :—
[*Set out exact words used.*]

4. The defendants in the issue of the said paper for March 12th, 1897, further falsely and maliciously caused to be written and printed and published of the plaintiff, and of him in the way of his said business, the words following, that is to say :—
[*Copy article of March 12th in full.*]

5. The defendants meant and were understood to mean thereby that the plaintiff conducted his business dishonestly; that he was in the habit of scattering circulars broadcast, and so wording such circulars as to attract the attention and excite the cupidity of parsons and other people not well acquainted with the ways of business; that he induced such people to open accounts with him by making false and fraudulent statements; that, in particular, he had by false and fraudulent statements induced the Rev. A. B. to pay over money to him, and that he had grossly deceived and defrauded the said Rev. A. B.; that he was a swindler, a rogue, and a liar; that he was unfit for and ought not to be trusted in his said business; and that no respectable bank ought to allow him either to open or keep an account with them, as by so doing they would be lending their name to a fraud and a lie.

6. The plaintiff has been thereby injured in his credit and reputation and in his said business, and has been brought into public hatred, odium, and contempt.

And the plaintiff claims 500*l.* damages.

Upon delivery of the Statement of Claim the defendant should consider whether he should take out a summons for particulars of the names of the persons to whom and the places where the words complained of have been published and of the special damage if any alleged by the plaintiff.

In an action for slander he is clearly entitled to particulars of the persons to whom the slander is alleged to have been uttered (*m*), and an order for such particulars will be made before defence (*n*).

In the words of Pollock, B. (*o*), "it may be necessary

(*m*) *Bradbury* v. *Cooper* (1883), 12 Q. B. D. 94.
(*n*) *Roselle* v. *Buchanan* (1886), 16 Q. B. D. 656.
(*o*) *Gouraud* v. *Fitzgerald* (1889), 37 W. R. at p. 55.

for the defendants to know the place and the time, and before whom the alleged slander was uttered."

In *Williams* v. *Ramsdale* (*p*), " the best particulars the plaintiff can give of the persons present" were ordered. Such particulars were, however, refused in an action for libel (*q*), and such refusal was upheld by the Court of Appeal (*r*). The reason of such refusal was, however, expressly stated to be that the application was made too late; and it is submitted that upon an application of this kind there is no ground for making any distinction between actions of libel and slander, and that in both cases a defendant is entitled to particulars provided that his application is made promptly.

Where the Statement of Claim alleges that by reason of the publication of the words complained of the plaintiff has been injured in his business or trade, the defendant is entitled to particulars of the special damage alleged, and it is always wise to ascertain exactly what the plaintiff intends to prove under these words. If the defendant is applying for particulars of other matters in the Statement of Claim he can include in his summons an application for "particulars of special damage if any alleged by plaintiff in his Statement of Claim." If he is not taking out any such summons, his solicitors should write to the plaintiff's solicitors asking for an undertaking that the plaintiff will not offer any evidence of special damage at the trial. If such an undertaking is refused, the defendant should take out a summons.

The following form may be found useful in settling a summons for particulars:—

[*Summons for Particulars.*]

Let all parties concerned attend the Master in Chambers, Central Office, Royal Courts of Justice, Strand, London, on Monday, March 22nd, 1897, at 1.30 o'clock in the afternoon,

(*p*) (1888), 36 W. R. 125.
(*q*) *Gouraud* v. *Fitzgerald* (1889), 37 W. R. 55.
(*r*) 37 W. R. 265.

on the hearing of an application on the part of the defendant for an order that the plaintiff do deliver to the defendant within seven days particulars in writing stating when, where, and to whom the libels alleged in paragraphs 3, 4, and 5 of the Statement of Claim were respectively written and published, and also particulars of the special damage alleged in paragraph 7 thereof, and that in default of delivery of such particulars the plaintiff be precluded from giving any evidence in support of the said paragraphs at the trial of this action, and that the defendant have ten days further time to deliver his Defence after the delivery of the said particulars.

Dated the ——— day of ———, 1897.

This summons was taken out by ———, of ———, solicitors for the defendant.

To the plaintiff, or to Messrs. ———, his solicitors.

Such particulars should be settled with the greatest care; and where the words complained of have been published to a large number of persons, and the plaintiff is uncertain whether he may not be able before the case comes on for trial to discover other publications than he is at present aware of, his particulars should be drafted with a view to enable him to deliver further particulars of such other publications in the event of his obtaining evidence thereof at a later stage of the proceedings.

The following is an example of particulars delivered in pursuance of a master's order upon the hearing of such a summons as that set out above:—

Particulars.

Delivered pursuant to the order of Master Archibald, dated March 22nd, 1897. The following are the particulars, showing when, where, and to whom the libels in paragraphs 3, 4, and 5 of the Statement of Claim were respectively written and published, and of the special damage mentioned in paragraph 7 of the Statement of Claim:—

1. The libel set out in paragraph 3 of the Statement of Claim was contained in a letter written by the defendant, and published by him, to A. B. in Bath on March 1st, 1897.

2. The libel set out in paragraph 4 was shown by the defendant to C. D. at the defendant's house at Templeton on March 2nd, 1897.

3. The libel set out in paragraph 5 was, &c.

4. The plaintiff believes, and will invite the jury to believe, that the defendant showed a copy of the said libels to divers other persons at present unknown to the plaintiff.

5. The special damage in paragraph 7 of the Statement of Claim consists of the verbal refusal at ——— on March 4th, 1897, of A., B., and C., former customers of the plaintiff, to give him any further orders.

In settling the Defence, the defendant should consider which of the defences mentioned on pp. 80, 81, *supra*, ought to be set up. If he decides to pay money into Court, he cannot plead any other defence denying liability (*s*).

Thus in *Mackay* v. *Manchester Press Co.* (*t*), where a general payment in was made in a libel action, with a Defence partly denying the innuendo in the Statement of Claim, the defendants were ordered to amend their defence by stating to which part of the Statement of Claim the payment into Court was intended to apply. Nor can the defendant plead an apology under sect. 2 of Lord Campbell's Act (*u*) with any other defence denying liability, for it is necessary to pay money into Court by way of amends at the time any plea under that section is delivered (*v*).

In *Gray* v. *Bartholomew* (*x*) it was held by the Court of Appeal that where the defendant pays money into Court, but at the trial the jury find a verdict for the plaintiff for less than the amount paid in, the judge has power under Ord. XXII., Rule 5, to direct the money paid in, less the amount recovered, to be paid out to defendant.

On the other hand, in *Dunn* v. *The Devon and Exeter Const. Newspaper Co. Ltd.* (*y*), it was held by Wills, J., that where the action is against a newspaper and the defendant pleads an apology under sect. 2 of Lord Campbell's Act (8 & 9 Vict. c. 75), and pays money into

(*s*) Ord. XXII., r. 1.
(*t*) (1889), 6 Times L. R. 16.
(*u*) 3 & 4 Vict. c. 96.
(*v*) 8 & 9 Vict. c. 75, s. 2.
(*x*) (1895), 1 Q. B. 209. See also *Best* v. *Osborne & Co.* (1896), 12 Times L. R. 419.
(*y*) (1894), 10 Times L. R. 335; (1895), 1 Q. B. 211, n.

Court, and the jury find a verdict for the plaintiff for less than the amount paid into Court, the plaintiff is, notwithstanding the verdict of the jury, entitled to the whole amount paid in. This decision was however doubted by Lord Esher, M. R., in *Gray* v. *Bartholomew* (*supra*), and it is respectfully submitted would not be upheld.

It frequently happens that a defendant can rely on two or more different defences, but such a course is not always desirable. For instance, if the defendant has undoubted evidence to prove that he never spoke any of the words complained of, it is unwise to plead privilege, as such a plea rather suggests that he did in fact utter the words complained of. Under such circumstances it is better to rely solely upon the defence that he never uttered the words. Again, if there is a clear defence of qualified privilege, and no evidence of malice, it would be foolish to justify, as such a course, if persisted in at the trial, affords some evidence of malice (*z*). And in any case it is dangerous to justify, unless the defendant is perfectly sure of his ground; for if he fails at the trial, such a plea will most certainly aggravate the damages.

In pleading to the allegation in the Statement of Claim that the defendant falsely and maliciously wrote [or spoke] and published the words complained of, "there is . . . no good done by a traverse of the allegation that the defendant published falsely; but it is, on the other hand, mischievous, as under it a defendant might set up a defence of truth, as a justification; and Ord. XIX., Rule 18, shows that a plaintiff is entitled to know if such a defence is contemplated" (*a*). Nor is it sufficient to deny generally in the Defence that the "defendant wrote or published the same maliciously, as alleged." The facts must be set out upon which the defendant relies, either to show justification or privilege (*b*)

(*z*) *Simpson* v. *Robinson* (1848), 18 L. J. Q. B. 73.
(*a*) *Per* Field, J., in *Belt* v. *Lawes* (1882), 51 L. J. Q. B. at p. 361.
(*b*) *Belt* v. *Lawes* (1882), 51 L. J. Q. B. 359.

The Defence must not be embarrassing. Thus, in *Fleming* v. *Dollar* (c), where the Defence to an action for libel, after admitting publication, alleged that certain of the words complained of were fair comment, and that the rest were true, and then set up a justification with an admission that the same was not complete, and pleaded payment of 40s. into Court in satisfaction, it was held that such a Defence was contrary to Ord. XXII., and embarrassing, and must be struck out. In *Davis* v. *Billing* (d), where by his Defence the defendant admitted that a certain passage in an alleged libel was libellous, and paid 40s. into Court and apologized, the Court of Appeal ordered the Defence to be amended, on the ground that the defendant could not separate one part of the alleged libel from another. Where, in an action for libel, par. 1 of the Statement of Claim stated the libel, par. 2 stated facts upon which the plaintiff would rely at the trial as showing malice, and referred to an appendix, the Court on an application to strike out par. 2 and the appendix struck out the latter (allowing it to be delivered as particulars) but left in par. 2 (e). Again, the defendant may not in his Defence set out his version of the words used and then justify those words (f), nor may he put a meaning upon the words which is not alleged in the Statement of Claim, and which they are not reasonably capable of bearing, and then seek to justify the words in that sense (g).

The Defence must confine itself to material facts. In *Wood* v. *Durham* (h), a jockey sued in respect of an alleged libel charging him with dishonest riding. The defendant pleaded justification, and afterwards applied to amend his Defence by adding a paragraph to the effect that plaintiff

(c) (1889), 23 Q. B. D. 388.
(d) (1891), 8 Times L. R. 58.
(e) *Glossop* v. *Spindler* (1885), 29 Sol. Jour. 556.
(f) *Rassam* v. *Budge* (1893), 1 Q. B. 571; 9 Times L. R. 247; W. N. 52.
(g) See the observations of Field, J., as reported in *Wood* v. *Durham* (1888), 4 Times L. R. at p. 556.
(h) (1888), 21 Q. B. D. 501.

at the date of publication was commonly reputed to have been in the habit of dishonestly riding in horse races. The application was refused on the ground that as general evidence of the plaintiff's bad reputation, if admissible, could only be given in reduction of damages, the paragraph did not contain a statement of material facts, but was merely a " denial or defence . . . as to damages " within the meaning of Ord. XXI., Rule 4.

The following precedents may assist the practitioner:—

No. 1.—*Defence to an Action for Libel against the Proprietors of a Newspaper—Fair comment—Justification.*

1. The defendants admit that they are the proprietors of a weekly newspaper called " The ———."
2. The defendants deny that they published the said words as alleged or with any of the meanings in the Statement of Claim alleged, or with any defamatory meaning.
3. The said words, if defamatory, do not refer to the plaintiff.
4. In so far as they consist of allegations of fact, the said words are true in substance and in fact, and in so far as they consist of expressions of opinion they are fair comments made in good faith and without malice upon the said facts, which are a matter of public interest (*i*).

No. 2.—*Defence—Libel in Newspaper—Fair Report—Fair Comment—Justification.*

1. The defendants are the proprietors of a weekly newspaper called " The Fly-Fisher."
2. The defendants admit that they printed and published in their said newspaper the words set out in paragraph 1 of the Statement of Claim, but deny that they did so with any of the meanings in the said paragraph alleged. The said words are incapable of the said alleged meanings or any other defamatory meaning.
3. The said words without the said alleged meanings are no libel.
4. The said words form part of a fair and accurate report in the said newspaper of proceedings publicly heard before a Court exercising judicial authority (namely, the action of

(*i*) See *Penrhyn* v. *The Licensed Victuallers' Mirror* (1890), 7 Times L. R. 1.

A. v. B., tried in the High Court of Justice before Mr. Justice H. and a jury on March 9th, 1897), which said report was published contemporaneously with such proceedings (k).

5. The said words form part of a fair and accurate report of judicial proceedings publicly heard in the High Court of Justice (namely, the action mentioned in the preceding paragraph), and were published *bonâ fide* and without malice (l).

6. The said words are fair and *bonâ fide* comment on matters of public interest, namely, the said judicial proceedings, and the promotion and registration of the E. M. F. Co., and were published by the defendants *bonâ fide* for the benefit of the public and without any malice towards the plaintiffs.

7. The said words, without the said alleged meanings and according to their natural and ordinary signification, are true in substance and in fact.

No. 3.—*Defence by Shareholder to Action for Libel contained in Circular—Privilege.*

1. The defendant does not admit that he caused any of the words set out in paragraph 2 of the Statement of Claim to be printed or published.

2. The defendant does not admit that he caused any of the said words to be printed or published of or concerning the plaintiff.

3. The defendant never caused any of the said words to be printed or published with any of the meanings alleged. The said words are incapable of the said meanings or of any other defamatory meaning.

4. The defendant was one of the largest shareholders in the A. Co., and printed and published the said words (if at all, which is not admitted) in the form of a circular. And the defendant prepared and issued the said circular in the *bonâ fide* belief that every statement therein contained was true and without malice towards the plaintiff, and with the honest desire to protect the interest of himself, the other shareholders, and the creditors of the said company. And the said circular was published by the defendant to the said shareholders and creditors, who had a corresponding interest with the defendant in the matters therein referred to, and

---

(k) This raises the statutory defence afforded by sect. 3 of the Law of Libel Amendment Act, 1888, see pp. 107, 108, *supra*.

(l) This raises the old common law defence of qualified privilege. See p. 114, *supra*.

as was reasonably necessary and proper for the protection of
the said interests to certain compositors and printers and to
no one else, and is therefore privileged.

No. 4.—*Defence—Libel in Newspaper—Apology before Action
under sect. 2 of Lord Campbell's Act (6 & 7 Vict. c. 96).*

1. The defendants admit that they printed and published
the words set out in paragraph 1 of the Statement of Claim.

2. The said words were contained in a public newspaper
called "The Poolewe Record," which is published by the
defendants once a week, namely, on Saturday. The said
words were inserted in the issue of such newspaper for
Saturday, March 20th, 1897, without malice and without
gross negligence.

3. Before the commencement of this action, to wit, in the
issue of their said newspaper immediately following that in
which the said words appeared, that is, in the issue for
Saturday, March 27th, 1897, the defendants inserted a full
apology for the said words, according to the statute in such
case made and provided, in the words following, that is to
say [*here copy the apology in extenso*].

4. The defendants deny each and every allegation contained in paragraph 2 of the Statement of Claim. They
bring the sum of 40s. into Court by way of amends for the
injury sustained by the plaintiff by the publication of the
said words, and say that that sum is sufficient to satisfy
the plaintiff's claim in this action.

No. 5.—*Defence—Libel in book sold by Booksellers.*

1. The defendants never published any of the words set
out in the Statement of Claim.

2. The defendants never published any of the said words
of the plaintiff.

3. The defendants never published any of the said words
with the meanings alleged.

4. The defendants admit that in February, 1897, they sold
at their premises in Book Street, in the City of London,
certain copies of the book mentioned in the Statement of
Claim, which contained the words set out in paragraph 2
thereof, but by reason of the facts stated in paragraph 5
hereof, the defendants say that they never published the
said words.

5. The defendants are booksellers carrying on a large
business in Book Street aforesaid. The said copies of the

said book were sent by the publishers thereof to the defendants' servants and sold by them in the ordinary course of the defendants' said business and not otherwise, and this is the alleged publication. Neither the defendants nor their servants knew at the time when they sold the said copies, nor ought they to have known, what were the contents thereof, nor that the said copies contained any libel on the plaintiff or were likely to contain any libellous matter. Such want of knowledge was not the result of any negligence on the part of the defendants or their servants (*m*).

No. 6.—*Defence—Libel in Newspaper—Payment into Court.*

The defendants admit that they are the printers and publishers of a newspaper called the " A—— Gazette," and published in the issue of the said newspaper for February 12th, 1897, the words set out in paragraph 2 of the Statement of Claim. They deny that the said words bear the meanings alleged in the said paragraph, but they admit that they are libellous in their natural signification, and that they refer to the plaintiff, and the defendants bring into Court the sum of ten guineas, and say that sum is sufficient to satisfy the plaintiff's claim in respect of the said words without the said alleged meanings, which are denied.

No. 7.—*Defence—Slander—Words of Heat.*

1. The defendant admits that he spoke and published the words set out in paragraph 2 of the Statement of Claim, but denies that he spoke or published them with the meanings in the said paragraph alleged.
2. The said words are merely words of heat, and were uttered by the defendant in anger, as every one who heard the words well knew; they did not mean, and were not understood to mean, that the plaintiff had committed any criminal offence.
3. The said words are incapable of any of the said meanings, or of any other defamatory or actionable meaning.
4. The defendant will object that the said words are not actionable without proof of special damage, and that none is alleged.

Where the defendant has pleaded that the words are true, the plaintiff is entitled to particulars of the matters

(*m*) See pp. 16, 65–66, *supra*, and cases there cited.

upon which the defendant intends to rely in support of such plea (*n*), in order that the plaintiff may know what case he will have to meet at the trial (*o*).

Thus, in *Hennessy* v. *Wright* (*p*), where the defendant pleaded that the alleged libels were reports of public meetings "and were true in substance and in fact," it was held that the plaintiff was entitled to know whether this meant that the defendant had truly reported what was said, or that what he had reported was true.

If the charge is general, and the defendant justifies, he must give specific instances in his pleadings or particulars (*q*). "The plea ought to state the charge with the same precision as an indictment" (*r*), and "if the instances are not put into the plea, the particulars must be as precise as would be necessary in an indictment" (*s*). Thus, in *Foster* v. *Perryman* (*t*), defendant was ordered to give particulars of the passages in the plaintiff's life to which he referred, and upon which he intended to rely at the trial in support of his plea of justification. In *Devereux* v. *Clarke* (*u*), defendant, who had published a review stating that the plaintiff was, by his own showing in a book he had published, a liar, was ordered to point out the passages in the plaintiff's book whereon he relied.

On the other hand, if the charge is specific, for example, that defendant cheated at cards on certain specified occasions, particulars are unnecessary (*x*).

Where the defendant has not justified he cannot, it seems, under Ord. XXXVI., Rule 37, or otherwise, give any evidence in mitigation of damages going to prove the

---

(*n*) *Oakey-Hall* v. *Bryce* (1890), 6 Times L. R. 344; *Zierenberg* v. *Labouchere* (1893), 2 Q. B. 183.
(*o*) *Underwood* v. *Parks* (1744), Str. 1200.
(*p*) (1888), 57 L. J. Q. B. 594.
(*q*) *Zierenberg* v. *Labouchere* (1893), 2 Q. B. 183.
(*r*) Per Parke, B., in *Hickinbotham* v. *Leach* (1842), 10 M. & W. at p. 363.
(*s*) Per Lord Esher, M. R., in *Zierenberg* v. *Labouchere* (1893), 2 Q. B. at p. 187.
(*t*) (1891), 8 Times L. R. 115.
(*u*) (1891), 2 Q. B. 582.
(*x*) *Cumming* v. *Green* (1891), 7 Times L. R. 409. See pp. 84, 85, *supra*.

truth of the words complained of. There appears to be no reported case on the subject, but in the unreported case of *Penny* v. *Stubbs*, tried on February 19th, 1892, Vaughan Williams, J., held that the defendant, having admitted that he had called the plaintiff a perjurer, and not having justified, could not give evidence under Ord. XXXVI., Rule 37, to prove that the plaintiff had made statements in the witness-box in another action which were not in fact true.

Generally speaking, in an action for libel or slander, the Reply is a mere joinder of issue; but sometimes it is desirable to raise an objection in point of law, as in paragraph 3 of the following Reply to a Defence of fair comment and privilege:—

Reply.

1. The plaintiff joins issue with the defendant upon his Defence.

2. The words complained of are not fair or *bonâ fide* comment on any matter of public interest. They are not comments, but false statements on matters of fact.

3. The plaintiff will object that the facts alleged in paragraph 4 of the Defence are not sufficient in law to render the occasion privileged.

It is submitted that in replying to a Defence of privilege, in which the defendant has pleaded that he published the words without malice, it is sufficient merely to join issue (for this puts in issue the question of malice), and that it is not necessary to reply specially that the defendant in publishing the words complained of was actuated by express malice.

The right to all relevant discovery would seem to be less absolute than in other actions (*y*); for example, the general rule allowing a party discovery for the purpose of giving particulars would probably be applied with some caution to a defendant required to give particulars

---

(*y*) *Hennessy* v. *Wright* (1888), 24 Q. B. D. 445, n.; *Parnell* v. *Walter* (1890), 24 Q. B. D. 441; *Zierenberg* v. *Labouchere* (1893), 2 Q. B. 183.

of justification (z). Thus, in *Zierenberg* v. *Labouchere* (a), Lord Esher, M. R., pointed out that as a general rule, "the defendant is not entitled to discovery for the purpose of finding out whether he has a defence or not." And where the defendant puts in a plea of justification, and delivers particulars in support of his plea, the issues to be tried under that plea are limited to the matters referred to in the particulars; and the defendant can only obtain discovery of documents relating to those matters (b).

As mentioned above (c), the plaintiff sometimes finds himself in a difficulty where he has no copy of the libel, and the original is in the possession of the defendant who claims in his affidavit of documents that it is privileged from production. The claim of this kind most commonly met with in practice is where the document in question is a letter passing between a solicitor and his client, and the question whether such a document is privileged from inspection is often one of considerable difficulty. The mere fact that the letter passed between a solicitor and his client does not make it privileged (d); it is necessary to show that it was a professional communication of a confidential character made for the purpose of obtaining or giving legal advice (e). If the defendant's affidavit goes this length no order will be made for production, and it would seem that the privilege applies whether the action be brought by or against the solicitor (f), or by or against his client (g).

It is not, however, always easy to say whether a particular letter is or is not "a professional communication of a confidential character."

(z) See *Gourley* v. *Plimsoll* (1873), L. R. 8 C. P. 362.
(a) (1893), 2 Q. B. at p. 188.
(b) *Yorkshire Prov. Life Ins. Co.* v. *Gilbert and Rivington* (1895), 2 Q. B. 148.
(c) Pages 212–213.
(d) *Penruddock* v. *Hammond* (1847), 11 Beav. 61; *Gardner* v. *Irvin* (1878), 4 Ex. Div. 53.
(e) *Gardner* v. *Irvin, supra*; *O'Shea* v. *Wood* (1891), L. R. P. D. 286.
(f) *Procter* v. *Smiles* (1886), 2 Times L. R. 474; *Ward* v. *Marshall* (1887), 3 Times L. R. 578.
(g) *O'Shea* v. *Wood* (1891), L. R. P. D. 286.

On the one hand, a letter containing a statement of facts written by a client to his solicitor for the purpose of obtaining such solicitor's advice thereon, and the solicitor's letter in reply thereto, come within the description, and will, therefore, be privileged from production in any action, whether such letter was written with reference to that particular action or not (*h*).

On the other hand, " letters containing mere statements of fact are not privileged " (*i*).

If a defendant swears that the alleged libel is " a professional and confidential communication between solicitor and client," it is generally useless for the plaintiff to take out a summons for production, or for a further and better affidavit of documents (*k*). He must be content to go to trial, trusting to the evidence of those persons to whom the defendant showed the libel; and if at the hearing the defendant declines to produce the alleged libel, and insists on still claiming that it is privileged from production, the plaintiff will be entitled to call such persons for the purpose of giving secondary evidence of its contents (*l*).

Thus, in *Procter* v. *Smiles* (*m*), where the defendants were solicitors, it was held that they could not be compelled to produce certain documents of which they were in possession merely as solicitors for their client; and in *Lowden* v. *Blakey* (*n*), a draft advertisement, submitted by a party for the approval of his counsel, was held privileged from production in a libel action subsequently brought against such party upon the advertisement as published.

(*h*) *Wilson* v. *Rastall* (1792), 4 T. R. 753, 760 ; *Goodall* v. *Little* (1850), 1 Sim. N. S. 155; *Minet* v. *Morgan* (1873), L. R. 8 Ch. 361.
(*i*) Per Kay, L. J., in *O'Shea* v. *Wood* (1891), L. R. P. D. at p. 290.
(*k*) See, however, *Russell* v. *Jackson* (1851), 9 Hare 392 ; *Postlethwaite* v. *Rickman* (1887), 35 Ch. D. 725; *Williams* v. *Quebrada R. &c. Co.* (1895), 2 Ch. 751.
(*l*) *Marston* v. *Downes* (1834), 1 A. & E. 31; 6 C. & P. 381; *Mills* v. *Oddy* (1834), 6 C. & P. 728; *Doe* v. *Ross* (1840), 7 M. & W. 102; *Doe* v. *Clifford* (1847), 2 C. & Kir. 448; *Newton* v. *Chaplin* (1850), 10 C. B. 356.
(*m*) (1886), 55 L. J. Q. B. 467.
(*n*) (1889), 23 Q. B. D. 332.

So, too, the plaintiff may be unable to obtain discovery if the alleged libel is contained in an official document (*o*).

It has been held by the Court of Appeal (*p*) that under Order XXXI., Rule 7, all or any of a set of interrogatories may be set aside as being unreasonably or vexatiously exhibited, or may be struck out as being prolix, oppressive, unnecessary, or scandalous; and, further, that if the interrogatories as a whole come within this description, they may all be set aside, or struck out, although some of them, taken alone, would be unobjectionable.

Thus, in *Hindlip* v. *Mudford* (*q*), where the defendants had not justified, but pleaded fair comment, and then administered interrogatories as to the truth of the libel, such interrogatories were ordered to be struck out.

The general rule is this—that the interrogatory must be answered if the answer will " disclose anything which can be fairly said to be material to enable (the party interrogating) either to maintain his own case or to destroy the case of his adversary " (*r*).

The party interrogated may object to answer any one or more of the interrogatories on any of the following grounds :—

1. *That to do so would tend to criminate him.*

The interrogatory cannot be struck out on this ground, but the objection must be taken in the answer in precisely the same way as in the case of any other interrogatory (*s*).

That the answer would tend to criminate others than the person interrogated is not a valid objection, unless

(*o*) See p. 213, *supra*, and the cases there cited.
(*p*) *Oppenheim & Co.* v. *Sheffield* (1893), 1 Q. B. 5; disapproving *Sammons* v. *Bailey* (1890), 24 Q. B. D. 727.
(*q*) (1890), 6 Times L. R. 367.
(*r*) Per Lord Esher, M. R., in *Hennessy* v. *Wright* (1888), 24 Q. B. D. at p. 447.
(*s*) *Allhusen* v. *Labouchere* (1878), 3 Q. B. D. 654; *Fisher* v. *Owen* (1878), 8 Ch. D. 645; disapproving *Atherley* v. *Harvey* (1877), 2 Q. B. D. 524, where interrogatories asking defendant in effect whether he published the libel were struck out.

the Court is satisfied that the interrogatory is not put *bonâ fide* for the purposes of the action (*t*).

2. *That it is irrelevant.*

Thus, in an action against the proprietor of a newspaper, if the defendant admits the publication of the words complained of, he need not answer interrogatories as to the names of the persons from whom his information has been obtained (*u*), or the steps he has taken to test that information (*x*), or the name of the writer of the libellous article (*y*), or the possession of the manuscript (*z*); for such interrogatories are "not material to enable the plaintiff either to maintain his own case or to destroy his adversary's" (*a*).

Again, although the defendant must answer an interrogatory asking him whether the words complained of were not intended to apply to the plaintiff, he need not answer the further question, "If they were not intended to apply to the plaintiff, to whom were they intended to apply?" (*b*).

Documents required merely for the purpose of comparing handwriting may be relevant; thus, where the defendant denied that he had written the letter containing the alleged libel, it was held that the plaintiff was entitled to ask him if he had written another letter, that the writing might be compared (*c*).

Where the plaintiff in an action for libel against the proprietors of a newspaper interrogates the defendants as to how many copies were printed and published of the

---

(*t*) *M'Corquodale v. Bell* (1876), W. N. 39.
(*u*) *Tangyes v. Inman Co.* (1889), 88 L. T. Jo. 32; *Parnell v. Walter* (1890), 24 Q. B. D. 441.
(*x*) *Parnell v. Walter* (1890), 24 Q. B. D. 441; *Mackenzie v. Steinkopf* (1890), 6 Times L. R. 141.
(*y*) *Gibson v. Evans* (1889), 23 Q. B. D. 384; *Hennessy v. Wright, No. 2* (1888), 36 W. R. at p. 880.
(*z*) *British Co. v. Wright* (1884), 32 W. R. 413; *Hennessy v. Wright* (1888), 57 L. J. Q. B. 594.
(*a*) Per Lord Coleridge, L. C. J., in *Gibson v. Evans* (1889), 23 Q. B. D. at p. 387.
(*b*) *Wilton v. Brignell* (1875), W. N. 289.
(*c*) *Jones v. Richards* (1885), 15 Q. B. D. 439; and see *Wilson v. Thornbury* (1874), 17 Eq. 517.

issue of the newspaper which contained the alleged libel, it is usually sufficient for the defendants to answer that a considerable number of copies of that issue were printed and published (*d*). But there may be circumstances in which the defendants would be required to answer the interrogatory more definitely, for instance, " if in such a case it could be shown that the place where the newspaper circulated was obscure, and nothing would be known as to the extent of its circulation, it might be that such an interrogatory would be proper " (*e*).

Where the defendant has in pursuance of Ord. XXXVI., Rule 37, furnished particulars to the plaintiff of matters as to which he intends to give evidence in mitigation of damages, he is entitled to administer interrogatories to the plaintiff as to the matters referred to (*f*). So, too, where it is an issue in the case whether the occasion is privileged, interrogatories are admissible for the purpose of proving or disproving that the defendant has been actuated by malice (*g*).

3. *That it is fishing.*

Interrogatories administered by a party "in order that he may find out something of which he knows nothing now, which might enable him to make a case of which he has no knowledge at present, . . . come within the description of fishing interrogatories, and on that ground cannot be allowed " (*h*).

Thus, in an action for slander, where the plaintiff was accused of using blasphemous words, it was held that he need not answer interrogatories directed to prove that, if he had not used the exact words alleged, he had in fact used language of much the same nature (*i*).

(*d*) *Whittaker* v. *Scarborough Post Newspaper Co.* (1896), 2 Q. B. 148; overruling on this point *Parnell* v. *Walter* (1890), 24 Q. B. D. 441.
(*e*) *Ibid.* per Lord Esher, M. R., at p. 150.
(*f*) *Scaife* v. *Kemp* (1892), 2 Q. B. 319.
(*g*) *Cooper* v. *Blackmore* (1886), 2 Times L. R. 746; *Martin and Wife* v. *Trustees of the British Museum and Thompson* (1893), 10 Times L. R. 215.
(*h*) Per Lord Esher, M. R., in *Hennessy* v. *Wright* (1888), L. R. 24 Q. B. D. at p. 448.
(*i*) *Pankhurst* v. *Hamilton* (1886), 2 Times L. R. 682.

4. *On the ground of legal professional privilege.*

For example, in an action for libel, the defendants were held protected from answering as to statements in their particulars of justification, on the ground that their only information had been procured as solicitors with a view to litigation (*k*).

5. *That it seeks to inquire the names of witnesses to be called or the evidence to be adduced at the trial.*

Thus, in an action for selling newspapers containing libels, interrogatories asking the defendants what precautions they took to ascertain whether newspapers contained libels were disallowed, as asking them how they were going to make out their case (*l*).

It should be noticed that, although the person interrogated may object to answer on the ground that to do so would disclose the names of persons whom he is going to call as witnesses at the trial, such objections will only be allowed when, as is usually the case, the names in question do not form any substantial part of the material facts in issue.

Where the name is a material fact it must be disclosed, and it is no answer that in giving the information the party may disclose the names of his witnesses.

Thus, in *Marriot* v. *Chamberlain* (*m*), the defendant pleaded that the libel was true. The substance of the libel was that the plaintiff had fabricated a story to the effect that a certain circular letter, purporting to be signed by the defendant, had been sent round to the defendant's competitors in business. The plaintiff had, in speeches and letters, stated that he had seen a copy of the alleged letter, that two of such letters were in existence, in possession respectively of a firm of bankers and a firm of manufacturers at Birmingham, and that his informant in the matter was a solicitor of high standing at Birmingham. In interrogatories administered by the

(*k*) *Procter* v. *Smiles* (1886), 55 L. J. Q. B. 467.
(*l*) *Ridgway* v. *Smith and Son* (1890), 6 Times L. R. 275.
(*m*) (1886), 17 Q. B. D. 154. See also *Humphries & Co.* v. *The Taylor Drug Co.* (1888), 39 Ch. D. 693.

defendant, the plaintiff was asked to state the name and address of his informant in whose hands he had seen the copy of the letter, and the names and addresses of the persons to whom the letter had been sent, and in whose possession the two letters were; but he refused to do so, on the ground that he intended to call those persons as witnesses at the trial. It was held that the defendant was entitled to discovery of the names and addresses of such persons, as being a substantial part of facts material to the case, upon the issue of the plea of justification.

It is, of course, legitimate to explain or qualify an answer; for instance, the defendant in a libel action was held justified in adding to his answer that he published the libel honestly and without malice (*n*).

6. *That it inquires as to the contents of a written document, unless the party interrogated has admitted that such document has been lost or destroyed.*

"I do not think," said Bowen, L. J., in *Dalrymple* v. *Leslie* (*o*), "that any law or authority exists by which a person can be compelled to set out his imperfect recollection of a document not produced for his inspection, which is not suggested to be lost or beyond the jurisdiction of the Court, or which, for anything that appears to the contrary, might even be in the possession of the interrogating party."

In accordance with the above rule, interrogatories asking the owner of a newspaper, who admitted responsibility for the libel, as to the contents of the manuscript, were not allowed (*p*).

An application for a new trial must be made by motion to the Court of Appeal (*q*). By Ord. XXXIX. Rule 4, the Notice of Motion is required to be a fourteen days' notice. If the trial has taken place in London or Middlesex, such notice must be served within eight days after the trial;

(*n*) *Malone* v. *Fitzgerald* (1886), 18 L. R. Ir. 187.
(*o*) (1881), 8 Q. B. D. at p. 8.
(*p*) *Hennessy* v. *Wright* (1888), 24 Q. B. D. 445, n.
(*q*) Rule of the Supreme Court, August, 1890.

if the trial has taken place elsewhere than in London or Middlesex, within seven days after the last day of sitting on the circuits for England and Wales during which the trial has taken place.

The Notice of Motion should state the grounds upon which a new trial is asked, *e.g.*, if misdirection is alleged, particulars must be given (*r*). The following is an example of such a Notice of Motion :—

Take notice that the Court will be moved on ——, the —— day of ——, 1897, at 10.30 in the forenoon, or so soon thereafter as counsel can be heard, by Mr. ——, of counsel on behalf of the defendant, for an order that the verdict obtained in this action be set aside and judgment entered for the defendant, on the ground that there was no evidence fit to be submitted to the jury in support of the plaintiff's case, or in the alternative that a new trial be had between the parties on the grounds—

1. That the verdict was against the weight of evidence.
2. That the damages were excessive.
3. That the judge misdirected the jury—

    (*a*) In not directing them that there was no evidence of publication.

    (*b*) In not directing them that the occasion was privileged, and the action could not be maintained without evidence of malice.

    (*c*) In not sufficiently explaining the nature of the privilege, and that the onus lay upon the plaintiff of showing that the defendant did not believe in the truth of the charges.

    (*d*) In leaving to them the question whether or not the occasion of the communications complained of was privileged.

And that in the meantime further proceedings be stayed.

As to the grounds upon which a new trial will be granted, see pp. 178–182, *supra*.

(*r*) *Pfeiffer* v. *Midland Ry. Co.* (1886), 18 Q. B. D. 243; *Murfitt* v. *Smith* (1887), 12 P. D. 116.

APPENDIX B.—*STATUTES.*

CONTENTS.

	PAGE
32 Geo. 3, c. 60 (Fox's Act)	241, 242
39 Geo. 3, c. 79	242, 243
60 Geo. 3 & 1 Geo. 4, c. 8	243–245
6 & 7 Will. 4, c. 76, s. 19	245, 246
2 & 3 Vict. c. 12	246, 247
3 & 4 Vict. c. 9	247, 248
6 & 7 Vict. c. 96 (Lord Campbell's Act)	249–252
8 & 9 Vict. c. 75	253, 254
9 & 10 Vict. c. 33	254, 255
11 & 12 Vict. c. 12	255, 256
20 & 21 Vict. c. 83	256–258
44 & 45 Vict. c. 60 (Newspaper Libel and Registration Act, 1881)	259–264
51 & 52 Vict. c. 64 (Law of Libel Amendment Act, 1888)	265–268
52 & 53 Vict. c. 18 (Indecent Advertisements Act, 1889)	268, 269
54 & 55 Vict. c. 51 (Slander of Women Act, 1891)	269
58 & 59 Vict. c. 40 (Corrupt and Illegal Practices Prevention Act, 1883)	270, 271

Fox's Act, 32 Geo. III. c. 60.

An Act to remove doubts respecting the Functions of Juries in cases of Libel. [A.D. 1792.]

On the trial of an indictment for a libel the jury may give a general verdict upon the whole matter put in issue, and shall not be required by the Court to find the defendant guilty merely on proof of the publication and of the sense ascribed to it in the information.]—Whereas doubts have arisen whether on the trial of an indictment or information for the making or publishing any libel, where an issue or issues are joined between the king and the defendant or defendants, on the plea of not guilty pleaded, it be competent to the jury impanelled to try the same to give their verdict upon the whole matter in issue: Be it therefore declared and enacted by the king's most excellent Majesty, by and with the advice and consent of the Lords spiritual and temporal, and Commons, in the present

Parliament assembled, and by the authority of the same, that on every such trial, the jury sworn to try the issue may give a general verdict of guilty or not guilty upon the whole matter put in issue upon such indictment or information; and shall not be required or directed, by the Court or judge before whom such indictment or information shall be tried, to find the defendant or defendants guilty, merely on the proof of the publication by such defendant or defendants of the paper charged to be a libel, and of the sense ascribed to the same in such indictment or information (*a*).

2. *But the Court shall give their opinion and directions on the matter in issue as in other criminal cases.*]—Provided always, that, on every such trial, the Court or judge before whom such indictment or information shall be tried, shall, according to their or his discretion, give their or his opinion and directions to the jury on the matter in issue between the king and the defendant or defendants, in like manner as in other criminal cases.

3. *Jury may find a special verdict.*]—Provided also, that nothing herein contained shall extend or be construed to extend to prevent the jury from finding a special verdict, in their discretion, as in other criminal cases (*a*).

4. *Defendants may move in arrest of judgment, as before passing this Act.*]—Provided also, that in case the jury shall find the defendant or defendants guilty, it shall and may be lawful for the said defendant or defendants to move in arrest of judgment on such ground and in such manner as by law he or they might have done before the passing of this Act; anything herein contained to the contrary notwithstanding.

---

39 GEO. III. c. 79. [A.D. 1799.]

28. *Not to extend to papers printed by authority of Parliament.*]—Nothing in this Act contained shall extend, or be construed to extend, to any papers printed by the authority and for the use of either House of Parliament.

29. *Printers to keep a copy of every paper they print, and write thereon the name and abode of their employer.—Penalty of 20l. for neglect or refusing to produce the copy within six months.*]—Every person who shall print any paper for hire, reward, gain, or profit, shall carefully preserve and keep one copy (at least) of every paper so printed by him or her, on

(*a*) See pp. 205, 206, *supra*.

which he or she shall write, or cause to be written or printed, in fair and legible characters, the name and place of abode of the person or persons by whom he or she shall be employed to print the same, and every person printing any paper for hire, reward, gain, or profit, who shall omit or neglect to write, or cause to be written or printed as aforesaid, the name and place of abode of his or her employer on one of such printed papers, or to keep or preserve the same for the space of six calendar months next after the printing thereof, or to produce and show the same to any justice of the peace, who, within the said space of six calendar months, shall require to see the same, shall for every such omission, neglect, or refusal, forfeit and lose the sum of twenty pounds (c).

31. *Not to extend to impressions of engravings, or the printing names and addresses.*]—Nothing herein contained shall extend to the impression of any engraving, or to the printing by letterpress of the name, or the name and address, or business or profession, of any person, and the articles in which he deals, or to any papers for the sale of estates or goods by auction or otherwise.

34. *Prosecutions to be commenced within three months after penalty is incurred.*]—No person shall be prosecuted or sued for any penalty imposed by this Act, unless such prosecution shall be commenced, or such action shall be brought, within three calendar months next after such penalty shall have been incurred.

35. *Recovery of penalties.*]—And any pecuniary penalty imposed by this Act, and not exceeding the sum of twenty pounds, shall and may be recovered before any justice or justices of the peace for the county, stewartry, riding, division, city, town, or place in which the same shall be incurred, or the person having incurred the same shall happen to be, in a summary way.

36. *Application of penalties.*]—All pecuniary penalties hereinbefore imposed by this Act shall, when recovered in a summary way before any justice (d), be applied and disposed of in manner hereinafter mentioned; that is to say, one moiety thereof to the informer before any justices, and the other moiety thereof to his Majesty, his heirs and successors (e).

(c) See p. 208, *supra*.
(d) See 9 & 10 Vict. c. 33, s. 1, at p. 254, *infra*.
(e) The above sections are re-enacted by 32 & 33 Vict. c. 24, Sched. II.

60 GEO. III. & 1 GEO. IV. c. 8.

[30th Dec. 1819.]

Court to make order for the seizure of copies of the libel in possession of the persons against whom verdicts shall have been had, &c.—Evidence of possession being given upon oath.—In case of refusal of admission, proceedings.]—Whereas it is expedient to make more effectual provision for the punishment of blasphemous and seditious libels: be it enacted by the king's most excellent Majesty, by and with the advice and consent of the Lords spiritual and temporal, and Commons, in this present Parliament assembled, and by the authority of the same, that from and after the passing of this Act, in every case in which any verdict or judgment by default shall be had against any person for composing, printing, or publishing any blasphemous libel, or any seditious libel, tending to bring into hatred or contempt the person of his Majesty, his heirs, or successors, or the Regent, or the government and constitution of the United Kingdom as by law established, or either House of Parliament, or to excite his Majesty's subjects to attempt the alteration of any matter in church or state as by law established otherwise than by lawful means, it shall be lawful for the judge, or the Court before whom or in which such verdict shall have been given, or the Court in which such judgment by default shall be had, to make an order for the seizure and carrying away and detaining in safe custody in such manner as shall be directed in such order, all copies of the libel which shall be in the possession of the person against whom such verdict or judgment shall have been had, or in the possession of any other person named in the order for his use; evidence upon oath having been previously given to the satisfaction of the Court or judge that a copy or copies of the said libel is or are in the possession of such other person for the use of the person against whom such verdict or judgment shall have been had as aforesaid; and in every such case it shall be lawful for any justice of the peace, or for any constable, or other peace officer acting under any such order, or for any person or persons acting with or in aid of any such justice of the peace, constable, or other peace officer, to search for any copies of such libel in any house, building, or other place whatsoever belonging to the person against whom any such verdict or judgment shall have been had, or to any other person so named in whose possession any copies of any such libel belonging to the person against whom any such verdict or judgment shall have been had, shall be; and in case admission shall be refused, or not obtained within a reasonable time after it shall have been first demanded, to enter by force by day into any such house, building, or place whatsoever, and to carry away all copies of the libel there found, and to detain the same in safe custody until the same shall be restored under the provisions of this Act, or disposed of according to any further order made in relation thereto (*a*).

2. *In what case copies of libels seized restored without fee, &c., or disposed of as Court shall direct.*]— And be it further enacted, that if in any such case as aforesaid, judgment shall be arrested, or if, after judgment shall have been entered, the same shall be reversed upon any writ of error, all copies so seized shall be forthwith returned to the person or persons from whom the same shall have been so taken as aforesaid, free of all charge and expense, and without the payment of any fees whatever: and in every case in which final judgment shall be entered upon the verdict so found against the person or persons charged with having composed, printed, or published such libel, then all copies so seized shall be disposed of as the Court in which such judgment shall be given shall order and direct.

4. *Second offence.—Punishment.*]—And be it further enacted, that if any person shall, after the passing of this Act, be legally convicted of having after the passing of this Act composed, printed, or published any blasphemous libel or any such seditious libel as aforesaid, and shall after being so convicted, offend a second time, and be thereof legally convicted before any commission of oyer and terminer or gaol delivery, or in his Majesty's Court of King's Bench, such person may, on such second conviction, be adjudged, at the discretion of the Court, either to suffer such punishment as may now by law be inflicted in cases of high misdemeanors, or to be banished from the United Kingdom and all other parts of his Majesty's dominions, for such term of years as the Court in which such conviction shall take place shall order.

---

6 & 7 WILL. IV. c. 76. [A.D. 1836.]

19. *Discovery of proprietors, printers, or publishers of newspapers may be enforced by bill, &c.*]—If any person shall file any bill in any Court for the discovery of the name of any person concerned as printer, publisher, or proprietor of any newspaper, or of any matters relative to the printing or publishing of any newspaper, in order the more effectually to

(*a*) See pp. 194, 195, *supra*.

bring or carry on any suit or action for damages alleged to have been sustained by reason of any slanderous or libellous matter contained in any such newspaper respecting such person, it shall not be lawful for the defendant to plead or demur to such bill, but such defendant shall be compellable to make the discovery required; provided always, that such discovery shall not be made use of as evidence or otherwise in any proceeding against the defendant, save only in that proceeding for which the discovery is made (*a*).

---

2 & 3 VICT. c. 12. [A.D. 1839.]

2. *Penalty upon printers for not printing their name and residence on every paper or book; and on persons publishing the same.*]—Every person who shall print any paper or book whatsoever, which shall be meant to be published or dispersed, and who shall not print upon the front of every such paper, if the same shall be printed on one side only, or upon the first or last leaf of every paper or book which shall consist of more than one leaf, in legible characters, his or her name and usual place of abode or business, and every person who shall publish or disperse, or assist in publishing or dispersing, any printed paper or book on which the name and place of abode of the person printing the same shall not be printed as aforesaid, shall for every copy of such paper so printed by him or her forfeit a sum not more than five pounds: Provided always, that nothing herein contained shall be construed to impose any penalty upon any person for printing any paper excepted out of the operation of the said Act of the thirty-ninth year of King George the Third, chapter seventy-nine, either in the said Act, or by any Act made for the amendment thereof (*b*).

3. *As to books or papers printed at the University Presses.*]— In the case of books or papers printed at the University Press of Oxford, or the Pitt Press of Cambridge, the printer, instead of printing his name thereon, shall print the following words, "Printed at the University Press, Oxford," or, "The Pitt Press, Cambridge," as the case may be.

4. *No actions for penalties to be commenced, except in the name of the Attorney or Solicitor-General in England or the*

(*a*) This section was re-enacted by 32 & 33 Vict. c. 24, Sched. II., and is still the law. The original statute, 6 & 7 Will. 4, c. 76, was entirely repealed, no reference, however, being made to this section.

(*b*) See p. 208, *supra*.

Queen's Advocate in Scotland.]—Provided always, that it shall not be lawful for any person or persons whatsoever to commence, prosecute, enter, or file, or cause or procure to be commenced, prosecuted, entered, or filed, any action, bill, plaint, or information in any of her Majesty's Courts, or before any justice or justices of the peace, against any person or persons for the recovery of any fine, penalty, or forfeiture made or incurred, or which may hereafter be incurred under the provisions of this Act, unless the same be commenced, prosecuted, entered, or filed in the name of her Majesty's Attorney-General, or Solicitor-General in that part of Great Britain called England, or her Majesty's Advocate for Scotland (as the case may be respectively); and if any action, bill, plaint, or information shall be commenced, prosecuted, or filed in the name or names of any other person or persons than is or are in that behalf before mentioned, the same and every proceeding thereupon had are hereby declared and the same shall be null and void to all intents and purposes (*c*).

---

3 & 4 VICT. c. 9.

An Act to give Summary Protection to Persons employed in the Publication of Parliamentary Papers.

[14th April, 1840.]

Proceedings, criminal or civil, against persons for publication of papers printed by order of Parliament to be stayed upon delivery of a certificate and affidavit to the effect that such publication is by order of either House of Parliament.]—Whereas it is essential to the due and effectual exercise and discharge of the functions and duties of Parliament, and to the promotion of wise legislation, that no obstructions or impediments should exist to the publication of such of the reports, papers, votes, or proceedings of either House of Parliament, as such House of Parliament may deem fit or necessary to be published; and whereas obstructions or impediments to such publication have arisen and hereafter may arise by means of civil or criminal proceedings being taken against persons employed by or acting under the authority of the Houses of Parliament or one of them, in the publication of such reports, papers, votes, or proceedings; by reason and for remedy whereof it is expedient that more speedy protection should be afforded to all persons acting under the authority aforesaid, and that all such civil or criminal proceedings should

---

(*c*) The above sections are re-enacted by 32 & 33 Vict. c. 24, Sched. II.

be summarily put an end to, and determined in manner hereinafter mentioned: Be it therefore enacted by the Queen's most excellent Majesty, by and with the advice and consent of the Lords spiritual and temporal, and Commons, in this present Parliament assembled, and by the authority of the same, that it shall and may be lawful for any person or persons who now is or are, or hereafter shall be, a defendant or defendants in any civil or criminal proceedings commenced or prosecuted in any manner soever, for or on account, or in respect of the publication of any such report, paper, votes, or proceedings by such person or persons, or by his, her, or their servant or servants by or under the authority of either House of Parliament, to bring before the Court in which such proceeding shall have been or shall be so commenced or prosecuted, or before any judge of the same (if one of the superior Courts at Westminster), first giving twenty-four hours' notice of his intention so to do to the prosecutor or plaintiff in such proceeding, a certificate under the hand of the Lord High Chancellor of Great Britain, or the Lord Keeper of the Great Seal, or of the Speaker of the House of Lords for the time being, or of the Clerk of the Parliaments, or of the Speaker of the House of Commons, or of the Clerk of the same House, stating that the report, paper, votes, or proceedings, as the case may be, in respect whereof such civil or criminal proceeding shall have been commenced or prosecuted, was published by such person or persons, or by his, her, or their servant or servants by order or under the authority of the House of Lords, or of the House of Commons, as the case may be, together with an affidavit verifying such certificate; and such Court or judge shall thereupon immediately stay such civil or criminal proceeding, and the same, and every writ or process issued therein shall be, and shall be deemed and taken to be, finally put an end to, determined, and superseded by virtue of this Act (*b*).

2. *Proceedings to be stayed when commenced in respect of a copy of an authenticated report, &c.*]—And be it enacted, that, in case of any civil or criminal proceeding hereafter to be commenced or prosecuted for or on account or in respect of the publication of any copy of such report, paper, votes, or proceedings, it shall be lawful for the defendant or defendants at any stage of the proceedings to lay before the Court or judge such report, paper, votes, or proceedings, and such copy, with an affidavit verifying such report, paper, votes, or proceedings, and the correctness of such copy, and the Court or judge shall immediately stay such civil or

(*b*) See pp. 106–107, 130, 131, *supra*.

criminal proceeding, and the same, and every writ and process issued therein, shall be deemed and taken to be finally put an end to, determined, and superseded by virtue of this Act (*b*).

3. *In proceedings for printing any extract, &c., it may be shown that extract was bonâ fide made.*]—And be it enacted, that it shall be lawful in any civil or criminal proceeding to be commenced or prosecuted for printing any extract from or abstract of such report, paper, votes, or proceedings, to give in evidence under the general issue such report, paper, votes, or proceedings, and to show that such extract or abstract was published *bonâ fide* and without malice; and if such shall be the opinion of the jury, a verdict of not guilty shall be entered for the defendant or defendants (*b*).

4. *Act not to affect privileges of Parliament.*]—Provided always, and it is hereby expressly declared and enacted, that nothing herein contained shall be deemed or taken, or held, or construed, directly or indirectly, by implication or otherwise, to affect the privileges of Parliament in any manner whatsoever.

Lord Campbell's Act (6 & 7 Vict. c. 96).

An Act to amend the Law respecting Defamatory Words and Libel. [24th August, 1843.]

Offer of an apology admissible in evidence in mitigation of damages.]—For the better protection of private character, and for more effectually securing the liberty of the press, and for better preventing abuses in exercising the said liberty, Be it enacted by the Queen's most excellent Majesty, by and with the advice and consent of the Lords spiritual and temporal, and Commons, in this present Parliament assembled, and by the authority of the same, that in any action for defamation it shall be lawful for the defendant (after notice in writing of his intention so to do, duly given to the plaintiff at the time of filing or delivering the plea in such action) to give in evidence, in mitigation of damages, that he made or offered an apology to the plaintiff for such defamation before the commencement of the action, or as soon afterwards as he had an opportunity of doing so, in case the action shall have been commenced before there was an opportunity of making or offering such apology (*c*).

(*b*) See pp. 106, 107, 130, 131, *supra*.
(*c*) See pp. 166, 167, *supra*.

2. *In an action against a newspaper for libel, the defendant may plead that it was inserted without malice and without neglect, and may pay money into Court as amends.*]—And be it enacted, that in an action for a libel contained in any public newspaper or other periodical publication, it shall be competent to the defendant to plead that such libel was inserted in such newspaper or other periodical publication without actual malice and without gross negligence, and that before the commencement of the action, or at the earliest opportunity afterwards, he inserted in such newspaper or other periodical publication a full apology for the said libel, or if the newspaper or periodical publication in which the said libel appeared should be ordinarily published at intervals exceeding one week, had offered to publish the said apology in any newspaper or periodical publication to be selected by the plaintiff in such action; *and that every such defendant shall, upon filing such plea, be at liberty to pay into Court a sum of money by way of amends for the injury sustained by the publication of such libel, and such payment into Court shall be of the same effect, and be available in the same manner and to the same extent, and be subject to the same rules and regulations as to payment of costs and the form of pleading, except so far as regards the pleading of the additional facts hereinbefore required to be pleaded by such defendant, as if actions for libel had not been excepted from the personal actions in which it is lawful to pay money into Court under an Act passed in the session of Parliament held in the fourth year of his late Majesty, intituled "An Act for the further Amendment of the Law, and better Advancement of Justice"* (d); and that to such plea to such action it shall be competent to the plaintiff to reply generally, denying the whole of such plea (e).

3. *Publishing or threatening to publish a libel, &c., with intent to extort money, punishable by imprisonment with hard labour.*]—And be it enacted, that if any person shall publish or threaten to publish any libel upon any other person, or shall directly or indirectly threaten to print or publish, or shall directly or indirectly propose to abstain from printing or publishing, or shall directly or indirectly offer to prevent the printing or publishing, of any matter or thing touching any other person, with intent to extort any money or security for money, or any valuable thing, from such or any other person, or with intent to induce any person to confer or procure for any person any appointment or office of profit or trust, every such offender, on being convicted thereof, shall be liable to

(d) The words in italics were repealed by the Civil Procedure Acts Repeal Act, 1879 (42 & 43 Vict. c. 59), Schedule, Part II.
(e) See pp. 156, 157, *supra.*

be imprisoned, with or without hard labour, in the common gaol or house of correction, for any term not exceeding three years; provided always that nothing herein contained shall in any manner alter or affect any law now in force in respect of the sending or delivery of threatening letters or writings.

4. *Punishment of false defamatory libel.*]—And be it enacted, that if any person shall maliciously publish any defamatory libel, knowing the same to be false, every such person, being convicted thereof, shall be liable to be imprisoned in the common gaol or house of correction for any term not exceeding two years, and to pay such fine as the Court shall award (f).

5. *Punishment of malicious defamatory libel.*]—And be it enacted, that if any person shall maliciously publish any defamatory libel, every such person, being convicted thereof, shall be liable to fine or imprisonment, or both, as the Court may award, such imprisonment not to exceed the term of one year (f).

6. *Proceedings upon the trial of an indictment or information for a defamatory libel.—Double plea.—Plea of not guilty in civil and criminal proceedings.*]—And be it enacted, that on the trial of any indictment or information for a defamatory libel, the defendant having pleaded such a plea as hereinafter mentioned, the truth of the matters charged may be inquired into, but shall not amount to a defence, unless it was for the public benefit that the said matters charged should be published; and that to entitle the defendant to give evidence of the truth of such matters charged as a defence to such indictment or information, it shall be necessary for the defendant, in pleading to the said indictment or information, to allege the truth of the said matters charged in the manner now required in pleading a justification to an action for defamation, and further to allege that it was for the public benefit that the said matters charged should be published, and the particular fact or facts by reason whereof it was for the public benefit that the said matters charged should be published, to which plea the prosecutor shall be at liberty to reply generally, denying the whole thereof: and that if after such plea, the defendant shall be convicted on such indictment or information, it shall be competent to the Court, in pronouncing sentence, to consider whether the guilt of the defendant is aggravated or mitigated by the said plea, and by the evidence given to prove or to disprove the same; provided always, that the truth of the matter charged in the alleged libel complained of by such indictment or information shall in no case be inquired into without such plea of

(f) See pp. 183, 190, *supra*.

justification; provided also, that in addition to such plea it shall be competent to the defendant to plead a plea of not guilty; provided also, that nothing in this Act contained shall take away or prejudice any defence under the plea of not guilty, which it is now competent to the defendant to make under such plea, to any action or indictment, or information for defamatory words or libel (*g*).

7. *Evidence to rebut primâ facie case of publication by an agent.*]—And be it enacted, that whatsoever, upon the trial of any indictment or information for the publication of a libel under the plea of not guilty, evidence shall have been given which shall establish a presumptive case of publication against the defendant by the act of any other person by his authority, it shall be competent to such defendant to prove that such publication was made without his authority, consent, or knowledge, and that the said publication did not arise from want of due care or caution on his part (*h*).

8. *On prosecution for private libel defendant entitled to costs on acquittal.*]—And be it enacted, that in the case of any indictment or information by a private prosecutor for the publication of any defamatory libel, if judgment shall be given for the defendant, he shall be entitled to recover from the prosecutor the costs sustained by the said defendant by reason of such indictment or information; and that upon a special plea of justification to such indictment or information, if the issue be found for the prosecutor, he shall be entitled to recover from the defendant the costs sustained by the prosecutor by reason of such plea, such costs so to be recovered by the defendant or prosecutor respectively to be taxed by the proper officer of the Court before which the said indictment or information is tried.

9. *Interpretation of Act.*]—And be it enacted, that wherever throughout this Act, in describing the plaintiff or the defendant, or party affected or intended to be affected by the offence, words are used importing the singular number or the masculine gender only, yet they shall be understood to include several persons as well as one person, and females as well as males, unless when the nature of the provision or the context of the Act shall exclude such construction.

10. *Commencement and extent of Act.*]—And be it enacted, that this Act shall take effect from the first day of November next; and that nothing in this Act contained shall extend to Scotland.

(*g*) See pp. 189, 200, 202, *supra*.
(*h*) See pp. 201, 203, 204, *supra*.

8 & 9 VICT. c. 75.

An Act to amend an Act passed in the session of Parliament held in the sixth and seventh years of the reign of her present Majesty, intituled "An Act to amend the Law respecting Defamatory Words and Libel."

[31st July, 1845.]

In cases of action for libel in Ireland where defendant shall plead matters allowed by 3 & 4 Will. 4, c. 42, and pay money into Court, such payment to be of the effect as if required by said Act.]—Whereas by an Act passed in the session of Parliament held in the sixth and seventh years of the reign of her present Majesty, intituled "An Act to amend the Law respecting Defamatory Words and Libel," it is amongst other things enacted and provided that the defendant, in an action for a libel contained in any public newspaper, or other periodical publication, may plead certain matters therein mentioned, and may upon filing such plea be at liberty to pay into Court a sum of money by way of amends for the injury sustained by the publication of such libel; and it is thereby further enacted, that such payment into Court shall be of the same effect, and be available in the same manner and to the same extent, and be subject to the same rules and regulations as to payment of costs and the form of pleading, except so far as regards the pleading of the additional facts thereinbefore required to be pleaded by such defendant, as if actions for libel had not been excepted from the personal actions in which it is lawful to pay money into Court under an Act passed in the session of Parliament held in the fourth year of his late Majesty, intituled "An Act for the further amendment of the Law and the better Advancement of Justice;" and whereas the said Act of the fourth year of the reign of his late Majesty relates only to proceedings in the superior Courts in England, but by an Act passed in the session of Parliament held in the third and fourth years of the reign of her present Majesty, intituled "An Act for abolishing Arrest on Mesne Process in Civil Actions, except in certain cases, for extending the Remedies of Creditors against the Property of Debtors, and for the further Advancement of Justice" (*i*), in Ireland, a like provision is made for payment of money into Court in all personal actions pending in any of the Superior Courts in Ireland as is contained in the said Act of the fourth year of the reign of his late Majesty in regard to actions pending in the Superior Courts in England, with a like exception of actions for libel; and it

---

(*i*) 3 & 4 Vict. c. 105, s. 46, repealed by Stat. Law Rev. Act, 1875.

is expedient to prevent any doubts as to the application of the said recited Act of the sixth and seventh years of the reign of her present Majesty to actions pending in the Superior Courts in Ireland, which may be created by reason of the omission of a reference in the last-mentioned Act to the said Act of the third and fourth years of the reign of her present Majesty : Be it therefore enacted and declared by the Queen's most excellent Majesty, by and with the advice and consent of the Lords spiritual and temporal, and Commons, in this present Parliament assembled, and by the authority of the same, that where in any action pending in the Superior Courts in Ireland for a libel contained in any public newspaper or other periodical publication, the defendant shall plead the matters allowed to be pleaded by the said first-mentioned Act, and shall on filing such plea pay money into Court as provided by such Act, such payment into Court shall be of the same effect and be available in the same manner and to the same extent, and be subject to the same rules and regulations now in force, or hereafter to be made, as to payment of costs and the form of pleading, except so far as regards the pleading of the additional facts so required to be pleaded by such defendant, as if actions for libel had not been excepted from the personal actions in which it is lawful to pay money into Court under the said recited Act of the third and fourth years of the reign of her present Majesty.

2. *Defendant not to file such plea without paying money into Court by way of amends.*]—And be it declared and enacted, that it shall not be competent to any defendant in such action, whether in England or in Ireland, to file any such plea without at the same time making a payment of money into Court by way of amends, *as provided by the said Act* (*k*), but every such plea so filed without payment of money into Court shall be deemed a nullity, and may be treated as such by the plaintiff in the action (*l*).

9 & 10 Vict. c. 33.

[27th July, 1846.]

1. *Proceedings under 39 Geo. 3, c. 79, shall not be commenced unless in the name of the law officers of the Crown.*]—It shall

(*k*) Words in italics repealed by Civil Procedure Acts Repeal Act, 1879 (42 & 43 Vict. c. 59), Sched. Part II.
(*l*) See pp. 156, 224, *supra*.

not be lawful for any person or persons to commence, prosecute, enter, file, or cause or procure to be commenced, prosecuted, entered, or filed, any action, bill, plaint, or information in any of her Majesty's Courts, or before any justice or justices of the peace, against any person or persons for the discovery of any fine which may hereafter be incurred under the provisions of the Act of the thirty-ninth year of King George the Third, chapter seventy-nine, set out in this Act, unless the same be commenced, prosecuted, entered, or filed in the name of her Majesty's Attorney-General or Solicitor-General in England, or her Majesty's Lord Advocate in Scotland, and every action, bill, plaint, or information, which shall be commenced, prosecuted, entered, or filed in the name or names of any other person or persons than is in that behalf before mentioned, and every proceeding thereupon had, shall be null and void to all intents and purposes (*m*).

---

11 & 12 VICT. c. 12.

An Act for the better security of the Crown and Government of the United Kingdom.

[22nd April, 1848.]

3. *Offences declared felonies by this Act to be punishable by transportation or imprisonment.*]—And be it enacted, that if any person whatsoever, after the passing of this Act, shall, within the United Kingdom or without, compass, imagine, invent, devise, or intend to deprive or depose our most Gracious Lady the Queen, her heirs or successors, from the style, honour, or royal name of the imperial crown of the United Kingdom, or of any other of her Majesty's dominions and countries, or to levy war against her Majesty, her heirs or successors, within any part of the United Kingdom, in order by force or constraint to compel her or them to change her or their measures or counsels, or in order to put any force or constraint upon, or in order to intimidate or overawe both Houses or either House of Parliament, or to move or stir any foreigner or stranger with force to invade the United Kingdom, or any other of her Majesty's dominions or countries under the obeisance of her Majesty, her heirs or successors, and such compassings, imaginations, inventions, devices, or intentions, or any of them, shall express, utter, or declare, by publishing any printing or writing, or by open or advised

(*m*) See pp. 208, 243, *supra*. This section is re-enacted by 32 & 33 Vict. c. 24, Sched. II.

speaking, or by any overt act or deed, every person so offending shall be guilty of felony, and being convicted thereof, shall be liable, at the discretion of the Court, to be transported beyond the seas for the term of his or her natural life, or for any term not less than seven years, or to be imprisoned for any term not exceeding two years, with or without hard labour, as the Court shall direct.

---

20 & 21 VICT. c. 83.

An Act for more effectually preventing the Sale of Obscene Books, Pictures, Prints, and other articles.

[25th August, 1857.]

WHEREAS it is expedient to give additional powers for the suppression of the trade in obscene books, prints, drawings, and other obscene articles: Be it enacted by the Queen's most excellent Majesty, by and with the advice and consent of the Lords spiritual and temporal, and Commons, in this present Parliament assembled, and by the authority of the same, as follows:

1. *Justices, &c., may authorize search of suspected premises.*]—It shall be lawful for any metropolitan police magistrate or other stipendiary magistrate, or for any two justices of the peace, upon complaint made before him or them, upon oath, that the complainant has reason to believe, and does believe, that any obscene books, papers, writings, prints, pictures, drawings, or other representations, are kept in any house, shop, room, or other place, within the limits of the jurisdiction of any such magistrate or justices, for the purpose of sale or distribution, exhibition for purposes of gain, lending upon hire, or being otherwise published for purposes of gain, which complainant shall also state upon oath that one or more articles of the like character have been sold, distributed, exhibited, lent, or otherwise published as aforesaid, at or in connection with such place, so as to satisfy such magistrate or justices that the belief of the said complainant is well founded, and upon such magistrate or justices being also satisfied that any of such articles so kept for any of the purposes aforesaid are of such a character and description that the publication of them would be a misdemeanor, and proper to be prosecuted as such, to give authority by special warrant to any constable or police officer into such house, shop, room or other place, with such assistance as may be necessary, to enter in the day time, and if necessary to use force, by breaking open doors or

otherwise, and to search for and seize all such books, papers, writings, prints, pictures, drawings, or other representations as aforesaid, found in such house, shop, room, or other place, and to carry all the articles so seized before the magistrate or justices issuing the said warrant, or some other magistrate or justices exercising the same jurisdiction; and such magistrate or justices shall thereupon issue a summons, calling upon the occupier of the house or other place which may have been so entered, by virtue of the said warrant, to appear within seven days before such police stipendiary magistrate or any two justices in petty sessions for the district, to show cause why the articles so seized should not be destroyed; and if such occupier or some other person claiming to be the owner of the said articles shall not appear within the time aforesaid, or shall appear, and such magistrate or justices shall be satisfied that such articles, or any of them, are of the character stated in the warrant, and that such, or any of them, have been kept for any of the purposes aforesaid, it shall be lawful for the said magistrate or justices, and he or they are hereby required, to order the articles so seized, except such of them as he or they may consider necessary to be preserved as evidence in some further proceeding, to be destroyed at the expiration of the time hereinafter allowed for lodging an appeal, unless notice of appeal as hereinafter mentioned be given, and such articles shall be in the meantime impounded; and if such magistrate or justices shall be satisfied that the articles seized are not of the character stated in the warrant, or have not been kept for any of the purposes aforesaid, he or they shall forthwith direct them to be restored to the occupier of the house or other place in which they were seized.

2. *Tender of amends, &c.*—No plaintiff shall recover in any action for any irregularity, trespass, or other wrongful proceeding, made or committed in the execution of this Act, or in, under, or by virtue of any authority hereby given, if tender of sufficient amends shall have been made by or on behalf of the party who shall have committed such irregularity, trespass, or other wrongful proceeding, before such action brought; and in case no tender shall have been made, it shall be lawful for the defendant in any such action, by leave of the Court where such action shall depend, at any time before issue joined, to pay into Court such sum of money as he shall think fit, whereupon such proceeding, order, and adjudication shall be had and made in and by such Court as in other actions where defendants are allowed to pay money into Court.

3. *Limitation of actions.*—No action, suit, or information,

or any other proceeding of what nature soever, shall be brought against any person for anything done or omitted to be done in pursuance of this Act, or in the execution of the authorities under this Act, unless notice in writing shall be given by the party intending to prosecute such action, suit, information, or other proceeding to the intended defendant, one calendar month at least before prosecuting the same, nor unless such action, suit, information, or other proceeding shall be brought or commenced within three calendar months next after the act or omission complained of, or in case there shall be a continuation of damage, then within three calendar months next after the doing such damage shall have ceased.

4. *Appeal.*—Any person aggrieved by any act or determination of such magistrate or justices in or concerning the execution of this Act may appeal to the next general or quarter sessions for the county, riding, division, city, borough, or place in and for which such magistrate or justices shall have so acted, giving to the magistrate or justices of the peace whose act or determination shall be appealed against, notice in writing of such appeal and of the grounds thereof, within seven days after such act or determination, and before the next general or quarter sessions, and entering within such seven days into a recognizance with sufficient surety before a justice of the peace for the county, city, borough, or place in which such act or determination shall have taken place, personally to appear and prosecute such appeal, and to abide the order of, and pay such costs as shall be awarded by such Court of Quarter Sessions, or any adjournment thereof, and the Court at such general or quarter sessions shall hear and determine the matter of such appeal, and shall make such order therein as shall to the said Court seem meet; and such Court, upon hearing and finally determining such appeal, shall and may according to their discretion award such costs to the party appealing or appealed against as they shall think proper; and if such appeal be dismissed or decided against the appellant, or be not prosecuted, such Court may order the articles seized forthwith to be destroyed: provided always, that it shall not be lawful for the appellant on the hearing of any such appeal to go into or give evidence of any other grounds of appeal against any such order, act, or determination than those set forth in such notice of appeal.

5. *Limitation of Act.*]—This Act shall not extend to Scotland.

NEWSPAPER LIBEL AND REGISTRATION ACT, 1881.

44 & 45 VICT. c. 60.

An Act to amend the Law of Newspaper Libel, and to provide for the Registration of Newspaper Proprietors.

[27th August, 1881.]

WHEREAS it is expedient to amend the law affecting civil actions and criminal prosecutions for newspaper libel :

And whereas it is also expedient to provide for the registration of newspaper proprietors :

Be it enacted by the Queen's most excellent Majesty, by and with the advice and consent of the Lords spiritual and temporal, and Commons, in this present Parliament assembled, and by the authority of the same, as follows :

1. *Interpretation.*]—In the construction of this Act, unless there is anything in the subject or context repugnant thereto, the several words and phrases hereinafter mentioned shall have and include the meanings following ; (that is to say),

The word "registrar" shall mean in England the registrar for the time being of joint stock companies, or such person as the Board of Trade may for the time being authorize in that behalf, and in Ireland the assistant registrar for the time being of joint stock companies for Ireland, or such person as the Board of Trade may for the time being authorize in that behalf.

The phrase "registry office" shall mean the principal office for the time being of the registrar in England or Ireland, as the case may be, or such other office as the Board of Trade may from time to time appoint.

The word "newspaper" shall mean any paper containing public news, intelligence, or occurrences, or any remarks or observations therein printed for sale, and published in England or Ireland periodically, or in parts or numbers at intervals not exceeding twenty-six days between the publication of any two such papers, parts, or numbers (*n*).

Also any printed paper in order to be dispersed, and made public weekly or oftener, or at intervals not exceeding twenty-six days, containing only or principally advertisements (*n*).

The word "occupation" when applied to any person shall mean his trade or following, and if none, then his rank or usual title, as esquire, or gentleman.

The phrase "place of residence" shall include the street, square, or place where the person to whom it refers shall reside, and the number (if any) or other designation of the house in which he shall so reside.

The word "proprietor" shall mean and include as well

(*n*) See p. 109, *supra*.

the sole proprietor of any newspaper, as also in the case of a divided proprietorship the persons who, as partners or otherwise, represent and are responsible for any share or interest in the newspaper as between themselves and the persons in like manner representing or responsible for the other shares or interests therein, and no other person.

2. *Newspaper reports of certain meetings privileged.*]—Any report published in any newspaper of the proceedings of a public meeting shall be privileged, if such meeting was lawfully convened for a lawful purpose and open to the public, and if such report was fair and accurate, and published without malice, and if the publication of the matter complained of was for the public benefit; provided always, that the protection intended to be afforded by this section shall not be available as a defence in any proceeding, if the plaintiff or prosecutor can show that the defendant has refused to insert in the newspaper in which the report containing the matter complained of appeared a reasonable letter or statement of explanation or contradiction by or on behalf of such plaintiff or prosecutor (o).

3. *No prosecution for newspaper libel without fiat of Attorney-General.*]—No criminal prosecution shall be commenced against any proprietor, publisher, editor, or any person responsible for the publication of a newspaper for any libel published therein, without the written fiat or allowance of the Director of Public Prosecutions in England or her Majesty's Attorney-General in Ireland being first had and obtained (p).

4. *Inquiry by Court of summary jurisdiction as to libel being for public benefit or being true.*]—A Court of summary jurisdiction, upon the hearing of a charge against a proprietor, publisher, or editor, or any person responsible for the publication of a newspaper, for a libel published therein, may receive evidence as to the publication being for the public benefit, and as to the matters charged in the libel being true, and as to the report being fair and accurate, and published without malice, and as to any matter which under this or any other Act, or otherwise, might be given in evidence by way of defence by the person charged on his trial on indictment, and the Court, if of opinion after hearing such evidence that there is a strong or probable presumption that the jury on the trial would acquit the person charged, may dismiss the case (q).

5. *Provision as to summary conviction for libel.*]—If a Court

(o) This section was repealed by 51 & 52 Vict. c. 64, s. 2. See sect. 4 of that Act, p. 265, *infra*.

(p) This section was repealed by 51 & 52 Vict. c. 64, s. 8, *q. v.*, p. 267, *infra*.

(q) See pp. 188-190, *supra*.

of summary jurisdiction upon the hearing of a charge against a proprietor, publisher, editor, or any person responsible for the publication of a newspaper for a libel published therein, is of opinion that though the person charged is shown to have been guilty the libel was of a trivial character, and that the offence may be adequately punished by virtue of the powers of this section, the Court shall cause the charge to be reduced into writing and read to the person charged, and then address a question to him to the following effect: "Do you desire to be tried by a jury, or do you consent to the case being dealt with summarily?" and, if such person assents to the case being dealt with summarily, the Court may summarily convict him and adjudge him to pay a fine not exceeding fifty pounds (*r*).

Section twenty-seven of the Summary Jurisdiction Act, 1879, shall, so far as is consistent with the tenor thereof, apply to every such proceeding as if it were herein enacted and extended to Ireland, and as if the Summary Jurisdiction Acts were therein referred to instead of the Summary Jurisdiction Act, 1848.

6. *22 & 23 Vict. c. 17, made applicable to this Act.*]—Every libel or alleged libel, and every offence under this Act, shall be deemed to be an offence within and subject to the provisions of the Act of the session of the twenty-second and twenty-third years of the reign of her present Majesty, chapter seventeen, intituled "An Act to prevent vexatious indictments for certain misdemeanors."

7. *Board of Trade may authorize registration of the names of only a portion of the proprietors of a newspaper.*]—Where, in the opinion of the Board of Trade, inconvenience would arise or be caused in any case from the registry of the names of all the proprietors of the newspaper (either owing to minority, coverture, absence from the United Kingdom, minute subdivision of shares, or other special circumstances), it shall be lawful for the Board of Trade to authorize the registration of such newspaper in the name or names of some one or more responsible "representative proprietors."

8. *Register of newspaper proprietors to be established.*]—A register of the proprietors of newspapers as defined by this Act shall be established under the superintendence of the registrar (*s*).

9. *Annual returns to be made.*]—It shall be the duty of the printers and publishers for the time being of every newspaper to make or cause to be made to the Registry Office on or before the thirty-first of July one thousand eight hundred

(*r*) See pp. 190, 191, *supra*.   (*s*) See pp. 208–209, *supra*.

and eighty-one, and thereafter annually in the month of July in every year, a return of the following particulars according to the Schedule A. hereunto annexed; that is to say,

    (a) The title of a newspaper :
    (b) The names of all the proprietors of such newspaper together with their respective occupations, places of business (if any), and places of residence (*s*).

10. *Penalty for omission to make annual returns.*]—If within the further period of one month after the time hereinbefore appointed for the making of any return as to any newspaper such return be not made, then each printer and publisher of such newspaper shall, on conviction thereof, be liable to a penalty not exceeding twenty-five pounds, and also to be directed by a summary order to make a return within a specified time.

11. *Power to party to make return.*]—Any party to a transfer or transmission of or dealing with any share of or interest in any newspaper whereby any person ceases to be a proprietor or any new proprietor is introduced may at any time make or cause to be made to the Registry Office a return according to the Schedule B. hereunto annexed and containing the particulars therein set forth (*t*).

12. *Penalty for wilful misrepresentation in or omission from return.*]—If any person shall knowingly and wilfully make or cause to be made any return by this Act required or permitted to be made in which shall be inserted or set forth the name of any person as a proprietor of a newspaper who shall not be a proprietor thereof, or in which there shall be any misrepresentation, or from which there shall be any omission in respect of any of the particulars by this Act required to be contained therein whereby such return shall be misleading, or if any proprietor of a newspaper shall knowingly and wilfully permit any such return to be made which shall be misleading as to any of the particulars with reference to his own name, occupation, place of business (if any), or place of residence, then and in every such case every such offender being convicted thereof shall be liable to a penalty not exceeding one hundred pounds.

13. *Registrar to enter returns in register.*]—It shall be the duty of the registrar and he is hereby required forthwith to register every return made in conformity with the provisions of this Act in a book to be kept for that purpose at the Registry Office and called "the register of newspaper proprietors," and all persons shall be at liberty to search and

    (*s*) See pp. 208-209, *supra*.
    (*t*) See p. 209, *supra*.

inspect the said book from time to time during the hours of business at the Registry Office, and any person may require a copy of any entry in or an extract from the book to be certified by the registrar or his deputy for the time being or under the official seal of the registrar (*u*).

14. *Fees payable for registrar's services.*]—There shall be paid in respect of the receipt and entry of returns made in conformity with the provisions of this Act, and for the inspection of the register of newspaper proprietors, and for certified copies of any entry therein, and in respect of any other services to be performed by the registrar, such fees (if any) as the Board of Trade with the approval of the Treasury may direct and as they shall deem requisite to defray as well the additional expenses of the Registry Office caused by the provisions of this Act, as also the further remunerations and salaries (if any) of the registrar, and of any other persons employed under him in the execution of this Act, and such fees shall be dealt with as the Treasury may direct (*u*).

15. *Copies of entries in and extracts from register to be evidence.*]—Every copy of an entry in or extract from the register of newspaper proprietors, purporting to be certified by the registrar or his deputy for the time being, or under the official seal of the registrar, shall be received as conclusive evidence of the contents of the said register of newspaper proprietors, so far as the same appear in such copy or extract without proof of the signature thereto or of the seal of office affixed thereto, and every such certified copy or extract shall in all proceedings, civil or criminal, be accepted as sufficient *primâ facie* evidence of all the matters and things thereby appearing, unless and until the contrary thereof be shown (*u*).

16. *Recovery of penalties and enforcement of orders.*]—All penalties under this Act may be recovered before a Court of summary jurisdiction in manner provided by the Summary Jurisdiction Acts.

Summary orders under this Act may be made by a Court of summary jurisdiction, and enforced in manner provided by section thirty-four of the Summary Jurisdiction Act, 1879; and, for the purposes of this Act, that section shall be deemed to apply to Ireland in the same manner as if it were re-enacted in this Act.

17. *Definitions*].—The expression "a Court of summary jurisdiction" has in England the meanings assigned to it by the Summary Jurisdiction Act, 1879; and in Ireland means any justice or justices of the peace, stipendiary or other magistrate or magistrates, having jurisdiction under the Summary Jurisdiction Acts.

(*u*) See pp. 208-209, *supra*.

The expression "Summary Jurisdiction Acts" has as regards England the meanings assigned to it by the summary Jurisdiction Act, 1879; and as regards Ireland, means within the police district of Dublin metropolis the Acts regulating the powers and duties of justices of the peace for such district, or of the police of that district, and elsewhere in Ireland the Petty Sessions (Ireland) Act, 1851, and any Act amending the same.

18. *Provisions as to registration of newspaper proprietors not to apply to newspaper belonging to a joint stock company.*]—The provisions as to the registration of newspaper proprietors contained in this Act shall not apply to the case of any newspaper which belongs to a joint stock company duly incorporated under and subject to the provisions of the Companies Acts, 1862 to 1879 (x).

19. *Act not to extend to Scotland.*]—This Act shall not extend to Scotland.

20. *Short title.*]—This Act may for all purposes be cited as the Newspaper Libel and Registration Act, 1881.

The SCHEDULES to which this Act refers.

SCHEDULE A.

Return made pursuant to the Newspaper Libel and Registration Act, 1881.

Title of the Newspaper.	Names of the Proprietors.	Occupations of the Proprietors.	Places of business (if any) of the Proprietors.	Places of Residence of the Proprietors.

SCHEDULE B.

Return made pursuant to the Newspaper Libel and Registration Act, 1881.

Title of Newspaper.	Names of Persons who cease to be Proprietors.	Names of Persons who become Proprietors.	Occupation of new Proprietors.	Places of business (if any) of new Proprietors.	Places of Residence of new Proprietors.

51 & 52 VICT. c. 64.

An Act to amend the Law of Libel.
[24 December, 1888.]

WHEREAS it is expedient to amend the law of libel: Be it therefore enacted by the Queen's most excellent Majesty, by and with the advice and consent of the Lords Spiritual and Temporal, and Commons, in this present Parliament assembled, and by the authority of the same, as follows:

1. *Interpretation.*]—In the construction of this Act the word "newspaper" shall have the same meaning as in the Newspaper Libel and Registration Act, 1881 (*y*).

2. *Repeal of 44 & 45 Vict. c. 60, s. 2.*]—Section two of the Newspaper Libel and Registration Act, 1881, is hereby repealed (*z*).

3. *Newspaper reports of proceedings in Court privileged.*]— A fair and accurate report in any newspaper of proceedings publicly heard before any Court exercising judicial authority shall, if published contemporaneously with such proceedings, be privileged: Provided that nothing in this section shall authorize the publication of any blasphemous or indecent matter (*a*).

4. *Newspaper reports of proceedings of public meetings and of certain bodies and persons privileged.*]—A fair and accurate report published in any newspaper of the proceedings of a public meeting, or (except where neither the public nor any newspaper reporter is admitted) of any meeting of a vestry, town council, school board, board of guardians, board or local authority formed or constituted under the provisions of any Act of Parliament, or of any committee appointed by any of the above-mentioned bodies, or of any meeting of any commissioners authorized to act by letters patent, Act of Parliament, warrant under the Royal Sign Manual, or other lawful warrant or authority, select committees of either House of Parliament, justices of the peace in quarter sessions assembled for administrative or deliberative purposes, and the publication at the request of any Government office or department, officer of state, commissioner of police, or chief constable, of any notice or report issued by them for the information of the public, shall be privileged, unless it shall be proved that such report or publication was published or made maliciously: Provided that nothing in this section shall authorize the publication of any blasphemous or indecent matter: Provided

(*y*) See pp. 109, 112, 200, *supra.*   (*z*) See p. 260, *supra.*
(*a*) See p. 107 *et seq.*

also, that the protection intended to be afforded by this section shall not be available as a defence in any proceedings if it shall be proved that the defendant has been requested to insert in the newspaper in which the report or other publication complained of appeared a reasonable letter or statement by way of contradiction or explanation of such report or other publication, and has refused or neglected to insert the same: Provided further, that nothing in this section contained shall be deemed or construed to limit or abridge any privilege now by law existing, or to protect the publication of any matter not of public concern and the publication of which is not for the public benefit (*b*).

For the purposes of this section "public meeting" shall mean any meeting *bonâ fide* and lawfully held for a lawful purpose, and for the furtherance or discussion of any matter of public concern, whether the admission thereto be general or restricted (*c*).

5. *Consolidation of actions.*]—It shall be competent for a judge or the Court, upon an application by or on behalf of two or more defendants in actions in respect of the same, or substantially the same, libel brought by one and the same person, to make an order for the consolidation of such actions, so that they shall be tried together; and after such order has been made, and before the trial of the said actions, the defendants in any new actions instituted in respect to the same, or substantially the same, libel shall also be entitled to be joined in a common action upon a joint application being made by such new defendants and the defendants in the actions already consolidated (*d*).

In a consolidated action under this section the jury shall assess the whole amount of the damages (if any) in one sum, but a separate verdict shall be taken for or against each defendant in the same way as if the actions consolidated had been tried separately; and if the jury shall have found a verdict against the defendant or defendants in more than one of the actions so consolidated, they shall proceed to apportion the amount of damages which they shall have so found between and against the said last-mentioned defendants; and the judge at the trial, if he awards to the plaintiff the costs of the action, shall thereupon make such order as he shall deem just for the apportionment of such costs between and against such defendants (*e*).

6. *Power to defendant to give certain evidence in mitigation of damages.*]—At the trial of an action for a libel contained in

(*b*) See pp. 108, 109, 121-131, *supra*.
(*c*) See pp. 121-127, *supra*.
(*d*) See pp. 54, 171-173, *supra*.
(*e*) See pp. 54, 173, 174, *supra*.

any newspaper the defendant shall be at liberty to give in evidence in mitigation of damages that the plaintiff has already recovered (or as brought actions for) damages or has received or agreed to receive compensation in respect of a libel or libels to the same purport or effect as the libel for which such action has been brought (*f*).

7. *Obscene matter need not be set forth in indictment or other judicial proceedings.*]—It shall not be necessary to set out in any indictment or other judicial proceeding instituted against the publisher of any obscene libel the obscene passages, but it shall be sufficient to deposit the book, newspaper, or other documents containing the alleged libel with the indictment or other judicial proceedings, together with particulars showing precisely by reference to pages, columns, and lines in what part of the book, newspaper, or other documents the alleged libel is to be found, and such particulars shall be deemed to form part of the record, and all proceedings may be taken thereon as though the passages complained of had been set out in the indictment or judicial proceeding (*g*).

8. *Order of judge required for prosecution of newspaper proprietor, &c.*]—Section three of the forty-fourth and forty-fifth Victoria, chapter sixty, is hereby repealed, and instead thereof be it enacted that no criminal prosecution shall be commenced against any proprietor, publisher, editor, or any person responsible for the publication of a newspaper for any libel published therein without the order of a Judge at Chambers being first had and obtained.

Such application shall be made on notice to the person accused, who shall have an opportunity of being heard against such application (*h*).

9. *Persons proceeded against criminally a competent witness.*]—Every person charged with the offence of libel before any court of criminal jurisdiction, and the husband or wife of the person so charged, shall be competent, but not compellable, witnesses on every hearing at every stage of such charge (*i*).

(*f*) See pp. 61, 167, 171, *supra*.
(*g*) This provision is aimed at preventing the recurrence of cases like *Bradlaugh and Besant* v. *The Queen* (1878) (C. A.), 3 Q. B. D. 607; 48 L. J. M. C. 5; 26 W. R. 410; 38 L. T. 118; 14 Cox, C. C. 68, where the appellants were indicted for publishing an obscene book and were convicted, but the Court for the Crown Cases Reserved subsequently quashed the conviction on the technical ground that the obscene passages in the book had not been fully set out in the indictment, the book having been merely referred to therein by name.
(*h*) See pp. 187, 191, 198-200, *supra*.
(*i*) This provision effects in the case of libel what in all likelihood will, before long, be the law in regard to *all* criminal offences.

10. *Extent of Act.*]—This Act shall not apply to Scotland.
11. *Short titles.*]—This Act may be cited as the Law of Libel Amendment Act, 1888.

---

52 & 53 VICT. c. 18.

An Act to suppress Indecent Advertisements.

BE it enacted by the Queen's most excellent Majesty, by and with the advice and consent of the Lords Spiritual and Temporal, and Commons, in this present Parliament assembled, and by the authority of the same, as follows:

1. *Short title.*]—This Act may be cited as the Indecent Advertisements Act, 1889.

2. *Commencement of Act.*]—This Act shall come into operation on the first day of January, one thousand eight hundred and ninety.

3. *Summary proceedings against persons affixing, &c. indecent or obscene pictures or printed or written matter.*]—Whoever affixes to or inscribes on any house, building, wall, hoarding, gate, fence, pillar, post, board, tree, or any other thing whatsoever, so as to be visible to a person being in or passing along any street, public highway, or footpath, and whoever affixes to or inscribes on any public urinal, or delivers or attempts to deliver, or exhibits, to any inhabitant or to any person being in or passing along any street, public highway, or footpath, or throws down the area of any house, or exhibits to public view in the window of any house or shop, any picture or printed or written matter which is of an indecent or obscene nature, shall, on summary conviction in manner provided by the Summary Jurisdiction Acts, be liable to a penalty not exceeding forty shillings, or, in the discretion of the Court, to imprisonment for any term not exceeding one month, with or without hard labour.

4. *Summary proceedings against persons sending others to do the acts punishable under sect.* 3.]—Whoever gives or delivers to any other person any such pictures, or printed or written matter mentioned in section three of this Act, with the intent that the same, or some one or more thereof, should be affixed, inscribed, delivered, or exhibited as therein mentioned, shall, on conviction in manner provided by the Summary Jurisdiction Acts, be liable to a penalty not exceeding five pounds, or, in the discretion of the Court, to imprisonment for any term not exceeding three months, with or without hard labour.

5. *Certain advertisements declared indecent.*]—[This section

declares that advertisements of a certain specified nature shall be deemed to be printed or written matter within the meaning of section 3 of this Act.]

6. *Constable may arrest on view of offence.*]—Any constable or other peace officer may arrest without warrant any person whom he shall find committing any offence against this Act.

7. *Interpretation.*]—In this Act the expression " Summary Jurisdiction Acts "—
In England means the Summary Jurisdiction (English) Acts within the meaning of the Summary Jurisdiction Act, 1879 ;
In Scotland means the Summary Jurisdiction (Scotland) Acts, 1864 and 1881, and any Acts amending the same; and
In Ireland means within the police district of Dublin metropolis the Acts regulating the powers and duties of justices of the peace for such district, or of the police of such district, and elsewhere in Ireland the Petty Sessions (Ireland) Act, 1851, and any Act amending the same.

---

54 & 55 VICT. c. 51.

An Act to amend the Law relating to the Slander of Women.
[5th August, 1891.]

BE it enacted by the Queen's most excellent Majesty, by and with the advice and consent of the Lords Spiritual and Temporal, and Commons, in this present Parliament assembled, and by the authority of the same, as follows :

1. *Amendment of law.*]—Words spoken and published after the passing of this Act which impute unchastity or adultery to any woman or girl shall not require special damage to render them actionable (*a*).

Provided always, that in any action for words spoken and made actionable by this Act, a plaintiff shall not recover more costs than damages, unless the judge shall certify that there was reasonable ground for bringing the action (*a*).

2. *Short title and extent.*]—This Act may be cited as the Slander of Women Act, 1891, and shall not apply to Scotland.

(*a*) See pp. 19, 36, 37, *supra*.

58 & 59 VICT. c. 40.

An Act to amend the Corrupt and Illegal Practices Prevention Act, 1883.   [6th July, 1895.]

BE it enacted by the Queen's most excellent Majesty, by and with the advice and consent of the Lords Spiritual and Temporal, and Commons, in this present Parliament assembled, and by the authority of the same, as follows:

1. *Certain false statements concerning a candidate to be an illegal practice.*]—Any person who, or the directors of any body or association corporate which, before or during any parliamentary election, shall, for the purpose of affecting the return of any candidate at such election, make or publish any false statement of fact in relation to the personal character or conduct of such candidate, shall be guilty of an illegal practice within the meaning of the provisions of the Corrupt and Illegal Practices Prevention Act, 1883, and shall be subject to all the penalties for and consequences of committing an illegal practice in the said Act mentioned, and the said Act shall be taken to be amended as if the illegal practice defined by this Act had been contained therein (*a*).

2. *Evidence on hearing of charge under the Act.*]—No person shall be deemed to be guilty of such illegal practice if he can show that he had reasonable grounds for believing, and did believe, the statement made by him to be true. Any person charged with an offence under this Act, and the husband or wife of such person, as the case may be, shall be competent to give evidence in answer to such charge (*b*).

3. *Injunction against person making false statement.*]—Any person who shall make or publish any false statement of fact as aforesaid, may be restrained by interim or perpetual injunction by the High Court of Justice from any repetition of such false statement, or any false statement of a similar character, in relation to such candidate, and for the purpose of granting an interim injunction, *primâ facie* proof of the falsity of the statement shall be sufficient (*b*).

4. *Candidate exonerated in certain cases of illegal practice by agents.*]—A candidate shall not be liable, nor shall be subject to any incapacity nor shall his election be avoided, for any illegal practice under this Act committed by his agent other than his election agent, unless it can be shown that the candidate or his election agent, has authorized or consented to the committing of such illegal practice by such other agent, or has paid for the circulation of the

(*a*) See pp. 177, 185, *supra*.   (*b*) See p. 186, *supra*.

false statement constituting the illegal practice, or unless upon the hearing of an election petition the election court shall find and report that the election of such candidate was procured or materially assisted in consequence of the making or publishing of such false statements.

5. *Short Title.*]—This Act may be cited as the Corrupt and Illegal Practices Prevention Act, 1895, and shall be construed as one with the Corrupt and Illegal Practices Prevention Act, 1883, and that Act and this Act may be cited together as the Corrupt and Illegal Practices Prevention Acts, 1883 and 1895.

INDEX.

ABATEMENT,
    of a suit by death of plaintiff or defendant, 162.

ABSOLUTE PRIVILEGE,
    what constitutes, 96–97.
    cases of, are—
        (1) statements made in parliament, or in the course of judicial, naval, military, or state proceedings, 101–106.
        (2) reports, &c., published by order of parliament, 106, 107.
        (3) reports in a newspaper of proceedings in a Court of justice, if published contemporaneously with such proceedings, 107–114.

ABSTRACTS,
    of Parliamentary Reports, when privileged, 107.
    of reports of judicial proceedings, when privileged, 107, 116–118.

ABUSE,
    mere general words of, need not be justified if gist of libel is justified, 84.
    vulgar, if spoken, not actionable without special damage, 26.

ACCIDENTAL PUBLICATION,
    civil liability for, 16, 17, 37.
    criminal liability for, 202.

ACCORD AND SATISFACTION,
    what constitutes, 157.
    a good defence to an action, *ibid.*
    who may make an agreement of, *ibid.*
    must be for valuable consideration, *ibid.*

ACCURATE,
    and fair, what is, 116.
    reports must be, 119.

ACT,
    of state, 106.

ACTIO PERSONALIS MORITUR CUM PERSONÂ, 161.

INDEX.

ACTION,
    assessment of damages in a consolidated, 173.
    apportionment of costs   ,,   ,,   *ibid.*
    consolidation of, 171.
        can only be in cases of same or substantially the same libel, *ibid.*
    costs of, 177.
    fair and *bonâ fide* comments on, after conclusion, no libel, 87.
    must be brought within what time, 159.
        and where, 18, note (*f*).
    no comment on, till concluded, 87, 177.
    previous, a good defence, 158.
    report of, where privileged, 87, 97, 107 *et seq.*, 114 *et seq.*
    who is liable to, for libel in newspaper or journal, 61.

ACTION ON THE CASE, 4.
    rule as to proving damage in, 23.

"ACTIONABLE *per se*,"
    what words are, 19.

ACTIONS,
    limitation of, 159–161.
    consolidation of, 171.

ACTS,
    of public men, fair and *bonâ fide* comments on, 93, 94.

ADMINISTRATION ACTION,
    libel by receivers appointed in an, 162.

ADMINISTRATION OF JUSTICE,
    a matter of public interest, 94.
    articles in newspaper reflecting on, 84, 87, 92, 94, 177.
    fair and *bonâ fide* comments on, no libel, 87, 94.
    no comment allowed until trial is concluded, 87, 176.

ADMINISTRATORS,
    cannot sue or be sued for libel or slander, 161.
    of deceased plaintiff, position of, 162.

ADMIRALTY,
    report by Board of, privileged, 93.

ADMISSION,
    of improper evidence, when ground for new trial, 178.
    of reporters, 128.

ADULTERATION OF GOODS,
    to impute, to a tradesman, actionable *per se*, 35.

ADULTERY,
    words imputing, to a woman or girl, do not require proof of special damage to support action for slander, 19, 36–37.

ADVERTISEMENT,
    of cure may be criticised, 96.
    indecent, may be destroyed, 196.
    of tradesmen, may be criticised, 90.
    in public paper, no privilege for, when, 138, 139.

ADVOCATE,
  statements by, when privileged, 102-103.
AFFAIRS OF STATE,
  a matter of public interest, 93.
  fair and *bonâ fide* comments on, no libel, 88, 93, 94.
AFFIDAVITS,
  are privileged, 102.
AGENT,
  and principal, 15-17, 62-66, 203, 204.
  command of principal no defence, 64, 65.
  innocently publishing a libel, 15-17, 62-66, 187, 203, 204.
  company or corporation, when liable for libel or slander, published by, 77.
AGGRAVATION OF DAMAGES,
  evidence in, what may be given as, 163.
  facts in, are in practice inserted in Statement of Claim, 214.
AGREEMENT,
  to accept apologies from defendant, 157, 158.
ALIEN,
  enemy cannot sue, 74.
  friend can sue, 73.
  friend must generally give security for costs, 71.
AMENDS,
  evidence of, in mitigation of damages, 167.
AMUSEMENT,
  places of, are " of public interest," 95.
ANNUAL RETURN,
  of the title of a newspaper, and of names of proprietors, &c., printers and publishers to make, 209.
ANTICIPATION,
  restraint on, 69.
ANXIETY,
  when jury may consider, 166.
APOLOGY,
  as a defence under Lord Campbell's Act, 156, 157.
  may not be pleaded with a defence denying liability, 156.
  notice of intention to give evidence of, in mitigation of damages, 167.
  publication of, agreement to accept when executed is a good defence to an action, 157, 158.
  should be full and prominent, 157.
APPEAL, 162.
  is by way of motion for new trial, 178-182, 239-240.
APPORTIONMENT,
  of damages, in consolidated actions, 173.
  of costs, *ibid.*

INDEX.

ARCHITECT,
   libel on, 7.
   slander on, 34.

ART,
   fair and *bonâ fide* comments on, no libel, 96.

ASSESSMENT,
   of damages in a consolidated action, 173.

ASSIGNEE,
   of a bankrupt may not sue for libel on him, 76.

ASTERISKS,
   may be actionable if showing plaintiff was referred to, 5.

AUTHOR,
   fair and *bonâ fide* comment on work of, no libel, 88, 90, 95.
   liability of, for libel in newspaper, 63, 197, 198.

AUTHORITY,
   to another to publish a libel, as regards civil liability, 15–17, 62.
   to another to publish a libel, as regards criminal liability, 203, 204.

BAIL,
   for appearance at trial, magistrate will accept reasonable, 190.

BANKRUPT,
   may sue for libel or slander, 71, 76, 77.
   right of action of, does not pass to trustee, 76.

BANKRUPTCY,
   imputation of, to trader, actionable *per se*, 35.
   Act, 1882 .. 76.

BARRISTER,
   communications between client and, when protected from disclosure, 233, 234, 238.
   libel on, what is, 8.
   privilege of, 97, 102, 103.
   slander on, what is, 34.

BELIEF,
   in truth of charge, how far essential to qualified privilege, 97, 152, 155.
           no defence except in cases of qualified privilege, 37.
   in truth of libel, evidence of, in mitigation of damages, 169.

"BEYOND THE SEAS,"
   Statute of Limitations does not run, 160.
   what is, *ibid.*

"BLACK LISTS,"
   when privileged, 119–120, 138.

BLASPHEMOUS WORDS,
   not privileged in reports, 108, 113, 121, 128, 130.
   publication of, a crime, 194.
   what are, *ibid.*

BOARD OF ADMIRALTY,
report by, is privileged, 93.

BOARD OF DIRECTORS,
report of meeting of, not privileged, 129.

BOARD OF GUARDIANS,
fair and *bonâ fide* comments on, no libel, 95.
reports of meetings of, when privileged, 127.

BOARD OF TRADE,
powers of, under Newspaper Libel and Registration Act, 1881..
261-263.

BONÂ FIDE,
comment on matter of public interest, what is, 89-93.

BONA FIDES,
of defendant, no defence except on occasion of qualified privilege, 37, 38, 97, 139.
in cases of slander of title, 40, 41.
goods, 46, 47.
may be proved in mitigation of damages, 169.
required in all fair comments, 91.

BOOK.
fair and *bonâ fide* comment on, no libel, 88, 95.
libellous, sale of, by bookseller's servant, 15, 16, 64, 65, 201, 203, 204.
not within protection given to "newspapers" by the Acts of 1881 and 1888 .. 109.
obscene, statute for preventing sale of, 256-258.
may be seized and destroyed by order of magistrate, 196.
must bear the name and address of printer, 208.

BOOKSELLER,
liability of, for sale of libellous publication, 15, 16, 61, 65, 198, 203.
libel on, 4.
slander on, 35, 36.

BURDEN OF PROOF,
in slander of title, 39.
in slander of goods, 45.
in cases of privilege, plaintiff must prove malice, 97, 138, 150.
on party who alleges words did not bear their natural and ordinary meaning, 10.

BURGLARY,
a charge of, is actionable *per se*, 25.

BUSINESS,
loss of general, when sufficient to support action for slander, 21, 22.

BYSTANDERS,
presence of, does not always destroy privilege, 148.

CAMPBELL'S (LORD) ACT,
   defence of apology, and payment into Court under, 156, 211.
   defence under, *precedent* of, 229.
   offer of apology admissible as evidence in mitigation of damages under sect. 1..167.
   libel inserted without actual malice and without gross negligence and apology tendered, sect. 2..156, 224.
   liability of employer for acts of servant under sect. 7..203.
   defence that words complained of are true and for the public benefit under sect. 6..202.
   is not applicable to blasphemous, seditious, or obscene words, *ibid.*
   nor to hearing before magistrates, 189.
   payment into Court under sect. 2..156, 224.
   text of, 249—252.

CANDIDATE,
   false statements as to, 177-186.
   for parliament or public office, acts of, comments on, 93, 94.

" CANT " TERMS,
   construction of, 10.

CARDS,
   cheating at, 85, 231.

CARICATURE,
   may be a libel, 3.

CAUSES OF ACTION,
   joinder of, 52, 56, 57.
   which are separate and distinct cannot be joined, 53.

CERTIFICATE,
   of entry in register of newspapers, 209.
   that publication is by order of parliament, all proceedings stayed on, 106, 107.

CERTIORARI,
   writ of, *precedent* of statement of claim in action for libel moved into High Court by, 220.

CHALK MARKS,
   may be a libel, 3.

CHAMBERS,
   judge at, order of, when necessary for criminal prosecution, 198.
   report of proceedings in judge's, privileged, 114, 115.

CHARACTER,
   evidence of plaintiff's good, not admissible, unless attacked, 164.
                        bad, when admissible in mitigation of damages, 167, 170.
   of clerks or servants,—privileged communication, 142, 143.

CHRISTIANITY,
   publications against, 194.

CIRCULARS,
   of tradesmen, fair and *bonâ fide* comments on, no libel, 96.

CIRCUMSTANCES,
 of publication may aggravate damages, 163.

CIVIL PROCEEDINGS, defences to, 80, 81.
 (1) justification, 81–86.
 (2) fair and *bonâ fide* on matter of public interest, 88—96.
 (3) privilege, 96–149.
 (4) apology, 156.
 (5) accord and satisfaction, 157.
 (6) release, 158.
 (7) *res judicata*, 158, 159.
 (8) Statute of Limitations, 159—161.
 (9) death of plaintiff or defendant, 161, 162.
 hints as to conduct of, 207—240.

CLERGY AND CLERGYMEN,
 bishop's charge to, conditionally privileged, 137, 138.
 communication between curate and vicar conditionally privileged, 138
 communication between curate and incumbent of another parish conditionally privileged, 137.
 communication to bishop concerning, conditionally privileged, 144.
 communication between parishioner and vicar conditionally privileged, *ibid.*
 criminal information against newspaper for defamatory observations concerning, 184.
 libel on, 7, 8.
 slander on, when actionable, without proof of special damage, 32, 33.
 statement by, about church architect, when privileged, 146.

CLERK,
 character of, a privileged communication, 144.
 publication to a, 13.
 slanders on, actionable *per se*, 36.

CLIENT,
 and solicitor, communications between, to what extent privileged, 103.
 statements to protect, are privileged, when, 135, 138, 145.

CO-DEFENDANTS, 69.

COMMAND,
 of principal, no defence for agent, 16, 17, 64, 65, 198, 203.

COMMENT,
 bonâ fide belief in truth of, no defence, 89.
 definition of, 86, 87.
 distinction between report and, *ibid.*
 exaggerated, not necessarily unfair, 89.
 fair and *bonâ fide*, what is, 89, 90.
   on matter of public interest not privileged, but no libel, 88, 89.
 functions of judge and jury in regard to, 91.
 general rules to be observed, 89–91.
 must be on actual fact, 92.

COMMENT—*continued.*
    on administration of public institutions, 95.
    on advertisements, 96.
    on anything which invites public attention and criticism, *ibid.*
    on architecture, 96.
    on art, *ibid.*
    on authors, 95.
    on books, 90, 95.
    on conduct of public men, 94.
    on ecclesiastical matters, 95.
    on government, 93.
    on judicial proceedings, 94, 95.
        not allowed till proceedings terminate, 87, 177.
    on legal matters, 94.
    on literature, 86, 90, 95.
    on local affairs, 85, 95.
    on parliament and committees thereof, 93.
    on places of public amusement or entertainment, 95.
    on state matters, 93.
    when a contempt of court, 87, 162, 177.

COMMERCIAL TERMS,
    construction of, 10.

COMMISSION,
    proceedings of royal, may be criticised, 93.

COMMISSIONERS,
    meetings of, reports of, privileged, 127, 128.

COMMITTAL,
    for trial in prosecutions for libel, 188.

COMMITTEE,
    meetings, what reports of, privileged, 127, 128.
        may be criticised, 93, 94.
    of House of Parliament, petition to, may be criticised, 93.
    of lunatic,
        duties of, 74, 75.
        must be joined as co-plaintiff, 75.
        must obtain leave of Court before suing, 75.

COMMON INTEREST,
    communications as to matters of, conditionally privileged, 97, 98, 136–140.

COMMON LAW,
    if publication proved and matter libellous, magistrate must commit at, 187.
    master liable, civilly and criminally, at, for acts of servant, 62–66, 203, 204.
    privilege at, for reports of judicial proceedings, 114.

COMPANY,
    comments on, 96.
    joint stock, not bound to register newspaper belonging to it, 209.
    reports of meetings of shareholders of, not privileged, 129.
    when action maintainable by or against, 77.

COMPENSATION,
> from other sources, may be proved in mitigation of damages, when, 167.

COMPETITION,
> in trade, no ground of action, 49.

COMPOSER,
> of libel, liability of, 65, 198, 199.

COMPOSITOR,
> liability of, 65, 198.

CONDUCT,
> of defendant may aggravate damages, 163, 164.
> of a civil action, 207-240.
> of criminal proceedings, 186-193.

CONFIDENTIAL COMMUNICATIONS,
> when privileged, 140.

CONSIDERATION,
> necessary, to accord and satisfaction, 157.

CONSOLIDATION,
> of actions, 54, 171.
>> assessment of damages in, 173.

CONSTRUCTION,
> function of the innuendo, 11, 214.
> of libel, duties of judge and jury in a civil action, 9, 10.
>> in a criminal case, libel or no libel a question for the jury, 205, 206.

CONTAGIOUS DISEASE,
> verbal imputation of, actionable without proof of special damage, 19, 27.

CONTEMPORANEOUS,
> report of trial to be absolutely privileged must be, 107 *et seq.*
> what is, 113-114.

CONTEMPT OF COURT,
> comment on case before conclusion thereof may be, 87, 162, 177.

CONTRACT,
> as to printing a libel, not enforceable, 60.

CONTRADICTION,
> letter of, effect of refusal to publish, 121, 128, 130.

CONTRIBUTION,
> none between tort feasors, 59.

CONTROVERSY,
> newspaper, a matter of public interest, 95.

CONVICTION,
> of criminal court, accusation of, whether libellous, 83, and see cases cited in foot-note (*y*) on p. 83.
> summary, before magistrate, 191, 196.

CO-PLAINTIFFS, 69.

COPYING,
 libels from another newspaper, evidence of, when admissible in mitigation of damages, 61, 166, 167, 169–171.
 no defence, 61, 169.
 position of defendant who has incurred liability in, 61, 167, 169–174.

CORPORATION,
 comments on, 95.
 liability of, on a privileged occasion, *quære*, 79–80.
 malice of, *ibid.*
 when action maintainable by or against, 77–79.

CORRUPT PRACTICES PREVENTION ACT, 1895 .. 177, 185–186.

COSTS,
 apportionment of, in consolidated action, 173.
 in action by or against a married woman, 68.
 "good cause" for depriving of, what is, 177, 178.
 if action tried with jury, follow the event, unless for good cause judge otherwise orders, 177.
 in discretion of judge, if action tried without a jury, 177.
 of action by and against infant, who is liable for, 74.
 provided for by 54 & 55 Vict. c. 57 .. 37.
 security for, 58, 59, 211.

COUNCIL,
 county or town, fair and *bonâ fide* comments on proceedings of, no libel, 95.
 reports of, privileged, 127, 128.

COUNSEL,
 communications between client and, when protected from disclosure, 233, 234, 238, to what extent privileged, 103.
 libel on, 8.
 privilege of, 97, 102, 103.
 report of speech of, 84.
 slander on, 34.

COUNTY COUNCIL MEETING,
 fair and *bonâ fide* comments on, no libel, 95.
 for granting licences not a Court recognized by law, 105.
 reports of, privileged, 127, 128.

COUNTY COURT,
 no jurisdiction in libel except by consent, 18, note (*f*).
 remission of actions to, 58, 77, 211.

COUNTY COURT JUDGE,
 proceedings of, may be criticised, 94.
 report of proceedings before, privileged, 115.

COURT MARTIAL,
 proceedings of, are privileged, 106.

COURT OF APPEAL,
 jurisdiction of, as to new trial, and entering judgment in lieu thereof, 182.

COURT OF SUMMARY JURISDICTION,
    hearing before, 187-191.
    power to seize and destroy obscene publications, 196.
        summarily convict for publication of indecent advertisements, 196, 197.

COURTS OF JUSTICE,
    fair and *bonâ fide* comments on, no libel, 88, 94.
    proceedings in, what are, 114-115.
        comment on, what is, 94.
            when allowed, 87, 177.
            how different from report, 86-87.
    reports of, when privileged, and to what extent, 107-118.
    statements made before, when absolutely privileged, 101, 102.

CREDITORS,
    letters between, as to liquidation, when privileged, 138.
    meeting of, report of, not privileged, 129.

CRIME,
    general accusation of, actionable *per se*, 26.
    publication of libel is a, 183.
    statements made to prevent, 131, 132.
    words imputing, actionable *per se*, 25.
        justification of, 83, 84.

CRIMINAL INFORMATION,
    ex officio, 192-193.
    procedure in applying for, *ibid.*
    trial of, *ibid.*
    two kinds of, *ibid.*
    when granted, *ibid.*

CRIMINAL OFFENCE,
    imputation need not be of an indictable offence, 25.
    in accusations of, no need to prove special damage, 19.

CRIMINAL PROCEEDINGS,
    can be taken for libel, 183.
        before magistrate, 187-191.
        by indictment, 187.
        by information, 192.

CRIMINAL PROSECUTION,
    for libel, procedure on, 187-192.
    when order of judge required for, 198-200.

CRITIC,
    duties of, 86, 89, 90.

CRITICISM. *See* COMMENT.

CROWN OFFICE INFORMATION, 192, 193.

CROWN OFFICE RULES, 1886..193.

CUSTOM,
    loss of general, when evidence of is admissible and sufficient to support action for words not actionable *per se*, 21-23.

DAMAGE,
presumed in libel on proof of publication, 18.
special, must be proved in slander, except in four cases, 19.
special, what is, 20–24, 164–166.

DAMAGES,
assessment of, and apportionment of costs in consolidated action, 173–174.
evidence in aggravation of, for plaintiff, 163–166.
evidence in mitigation of, for defendant, 166–171.

DEAD,
libel on the, not actionable, 183.
    criminal proceedings for, *ibid.*

DEAF AND DUMB,
person, may publish slander, 3.

DEATH,
of plaintiff or defendant before verdict, effect of, 161.
of plaintiff after final judgment, effect of, 162.

DEBATES,
at meeting of board of guardians, report of, when privileged, 127–129.
at meeting of local authority, reports of, when privileged, *ibid.*
at public meeting, report of, when privileged, 121.
at school board meetings, reports of, when privileged, 127–129.
comments on, when allowed, 87, 93–96.
in Parliament, reports of, when privileged, 120, 121.
in county council meeting, reports of, when privileged, 128, note (*f*).
reports of, when privileged, 97, 106, 120–121, 127, 128, 130.

DECEASED PERSON,
libels on, 183.

DECLARATION,
in Lord Mayor's Court, *precedent* of, 219.

DEEDS OF ARRANGEMENT ACT, 1887..119.

DEFAMATORY WORDS,
actionable when published, 1, 13.
criminal proceedings for publication of, 183 *et seq.*
in certain cases not actionable in the interests of public policy, 96.
what are, 1–9, 183.

DEFENCE,
to an action, what is, 80.
  accord and satisfaction, 157.
  apology, 156.
  death of plaintiff or defendant, 161.
  fair and *bonâ fide* comment on a matter of public interest, 88.
  justification, 81.
  master's commands no defence, 15, 16, 64–65, 203, 204.
  previous action, 158
  privilege, 96–149.
  release, 158.

DEFENCE—*continued.*
    Statute of Limitations, 159.
    that words are not libellous, 1, 81, 201.
    that there has been no publication, 13, 81, 197, 198, 201.
    that words do not relate to the plaintiff, 3–4, 81, 201.
    must not be embarrassing, 226.
    of certain kinds, must be expressly raised, 81.
    precedents of, 227–230.
  to criminal proceedings, what is, 200–201.
    fair and *bonâ fide* comment on a matter of public interest, 201.
    privilege, 200.
    that publication was made without the authority or knowledge of the defendant, and did not arise from want of due care or caution on his part, *ibid.,* 203, 204.
    that words are true, and their publication is for the public benefit, 200.
    that there has been no publication, 185, 197–198, 201.
    that words are not libellous, 183, 201.
    that words do not relate to the complainant, 184, 201.

DEFENDANT,
    death of, destroys right of action, 161.
    out of jurisdiction, modes of suing, 210.
    when not liable, for publication of libel, 16.

DEFENDANTS,
    joint, no contribution between, or indemnity to, 59.
    who are liable as, *ibid.,* 158, 159.

DEFINITION,
    of libel and slander, 1.

DELIVERY,
    of libel to third person, when a publication, 13–17, 197–198.

DENIAL OF LIABILITY,
    cannot co-exist with payment into Court, 156.

DESTRUCTION,
    of obscene books or pictures by magistrate's order, 196.

DETAILS,
    of a charge, need not be justified in every case, 84.

DIRECTORS,
    report of meeting of board of, not privileged, 129.

DISABILITY,
    infancy, lunacy, beyond seas, 160.

DISCOVERY,
    of author of libel, 63, 208, 236.
    of printer, 208.
    of proprietor, 208, 209.
    of publisher, 208.
    of documents, 212.

DISEASE,
    contagious, words imputing, when actionable *per se,* 19, 27.

DISTINCTION,
    between report and comment, importance of, 86.
    between libel and slander, 3.

DISTRIBUTOR,
    of newspaper containing a libel, liability of, 16, 61, 197–198.

DIVISIBLE,
    when libel is, defendant can justify one part and admit liability as to another part, 86.

DOCTOR,
    libel on, 8.
    privileged communications as to, 144.
    slander on, 29, 33.
    Statement of Claim by, 215.

DOCUMENTS,
    discovery of, 212.
    which are absolutely privileged from production, 213.

DUMB,
    person may publish slander, 3.

DUTY,
    statements made in discharge of, are privileged, when, 100, 140, 141.

ECCLESIASTICAL MATTERS. *See* CLERGY.
    fair and *bonâ fide* comments on, no libel, 94, 95.

EDITOR,
    cannot be compelled to discover name of author, 208, 236.
    cannot recover from employer, 60.
    command of employer no defence to, 64, 65.
    duty of, 62, 63, 127.
    liability of, for libel in newspaper, 62, 63.
        proprietor for acts of, 60.
    no prosecution against, without judge's order, 198–200.

EFFIGY,
    may be a libel, 3.

ELECTION,
    false statements at an, 177, 186.

EMBARRASSING,
    when defence can be struck out as, 226.

EMPLOYER,
    liability of, to an action, 62 *et seq*.
        to criminal proceedings, 203 *et seq*

ENDORSEMENT,
    of writ, 211.

ENEMY, ALIEN,
    cannot sue here, 74.

ENTERTAINMENT,
    place of, comment on, 95.

ENTICEMENT,
    a statement obtained by, is privileged, when, 134, 135.

ENTRIES,
    copies of, in register of proprietors to be evidence, 209, 263.

ERRONEOUS BELIEF,
    no defence, 139.

EVIDENCE,
    as to meaning of libel, when allowed, 10.
    copies of entries in register to be, 209, 263.
    in aggravation of damages, 163–166.
    in mitigation of damages, 166–171.
    on hearing before magistrates, 187–191.
    of person proceeded against criminally, and husband or wife of such person admissible, 267.
    improper admission or rejection of, ground for new trial, 178.

EX OFFICIO,
    criminal information, what is, 192.
                        procedure on, 192, 193.

EX PARTE PROCEEDINGS,
    extracts from parliamentary reports, when privileged, 107.
                        registers kept pursuant to statute, 119.
    reports of, privileged, 115.

EXAGGERATION,
    even if gross, may still be "fair comment," 89, 90.
    if there is, plea of justification will fail, 83.
    not privileged, 139.

EXCESSIVE,
    damages, may be reduced, in lieu of new trial, 182.
    language, not always a proof of malice, 154.

EXECUTORS,
    cannot sue for libel on testator or be sued for libel published by him, 161.
    may appear on an appeal, when, 162

EXPLANATION,
    of report, refusal to publish, 121, 128.

EXTRACTS,
    from registers are privileged, when, 118, 119, 209, 263.
    from parliamentary reports are privileged, when, 107.

FAIR AND ACCURATE REPORT. *See* REPORT.

FAIR COMMENT. *See* COMMENT.

FALSITY,
    of words presumed in action for libel, 46.

FATHER,
    statements made to, *re* his child, may be privileged, 144.

FELONY,
    imputation of, actionable *per se*, 25, 26.
    justification of charge of, 83–84.

FEME SOLE, 68.

FICTITIOUS NAME,
    may show that plaintiff was referred to, 5.

FINE,
>for not making annual returns required by Newspaper Libel an Registration Act, 1881 .. 262.
>for publishing indecent advertisement, 268.
>for publishing libel, 183.
>>on summary conviction by magistrates, 191.

FIRM,
>actions by, 57.
>>joinder of, with actions by a partner, 57.

"FISHING,"
>interrogatories, not allowed, 237.

FOREIGN FIRM,
>issue of writ against, 72.
>judgment against, effect of, *ibid*.

FOREIGN PRINCIPAL,
>how to sue for libel published by agent here, 72, 210.

FORGERY,
>a charge of, is actionable *per se*, 25.

FORMER PUBLICATION,
>of same libel by others, no defence, 61, 169.
>>when admissible in evidence, 61, 170.

FOX'S LIBEL ACT (32 Geo. 3, c. 60), 205, 241, 242.

FRAUD,
>allegation of against a corporation, is actionable, 79.

GAMEKEEPER,
>slander on, 36.

GENERAL BUSINESS, LOSS OF,
>when sufficient to support action of slander, 22, 23, 50.

GENERAL VERDICT,
>jury may give, 205.

GESTURES,
>may be a slander, 1, 3.

GIRL,
>imputation of unchastity to, is actionable *per se*, 36.

GOOD CAUSE,
>for depriving plaintiff of costs, what is, 178.

GOOD CHARACTER,
>of plaintiff, evidence of, when admissible, 164.

GOOD FAITH,
>may be proved, in mitigation of damages, 169.

GOODS, SLANDER OF,
>what is, 44.
>what plaintiff must prove in action for, 45.

GOVERNMENT,
>everything concerning, may be criticised, 93.
>notices and reports, publication of, when privileged, 130.
>official communication to, generally privileged, 131, 132.

GRAND JURY, 191.
GUARDIAN *AD LITEM*,
 infant defends by, 74.
 when liable for costs, *ibid*.
GUARDIANS,
 fair and *bonâ fide* comment on proceedings of, no libel, 95.
 report of proceedings of board of, privileged, 129.
 statements made at meetings of board of, when privileged, 148, 149.
HANDBILL,
 of tradesman, may be commented on, 96.
HANDWRITING,
 primâ facie publication of libel, if manuscript in defendant's, 17.
"HATRED, RIDICULE, AND CONTEMPT," 6.
HEADING,
 of article may be libellous, 82, 117, 118.
  must be justified, *ibid*.
HUSBAND,
 and wife, joinder of, in actions, 68, 69.
 liability of, for wife's libel or slander, 70.
 libel uttered by, to wife, not published, 15.
 of person charged with crime of libel competent but not compellable witness, 267.

ILLEGAL PRACTICES PREVENTION ACT, 1895, 177, 185, 269.
IMPRISONMENT,
 for publication of libel, 183, 250, 251.
 for threatening to publish a libel, 250, 251.
INDECENT ADVERTISEMENTS, 197, 267, 268.
INDECENT MATTER,
 publication of, in report of judicial proceedings, not privileged, 108, 114.
  or in report of public meeting, 121.
INDECENT PUBLICATIONS,
 seizure and destruction of, by order of magistrates, 196.
INDEMNIFICATION,
 promise of, for publishing a libel, is void, 60.
INDEMNITY,
 from negligent editor or author of libel, proprietor cannot enforce, 59.
 from co-defendant in case of joint publication, unenforceable, 59.
INDICTABLE OFFENCE,
 a slander need not impute an, to be actionable *per se*, 25.
INDICTMENT,
 for libel, procedure on, 187–191.
 order of judge, when required for, 198–200.

U

INDORSEMENT OF WRIT,
  in actions of libel or slander, 211.
INFANCY,
  Statute of Limitations does not run in, 160.
INFANT,
  can sue and be sued, for libel and slander, 71, 74.
INFORMATION, CRIMINAL,
  ex officio, what is, 192, 193.
  procedure on, *ibid.*
  two kinds of, *ibid.*
INGRATITUDE,
  charge of, libellous, 6.
INITIALS,
  may show that plaintiff was referred to, 5.
INJUNCTION,
  Court has jurisdiction to restrain publication of libel by interim or final, 174–177.
  interim, when granted, 174–176.
INNOCENT AGENT,
  when excused for publication of libel, 15, 16, 65, 66.
INNUENDO,
  defined, 11, 12.
  when required, 11, 12, 214.
  when not required, 11, 12.
INQUIRY,
  answer to an, is privileged, when, 141.
  writ of, 162.
INSANITY,
  imputation of, libellous, 6.
INSOLVENCY,
  to impute, to a tradesman, is actionable *per se*, 35.
INSPECTION,
  of register of newspaper proprietors at Somerset House, 209.
INTENTION,
  of defendant immaterial in civil action, except in case of qualified privilege, 37.
    in criminal cases, 194, 201, 203.
INTEREST,
  statements made to protect self, when privileged, 133.
        common, when privileged, 136.
INTEREST, MATTER OF PUBLIC,
  matter of, what is, 93–96.
      fair and *bonâ fide* comments on, no libel, 88.
    administration of public institutions, 95.
    advertisements, 96.
    anything which invites public attention or criticism, *ibid.*
    architecture, 96.

INTEREST, MATTER OF PUBLIC—*continued.*
    art, 96.
    authors, 95.
    books, 90, 95.
    conduct of public men, 93, 94.
    ecclesiastical matters, 94, 95.
    government, 93.
    judicial proceeding, 94.
    legal affairs, 94, 95.
    literature, 90, 95.
    local affairs, 95, 129.
    Parliament, and committees thereof, 93.
    places of public amusement or entertainment, 95.
    State matters, 93.

INTERIM INJUNCTION,
    when granted, 45, 174, 176.

INTERLOCUTORY JUDGMENT, 162.

INTERPRETATION,
    of libellous words, in civil action, 10, 11.
                       on criminal trial, 183, 205.

INTERROGATORIES,
    grounds for refusing to answer, 235–239.
    may be struck out, when, 235.

IRRELEVANT MATTERS,
    may not be given in evidence, 168.

JEST,
    no defence to an action for defamation, 38.

JOINDER OF,
    causes of action, 52, 56.
                rules as to, 56, 57.
    defendants, 53, 55.
    parties, 51–55.
    partners, 57.
    plaintiffs, 51.

JOINT,
    defendants, 53–56, 173, 174.
    publication of libel, liability in cases of, 53–58, 59–62, 158, 173, 174.
    publishers, judgment in action against one bars action against others, 61.

JOURNAL,
    other than newspaper, reports in, 110, 112, 114–118.
    when a "newspaper" within meaning of Acts of 1881 and 1888 ..109.

JOURNALIST,
    defence to publication of libel by, 80, 81, 200, 201.
    libel on, 83.
    slander on, 34.

JUDGE,
discretion of, as to costs, 177.
duty of, in civil action, as to privilege, 99.
    as to publication, 17.
    as to comment, 88.
    as to meaning of words complained of, 9.
in criminal proceedings, 205, 206.
may tell the jury his personal opinion, 205.
of superior Court, everything said in office by, absolutely privileged, 102-104.
of inferior Court, everything said in office by, absolutely privileged, provided he has jurisdiction, 103, 104.

JUDGE IN CHAMBERS,
no appeal from decision of, under 51 & 52 Vict. c. 64, s. 8..199.
order of, required for criminal prosecution (by way of indictment) for newspaper libel, 198-200.

JUDGE'S CHAMBERS,
report of proceedings in, privileged, 114, 115.

JUDGMENT,
evidence of previous, when admissible in mitigation of damages, 171.
final, cannot be signed after plaintiff dies, 161, 162.
interlocutory, effect of plaintiff's death after, *ibid.*
previous, against same defendant a defence, 159.
    other defendant no defence unless joint publication, *ibid.*
report of, when privileged, 116-117.

JUDICIAL PROCEEDINGS,
ex parte reports of, privileged, 114.
fair and *bonâ fide* comments on, no libel, 94.
reports of, privilege of, when absolute, 96, 97, 107-113.
    qualified, 87, 97, 98, 114-118.
what are, 102-105, 114, 115.

JURISDICTION,
defendant out of, 71-74.
of Court, as to injunctions, 175.
publication out of, 73.

JURORS,
observations of, absolutely privileged, when, 104.

JURY,
functions of, in civil action, as to publication, 17.
    as to comment, 88, 91.
    in assessing damages, 164.
    in consolidated actions, 173.
    as to meaning of words complained of, 9-11, 205-206.
    as to privilege, 99.
    as to publication being for public benefit, 124.
in criminal cases, 205, 206.

INDEX. 293

JUSTICE OF THE PEACE,
  administration of law by, fair and *bonâ fide* comments on, no libel, 94.
  hearing before, procedure on, 187-191.
  reports of proceedings before, privileged, 105, 114, 115.
  words spoken by, when action lies for, 105.
  libel on, what is, 9.
  slander on, what is, 28-32.

JUSTIFICATION,
  as a defence to civil action, 81-86.
  in criminal proceedings, 184, 185, 200, 202.
  is a dangerous plea, 225.
  not allowed in blasphemous, seditious, or obscene libels, 197.
  of general abuse, not necessary if gist of libel justified, 84.
  of title to libellous article or paragraph, necessary, 82, 118.
  plea of, 231.
  where libel contained in report of trial, 84.
  whole libel must be proved substantially true, 82.
  where libel divisible part may be justified, and liability as to rest admitted, 86.

LAND AGENT,
  libel on, 7.
  slander on, 34.

LARCENY,
  a charge of, is actionable *per se*, 25.

"LAWFULLY HELD,"
  meaning of, in sect. 4 of Law of Libel Amendment Act, 1888..126.

LAWFUL OCCASION,
  what is in slander of goods, 46.

"LAWFUL PURPOSE,"
  meaning of, in sect. 4 of Law of Libel Amendment Act, 1888..126.

LEARNED PROFESSIONS,
  slanders on, actionable *per se*, 32.

LEAVE,
  of judge, needed to prosecute, when, 187, 198.

LEGAL MATTERS,
  comment on, 94, 95.

LEPROSY,
  a charge of, actionable *per se*, 27.

LETTER BEFORE ACTION,
  advisability of, 207.

LETTER BETWEEN SOLICITOR AND CLIENT,
  when privileged from discovery, 233, 234.

LETTER OF EXPLANATION,
  evidence of publication of, when admissible as evidence in mitigation of damages, 169.

INDEX.

LETTER OF EXPLANATION—*continued.*
   refusal to insert, effect of, 121, 128, 130.
   written to protect interest of writer, when privileged, 133, 134.

LIABILITY,
   denial of, cannot be pleaded with payment into court, 156, 224.
   for publication of libel, when avoided, 16.
   joint and several, 57, 58, 158, 159.

LIBEL,
   action for, without proof of special damage, 18.
   blasphemous, what is, 194.
   construction of, duty of judge and jury as to, 9.
   contract for printing, not enforceable, 60.
   criminal proceedings for, 183.
   defences to action for, 80.
      criminal proceedings for, 200, 201.
      precedents of, 227-230.
   definition of, 1, 183.
   distinguished from slander, 1, 3.
   evidence of other, when allowed in aggravation of damages, 164.
                     in mitigation of damages, 169-170.
   evidence of truth of, when admissible, 168, 188-190, 231-232.
   in a newspaper, who is liable for, 61-63, 65.
   injunction to restrain, 174-177.
   obscene, what is, 196-197.
   printer of, how to discover, 208.
   proprietor of newspaper containing, how to discover, 209.
   publication of, a crime, 183.
          what is, 13-17, 197-198.
   published abroad, when actionable here, 64, 65.
   repetition of, liability for, 66-68, 165.
   seditious, what is, 195.

LIBELLOUS WORKS,
   printer of, cannot recover for printing, 60.

LIMITATIONS,
   Statute of, 159.

LITERATURE,
   fair and *bonâ fide* comment on, is not a libel, 95.

LOCAL,
   affairs, fair and *bonâ fide* comments on, no libel, 95.
      reports of, when privileged, 121, 127-129.

LOCAL BOARD,
   proceedings of, fair and *bonâ fide* comments on, no libel, 95.
      reports of, privileged, 127-129.

LONDON COUNTY COUNCIL,
   is not a "Court recognized by law," 105

LORD CAMPBELL'S ACT,
   defence under, 156, 202, 249-252.

LORD MAYOR'S COURT,
   precedent of Declaration in, 219.

LUNACY,
    Statute of Limitations does not run in, 160.

LUNACY ACT,
    1890 .. 74.
    1891 .. 75.

LUNATIC,
    can sue or be sued, 71, 74-75.
    procedure in action by or against, 75.

MAGAZINE,
    joint liability of editor and printer of, for libel in, 59-63.
    not a newspaper within the meaning of the Law of Libel Amendment Act, 1888 .. 109.
    reports of judicial proceedings in, when privileged, 112, 114.
    reports of public meetings in, not privileged, 129.

MAGISTRATE. *See* JUSTICE OF THE PEACE.

MALICE,
    actual, rebuts qualified privilege, 97.
    burden of proof of, is on plaintiff, 150.
    definition of, *ibid*.
    may be inferred from excessive publication, etc., 153.
    only material in cases of qualified privilege, 97, 150-155.
    meaning of, in this work, 97, note (*n*).
    onus of proof on plaintiff in action for libel or slander, 97.
    proof of, essential in action for slander of title, 39-41, 43.
    proof of, how far essential in action for slander of goods, 46-48.
    what may be evidence of, 151-153.
    whether corporation can be guilty of, 79-80.

MARRIED WOMAN,
    can sue or be sued, 68-69.
    liability of husband for libel or slander by, 70.
    words imputing immorality to, 36-37.

MARRIED WOMEN'S PROPERTY ACT, 1882 .. 68.

MASTER,
    commands of, no defence for servant, 64-65.
    liability of, in civil action, for acts of servant, 62-64.
        in criminal proceedings for act of servant, 203.
    statements made to, by, or as to, servant, may be privileged, 144.
    statements made by, as to servant's character, 142-144.

MATTER OF PUBLIC INTEREST,
    administration of public institutions, 95.
    advertisements, 96.
    anything which invites public attention or criticism, *ibid*.
    architecture, 96.
    art, *ibid*.
    authors, 95.
    books, 90, 95.

MATTER OF PUBLIC INTEREST—*continued.*
conduct of public men, 93, 94.
ecclesiastical matters, 94, 95.
fair and *bonâ fide* comments on, no libel, 88.
government, 93.
judicial proceeding, 94.
legal affairs, 94, 95.
literature, 90, 95.
local affairs, 95, 129.
parliament, and committees thereof, 93.
places of public amusement or entertainment, 95.
public meeting, 121.
state matters, 93.
what is, 93–96.

MEANING,
of words in a civil action, who decides, 9, 10, 12.
on a criminal trial, who decides, 205, 206.

MEDICAL MAN,
libel on, 8.
privileged communications as to, 144.
slander on, 29, 33.

MEDICAL REMEDIES,
criticism on advertisements of, 85, 96.

MEETING,
public, what is a, 121, 266.
reports of, when privileged, 121–129.
comments on, 95.
statements made at, when privileged, 136, 137, 140, 148, 149.

MERCHANT,
libel on, 8.
slander on, 35.
goods manufactured by, 44.

MILITARY PROCEEDINGS,
statements in, are privileged, 101, 106.

MINUTES,
publication of, privileged, when, 145.

MISDIRECTION,
may be ground for a new trial, 178, 179.

MISMANAGEMENT,
allegation of, against a company, actionable, 79.

MISTAKE,
no defence to an action for defamation, 37.
publication by, 17.
small and accidental, does not affect fair comment, 92, 93.

MITIGATION OF DAMAGES,
evidence in, what may be given as, 24, 61, 67, 68, 166–171.
particulars of, when necessary to be given, 167.

MONEY,
>   payment of, into Court, cannot accompany denial of liability, 156, 202, 224.
>   must accompany plea of apology under Lord Campbell's Act, *ibid.*

MOTION,
>   for a rule for a criminal information, 193.

MURDER,
>   a charge of, is actionable *per se*, 25.

NAME,
>   of author of libel, editor cannot be compelled to discover, 208, 236.
>   of printer of libel, 208.
>   of proprietor of newspaper, 209.
>   of publisher, 208, 209.

NATURAL MEANING,
>   words must first be construed in, but special meaning may be shown, 9.

NAVAL PROCEEDINGS,
>   statements in, are absolutely privileged, 101, 106.

NEGLIGENCE,
>   of servant, master's liability for, in civil action, 62–64.
>   in criminal proceedings, 203, 204.
>   culpable, may aggravate damages, 163.

NEW TRIAL,
>   how to apply for, 239–240.
>   when granted, 178–182.

NEWSAGENTS,
>   liability of, 61, 64, 65, 198.

NEWSPAPER,
>   apology for libel in, as a defence, 80, 156, 202, 224.
>   comments in, on matter of public interest, what are, 93 *et seq.*
>   copying libels from another, no defence, 65, 169.
>   defences to action for libel in, 80.
>   criminal proceedings for libel in, 200–201.
>   definition of, in Law of Libel Amendment Act, 1888.. 109.
>   distributors of, 61, 64, 65, 198.
>   editor of, need not disclose name of author of libel, 208, 236.
>   interrogatories in action against, 236, 238.
>   libel in, what is, 1, 183.
>   liability of proprietor for libels in, 59, 61, 127, 198, 203.
>   publisher for libels in, 59, 61, 198, 202, 203.
>   editor for libels in, 59, 61, 169, 198, 203.
>   printer for libels in, 59, 61, 202, 203, 208.
>   author for libels in, 59, 61, 203.
>   proof of publication of, 13–17, 197–198, 207–209.
>   proprietors, register of, at Somerset House, 209.
>   receiver in bankruptcy conducting, 162.
>   report in, of judicial proceedings, 107, 112.

NEWSPAPER—*continued.*
   report in, of parliamentary proceedings, 120.
          of what meetings privileged, 121, 127-129.
   who are liable for libel in, 61.
   writers in, duties of, 86, 89-93.
          not liable for trivial mistakes, 93.

NEWSPAPER LIBEL AND REGISTRATION ACT, 1881, *text of*, in Appendix B., 259-264.

NEW TRIAL,
   when granted, 178-182.
   notice of motion for, *precedent of*, 240.
          time for service of, 239.
          what it must contain, 240.

NEXT FRIEND,
   infant sues by, 74.
   personally liable for costs, *ibid.*

NOTICE,
   that defendant intends to give certain evidence in mitigation of damages, when necessary, and form of, 167.
   to third party to preserve a libellous document, 210.
   seven days, under O. xxxvi. r. 37 .. 168.

NOTICE OF MOTION,
   for new trial, *precedent of*, 239.

NOTICES,
   publication of what, privileged, 130.
   what, may be criticised, 93-96.

OBSCENE PUBLICATION,
   on wall, hoarding, &c., punishable by summary conviction, 194-197.
   report of judicial proceeding, if it amount to, not privileged, 108, 110, 114, nor of public meeting, 121, 128.
   seizure and destruction of, by order of magistrate, 196.
   what is, *ibid.*

OFFICE,
   libel in way of, 7.
   slander in way of, is actionable *per se*, 27.
   what must be proved, *ibid.*
   words must touch or affect, 28.
   nature of, if legal, is immaterial, *ibid.*
   of profit and of credit, difference between, 30

OFFICIAL NOTICES AND REPORTS,
   publication of, when privileged, 106, 130.

OFFICER OF STATE, 130.

ONUS OF PROOF,
   lies where, 11.

OPPORTUNITY,
    of admission for reporters, 128.

ORDER,
    nisi, motion for, on application for criminal information, 193.
    of judge required for criminal prosecution for libel in newspaper, 187, 198–200.
    of magistrate as to seizure and destruction of obscene publications, 196.
    of Supreme Court, II. r. 4 .. 71.
        XI. r. 1 .. 71, 72, 210.
        XVI. r. 1 .. 51.
        r. 4 .. 54.
        XVII. r. 1 .. 161.
        XVIII., 52.
        XIX. r. 18 .. 225.
        XXI. r. 4 .. 227.
        XXII., 156.
        XXXI. r. 7 .. 235.
        XXXVI. r. 37 .. 167, *note* (*s.*), 168, 231, 232.
        XXXIX. r. 4 .. 239, r. 6 .. 179.
        XLVIII. A, 72.

OTHER LIBEL ACTIONS,
    consolidation of actions allowed in respect of same, or substantially the same, words, 171–173.
    evidence of, when admissible in mitigation of damages, 167, 171.

OTHER LIBELS,
    evidence of, not allowed merely in aggravation of damages, 164.
        when allowed in mitigation of damages, 167–171.

OTHERS LIABLE,
    consolidation of actions when for same, or substantially the same, libel, 171.
    evidence of, when admissible in mitigation of damages, 167–171.

PAINTINGS,
    fair and *bonâ fide* comments on, no libel, 96.

PAMPHLET,
    issued to the public, fair and *bonâ fide* comments on, no libel, 96.

PAPERS,
    parliamentary, authorized publication of, 106.
        extracts from or abstracts of authorized, 106, 107, 247, 248.

PARENT,
    statements made to, *re* child, may be privileged, 144.

PARISH MEETINGS,
    proceedings at, fair and *bonâ fide* comments on, 95.
        reports of, when privileged, 127–129.
    statements made at, when privileged, 136, 137, 140, 148, 149.

300 INDEX.

PARLIAMENT,
 extracts from, and abstract of papers, &c., issued by order of, when privileged, 106, 107.
 papers, &c., issued by order of, and verified copies thereof, absolutely privileged, 106, 107, 130, 131.
 petition to, fair and *bonâ fide* comments on, no libel, 93.
 proceedings in, &c., may be criticised, 93–94.
   reports of, when privileged, 120, 121.
 statements made in, absolutely privileged, 101.

PARLIAMENTARY ELECTIONS,
 false statements at, 177, 186.

PARLIAMENTARY PAPERS,
 authorized publication of, protected, 97, 106, 107, 130, 131.
   extracts from, and abstracts of, when protected, 106, 107.

PARTICULARS,
 precedent of, 223.
 summons for, 221–222.
 precedent of, 222–223
 when ordered, 221, 222.

PARTIES,
 joinder of, 51–55.
 to a suit, statements of, in Court, privileged, 102.

PARTNERS,
 action by, 57.
 previous action against one is good defence where liability is joint, 158–159.
 contra, where liability is several, *ibid*.

PAYMENT INTO COURT,
 must accompany plea of apology under Lord Campbell's Act, 156, 224.
 no plea denying liability can be pleaded if there be, *ibid*.

PERIODICAL PUBLICATION, 80, 109. *See* MAGAZINE.

PERJURY,
 charge of, 25, 83, 84, 92, 118, 168, 232.

PETITION AND PETITIONERS,
 to Parliament, fair and *bonâ fide* comments on, no libel, 93, 94.
 to Parliament, privileged, 101.

PICTURE,
 if publicly exhibited, fair and *bonâ fide* comments on, no libel, 96.
 may be a libel, 3.

PLACARD,
 publication of, containing indecent matter, punishable on summary conviction, 196–197.

PLACE OF ENTERTAINMENT,
 comment on, no libel, 95.

PLAGUE,
 charge of, actionable, *per se*, 27.

PLAINTIFF,
  disability of, prevents Statute of Limitations from running against, 159, 160.
  who may be joined as, 51.

PLEADING,
  precedents of, 212, 215–224, 227–230, 232.
  suggestions as to, 214–232.

PLEADINGS,
  are absolutely privileged, 102.

PLEAS,
  severance of, 86.

POLICE,
  affairs, everything concerning, may be criticised, 94.
  notices and reports, publication of, when privileged, 130.

POLITICAL MEETINGS,
  conduct of persons at, fair and *bonâ fide* comments on, no libel, 93, 94.
  proceedings at, reports of, when privileged, 121.

POOR LAW,
  administration of, fair and *bonâ fide* comments on, no libel, 95.

POST-CARD,
  publication presumed if libel on, 14.

PRAISE,
  ironical, may be a libel, 6, 118.

PRECEDENTS,
  of indorsement on writ, 211.
    Statements of claim, 215–221.
    Defences, 227–230.
    Reply, 232.
    particulars, 223.
    summons for particulars, 222.
    notice of motion for new trial, 240.

PRESS,
  writers for the, duties of, 86, 89–93, 117.
    liability of, 59, 61, 202, 203.
    defences open to, 80, 200–201.

PRESUMPTION,
  that defamatory words are false, 46, 212.

PREVIOUS ACTION,
  for same libel, evidence of, admissible in mitigation of damages, 167, 171.
  when a defence to an action, 158, 159.

PREVIOUS PUBLICATION,
  of same, or substantially the same, libel by others, when admissible as evidence, 167, 170, 171.

302 INDEX.

PRINCIPAL,
 commands of, no defence for servant, 64, 65, 203, 204.
 foreign, how to sue for libel published by agent here, 72, 210.
 liability of and defences open to, for acts of servant, in civil action, 59, 61, 62–64, 80.
 in criminal proceedings, 200, 201, 203, 204.

PRINTER,
 cannot maintain an action for his charges for printing a libel, 60.
 defences open to, 80, 200.
 how to discover, 208.
 liability of, 60, 64, 65, 200, 208.
 must make a return under Newspaper Libel and Registration Act, 1881..208.
 must print his name and address on every publication, *ibid.*
 must preserve name of his employer, *ibid.*
 rights of, against employer, on discovering libellous nature of copy, 60.
 must keep copy of printed paper for six months, 208.

PRINTING,
 libellous matter, no action maintainable for, 60.

PRIVATE LIFE,
 of public man, comments on, when allowed, 94.

PRIVATE MEETINGS,
 proceedings at, reports of, not privileged, 125.
 what are not, 121, 125–129.

PRIVILEGE,
 as a defence to a civil action, 96–98.
  criminal proceedings, 200, 201.
 duty of judge as to, 98.
 may be,
  (1.) *Absolute* — where no action lies, however untrue or malicious the statement may have been, 96, 97, 101–113.
    See ABSOLUTE PRIVILEGE.
  (2.) *Qualified*—where the *primâ facie* protection is rebutted by proof of actual malice, 97, 98, 106–149.
    See QUALIFIED PRIVILEGE.

PRIVILEGED OCCASION,
 distinguished from privileged communication, 99.
 position of a corporation on, *quære*, 80.

PROCEEDINGS,
 former, when a defence, 158, 159.
 in Court of Justice, may be criticised, 94.
 in Parliament, may be criticised, 93, 94.
 report of, in a Court of Justice, 107–118.
   in Parliament, 120, 121.

PROFESSION,
 in action for libel on member of, plaintiff need only prove he has practised such profession, 8–9.

PROFESSION—*continued*.
    in slander, plaintiff must prove he practised such profession when words were spoken, 9.
    libels on members of, 7–8.
    slanders on members of, special damage need not be proved, 32–34.

PROOF. *See* BURDEN OF PROOF.

PROPRIETOR OF NEWSPAPER,
    how to discover, 209.
    if limited company, not obliged to register, 209.
    liability to civil action for libels contained therein, 59, 61, 127.
    liability to criminal proceedings, 198, 203.
    register of, at Somerset House, open to public inspection, 209.
    registration of, defects of system of, 209.
    interrogatories, when he may refuse to answer, 236–238.

PROSECUTION,
    for libel, 183.
    procedure on, 187–193.
    when order of judge required for, 198–200.

PROSECUTIONS, DIRECTOR OF PUBLIC,
    fiat of, not necessary for criminal proceedings, 199.

PROTECTION,
    of reports, 97–98, 201.
    of writers for the press, 80, 200, 201.

PROVOCATION,
    by plaintiff's conduct in publishing previous libels, when admissible as evidence in mitigation of damages, 167–171.

PUBLIC ATTENTION AND CRITICISM,
    anything inviting, fair and *bonâ fide* comments on, no libel, 96.

PUBLIC GRIEVANCES,
    statements made to redress, privileged, 131–133.

PUBLIC BENEFIT,
    that words are true and that the publication thereof is for the, a defence under sect. 6 of Lord Campbell's Act, 200, 202.

PUBLIC ENTERTAINMENTS,
    fair and *bonâ fide* comments on, no libel, 95.

PUBLIC INTEREST. *See* MATTER OF PUBLIC INTEREST.

PUBLIC MEETING,
    proceedings at, may be criticised, 95.
        report of, 121, *et seq.*
    report of, when privileged, 121.
    what is a, 121, 122, 125, 126.

PUBLIC MEN,
    conduct of, in public affairs, fair and *bonâ fide* comments on, no libel, 93, 94.
    who are, 94.

PUBLIC POLICY,
fair and *bonâ fide* comment on, no libel, 94, 96.

PUBLICATION,
all concerned in, are liable, 59, 61, 64–65, 197.
as regards husband and wife, 15.
contemporaneous, what is, 113.
definition, 13.
excessive, may be evidence of malice, 153.
fresh, what is, 160, 161.
functions of judge and jury as to, in civil action, 17.
in civil action must be to third person, 13.
in criminal proceedings, need not be to third person, 185, 197, 198.
no action without, 13.
of comments on a pending trial may be restrained by injunction, whether they amount to a libel or not, 176–177.
of libel may be restrained by injunction, 174.
outside jurisdiction, 71.
previous, by other persons, no defence, 169.
    when admissible as evidence in mitigation of damages, 167, 171.
primâ facie case of, 16.
question for jury alone in criminal trial, 202.
what is, as regards a civil action, 13–17.
    criminal liability, 185, 197–198.
what necessary, in criminal cases, *ibid*.
when for public benefit, 126, 127.

"PUBLICATION FOR PUBLIC BENEFIT,"
meaning of, within sect. 4 of Law of Libel Amendment Act, 1888 ..126–127.
under sect. 4 of Libel Act of 1888, not absolutely necessary for defendant to prove, 122 *et seq*.

"PUBLISHED CONTEMPORANEOUSLY WITH SUCH PROCEEDINGS,"
meaning of, 112, 113.

PUBLISHER,
liability of, 59, 61, 199, 202, 203.
return under Newspaper Libel and Registration Act of 1881 ..208.

"PUFFING,"
no action lies for, 49.

PUNISHMENT,
for publishing a libel, 183, 251.
for publishing a libel, &c., with intent to extort money, &c., 250.
for publishing indecent advertisements, 196, 197.

"QUACK,"
to call a doctor a, is actionable, *per se*, 33.

QUALIFIED PRIVILEGE,
    where the *primâ facie* protection is rebutted by proof of actual malice, 97.
    under this head come—
        (a) Reports other than those in a newspaper of judicial proceedings, and reports in a newspaper of such proceedings, if not published contemporaneously with such proceedings, 97, 98, 113-118.
        (b) Extracts from registers kept pursuant to statute, 98, 118-120.
        (c) Reports of proceedings in Parliament, 98, 120, 121.
        (d) Reports of proceedings of public meetings, 98, 121-127.
        (e) Reports of Vestry meetings, &c., 98, 127-130.
        (f) Notices and reports published at request of Government office or authority, 98, 130-131.
        (g) Statements made to a public servant or other person in authority with the object of preventing or punishing crime or redressing a public grievance, 98, 131-133.
        (h) Statements made with the object of protecting some interest of the writer or speaker, and reasonably necessary for such purpose, 98, 133-136.
        (i) Statements made with the object of protecting an interest common to the writer or speaker and the person to whom the statement is made, 98, 136-140.
        (j) Statements made in discharge of a legal, moral, or social duty, 98, 140-149.

QUANTUM MERUIT, printer can sue for parts of book not libellous, 60.

REASONABLE AND PROBABLE CAUSE,
    want of, must be proved in an action of slander of goods, 47.

RECEIVERS,
    in an administration action, liability of, 162.

RECKLESSNESS,
    may be evidence of malice, 151, 152.

REDRESS OF GRIEVANCES,
    statements as to, privileged, when, 131.

REFUSAL,
    to insert a reasonable letter of explanation or contradiction, consequences of, 121, 128, 266.

REGISTER,
    certified copy of, evidence, 209, 263.
    no obligation on printers and publishers of newspaper owned by limited company to, 209.
    of newspaper proprietors, open to inspection of the public, 209.

REGISTRAR IN BANKRUPTCY,
    proceedings before, report of, 115.

RELEASE,
    what is, 158.
    a good defence to an action, *ibid.*

RELIGION,
    attack on, what is blasphemy, 194.

REMEDIES,
    civil, 18, 174.
    criminal, 183-193.
    for libel in newspaper, 59-62, 198, 203.
    for repetition of libel or slander, 23-25, 66-68.
    of and against aliens, 71-74.
                bankrupts, 71, 75-77.
                companies, 77-80.
                corporations, *ibid.*
                infants, 71, 74.
                lunatics, 71, 74-75.
                married women, 68, 69.

REMISSION OF ACTIONS,
    to County Court, when granted, 77.

REPETITION,
    of libel or slander, liability for, 23-25, 66-68.
                when evidence of, admissible in mitigation damages, 166-171.

REPLY,
    raising objection in law, *precedent of*, 232.

REPORT,
    defined, 86.
    differs from comment, *ibid.*
    may be criticised, when, 93-96.
    of judicial proceedings in newspaper, 97-98, 106-113.
                other than in a newspaper, 97, 98, 113-1
    of county council meetings, 127-129.
    of parliamentary proceedings, 120, 121.
    of public meetings, 98, 121-127.
    of other meetings, 127-129.
    of school board meetings, *ibid.*
    of vestry meetings, *ibid.*
    of proceedings of board of guardians, *ibid.*
                of parliamentary committee, *ibid.*
    title of, must not be libellous, 82, 118.
    publication of what, privileged, 87, 96-98.
                not privileged, 129.
    fair, what is, 116-118.

REPORTER,
    criminal prosecution against, no order of judge necessary, 199.
    defences open to, 80, 200, 202.
    duties of, 86, 87, 89-93, 116-118.
    employer's liability for libels of, 197, 202.
    liability of, in criminal prosecution, 198, 199, 200-202.

REPUBLICATION,
    of libel, by copying from another newspaper, no defence, 61, 169.
        when admissible in mitigation of damages, 61, 166, 167, 169–171.

REPUTATION,
    injury to, gist of action, 1, 81.
    of plaintiff, when admissible as evidence in aggravation of damages, 164.
    of plaintiff, when admissible as evidence in mitigation of damages, 67, 170.

RES JUDICATA,
    a good defence, 158–159.

RESTRAINT,
    of publication of libel by injunction, when granted, 174, 177.

RETORT,
    fact that libel complained of is a, admissible as evidence in mitigation of damages, 170.
        may sometimes amount to a defence, 133–136.

REVIEWS,
    of books, if fair and *bonâ fide,* no libel, 90, 95.

RULE NISI,
    in criminal information, 193.

RUMOURS,
    to same effect as libel, evidence of, inadmissible, 67, 170.

ROYAL COMMISSION,
    evidence given before, fair and *bonâ fide* comment on, no libel, 93.

SATISFACTION,
    accord and, what is, 157, 158.
        a good defence to an action, *ibid.*

SCHOOL BOARD,
    meeting of, proceedings at, fair and *bonâ fide* comments on, no libel, 95.
        reports of, privileged, 127.

SCHOOLMASTER,
    to impute incapacity to, actionable *per se,* 34.

SECONDARY EVIDENCE,
    not allowed, of documents absolutely privileged, 213.

SECONDARY MEANING, 10.

SECT,
    libel on, may be a crime, though not actionable, 183, 184.

SECURITY FOR COSTS,
    alien, if not resident here, is generally ordered to give, 71, 76, 211
    when plaintiff ordered to give, 58.

SEDITIOUS,
    words, publication of a crime, 194.
        what amounts to, 195.
        not privileged in reports, 108, 114, 121.

308 INDEX.

SELECT COMMITTEE,
    statements before, privileged, 101.

SELF-DEFENCE,
    statements made in, privileged when, 133.

SELF-INTEREST,
    statements made in, privileged when, 133.

SELLER,
    of newspaper containing a libel, 16, 61, 198, 199.

SERVANT,
    character of, privileged communication, 142–144.
    communication to master of, when privileged, 144.
    criminal liability of master for libel published by his, 203.
    liability of, for publishing libel by master's order, 59, 61, 64, 65, 198, 199.
    liability of master for libel by, 62–64, 77–99, 203.
    slanders on, 36.

SERVICE OF WRIT,
    out of jurisdiction, leave required, 71.

SEVERAL LIABILITY, 159.

SEVERANCE,
    of parts of a libel, 86.

SHAREHOLDERS,
    meetings of proceedings at reports of, not privileged, 129.

SIGNS,
    may constitute a libel, 3.

SLANDER,
    definition, 1.
    distinguished from libel, 2, 3, 18.
    company or corporation, when liable for, 77–80.
    gestures may be, 3.
    no action lies without proof of special damage except in four cases, 2, 19 *et seq.*
    repetition of, 66–68.
    when action will lie for, 19.
    when within the criminal law, 1, 2, 185.

SLANDER OF TITLE, 38–43.
    definition of, 38.
    what must be proved in action for, 39.

SLANDER OF GOODS, MANUFACTURED, 44–51.
    definition of, 44.
    what must be proved in action for, 45, 47.

SLANDER OF WOMEN ACT, 1891 .. 36. 37.

SMALLNESS OF DAMAGES,
    not always " good cause " to deprive a plaintiff of his costs, 178.

SOLICITOR,
> communications between client and, to what extent privileged, 103, when privileged from production, 233-234.
> libel on, 7, 8.
> not obliged to produce documents of client, 233-234.
> slander on, 33, 34.
> statements by, in course of judicial proceedings absolutely privileged, 102, 103, to third party, when privileged, 145.

SOMERSET HOUSE,
> register of newspaper proprietors at, 209.

SPECIAL DAMAGE,
> loss of general business may rank as, 22.
> may be proved in aggravation of damages, 164.
> must be proved in actions for Slander of Title, 39, 42-43.
> necessity of sometimes pleading, 22, 215.
> *precedent* of count for, 219.
> *precedent* of particulars, 222.
> what is, 2, 20, 21.
> where not necessary to prove, 19.

SPECIAL MEANING,
> words may be shown to have, 9, 11.

SPEECHES,
> reports of, when privileged, 96-98.
> when legitimate subject for criticism, 93, 94.

STATEMENTS OF CLAIM,
> how to draft, 212-215.
> *innuendo* required in, when, 12.
> *precedents* of, 215-221.

STATEMENTS,
> even of voluntary, may be privileged, 142.
> in discharge of a duty, privileged, when, 140, 141.
> when privileged, 96-98.

STATUE,
> may be a libel, 3.

STATUTE OF LIMITATIONS, 74, 159.

STATUTES. *See* Appendix of Statutes, 241, and Contents of such Appendix, *ibid.* *See also* Index to Statutes cited, xxxiii.

STIPENDIARY MAGISTRATE,
> power of, to destroy obscene publications, 196, 197.

STUPIDITY,
> is not malice, 155.

SUBPŒNA DUCES TECUM, 213.

SUBSCRIBERS TO CHARITY,
> proceedings at meeting of, report of, not privileged, 129.

SUMMARY JURISDICTION OF JUSTICES,
> to commit for trial, 187-191.
> to convict for advertisement of indecent matter, 196, 197.
> to convict for publication of trivial libel in a newspaper, 190-191.
> to issue warrant for apprehension of libeller, 187.
> to seize and destroy obscene publications, 196.
> to take bail, 190.

SUMMONS,
    before a magistrate, procedure on hearing of, 187-191.
    for particulars, 222-224.
                precedent of, 222, 223.
SURVEYOR,
    libel on, 7, 8.
    slander on, 34.

TELEGRAM,
    publication presumed if libel contained in, 14.
THEATRE,
    performances at, fair and *bonâ fide* comments on, no libel, 95-96.
"THE GREATER THE TRUTH, THE GREATER THE LIBEL," 185.
THIRD PARTY,
    defendant not liable for damages due to unreasonable conduct of, 165.
    where document containing libel is in possession of, how to proceed, 212, 213.
    accidental presence of, privilege not destroyed by, 148, 149.
    unnecessary publication to, destroys privilege, 132, 135, 138, 139, 149, 153.
TITLE,
    of article or paragraph, may be libellous, 82, 117, 118.
                must be justified, *ibid*.
TONE,
    of publication, may be evidence of malice, 153.
TORT FEASORS,
    no contribution between, 60.
TORTS,
    committed abroad, actionable here, when, 73.
TOWN COUNCIL,
    proceedings of, fair and *bonâ fide* comment on, no libel, 95.
    proceedings of, reports of, privileged, 12, 92, 127.
    statements made at meetings of, when privileged, 136, 137, 140, 148, 149.
TRADE COMPETITION,
    no ground for action, 49.
TRADE, PROFESSION, OR OFFICE,
    words affecting, actionable *per se*, 27.
    are libellous, when, 7.
TRADE JOURNAL,
    not a newspaper within 52 & 53 Vict. c. 96. .109-110.
    reports in, not privileged, 129.
TRADESMAN,
    libel on, 8.
    slander on, 35.
    slander of goods manufactured, or sold by, 44-51.
    advertisement of, may be criticised, 96.
TRIAL,
    before a magistrate, 187-191.
    of criminal information, 192.
    of indictment, 187-191.
    without pleadings, not advisable, 210.

TRIAL, NEW,
    on what grounds granted, 178-179.
    notice of motion of, *precedent of*, 240.
    time within which to apply for, 239.
TRUSTEE IN BANKRUPTCY, 76.
TRUTH,
    a defence to a civil action, 81-86.
    belief in, of words complained of, no defence unless occasion privileged, 37, 68, 91, 92, 139.
    not admissible as evidence in mitigation of damages, 168.
    no defence to criminal proceedings unless publication was for public benefit, 200, 202.
    of libel, when magistrate can receive evidence of, 188, 189.
TYPEWRITER,
    publication to, 13.

UNCERTAINTY,
    of plaintiff, defeats action, 5.
UNCHASTITY,
    imputation of, to woman or girl, actionable without proof of special damage, 19, 36, 165, 211-212, 269.
UNLAWFUL MEETINGS,
    proceedings at, reports of, not privileged, 126.
    what are, *ibid*.

VENEREAL DISEASE,
    a charge of, actionable *per se*, 27.
VENDOR,
    of newspaper or book containing a libel, liability of, 16, 61, 198, 199.
VERBATIM,
    report to be fair and accurate, need not be, 116.
VERDICT,
    of jury in civil action, 9, 17.
    of jury in criminal case, 191, 205.
VESTRY CLERK,
    libel on, 7, 8.
VESTRY MEETINGS,
    proceedings at, fair and *bonâ fide* comments on, no libel, 94, 95.
    proceedings at, reports of, privileged, 127.
    statements made at, when privileged, 136, 137, 140, 148, 149.
VETERINARY SURGEON,
    libel on, 7, 8.
    slander on, 34.
VEXATIOUS INDICTMENTS ACT,
    all libels now within, 190.
    binding over to prosecute, *ibid*.
VIOLENT LANGUAGE,
    may be evidence of malice, 153.
    not always so, 154.
VOLUNTARY STATEMENTS,
    may be privileged, 142.
    not necessarily evidence of malice, 154.

VULGAR ABUSE,
  not actionable *per se*, 26.

WIFE. *See* MARRIED WOMAN.

WITNESS,
  name of, need not generally be disclosed in answer to interrogatories, 238.
  statements of, when absolutely privileged, 101–106.

WORDS,
  defamatory,
    action on the case for, 38, 39, 44.
    actionable *per se*, 19.
    construction of, duty of judge and jury as to, in civil action, 9, 10.
    construction of, duty of judge and jury as to, in criminal trial, 205, 206.
    commercial terms, 10.
    defences to action for, 80.
        criminal proceedings for, 200, 201.
    injunction to restrain, when granted, 174–177.
    ironical, may be a libel, 6, 118.
    must be taken in their natural sense, 10–11.
    of a cant or slang character, 10.
    publication of, duty of judge and jury as to, in criminal trial, 197.
    publication of duty of judge and jury as to, in civil action, 17.
    published outside jurisdiction, 71, *et seq.*
    what are, 1–10.
    when action lies for, 1–18.
    when criminal proceedings lie for, 183, *et seq.*
  blasphemous, 194.
  seditious, 195.
  obscene, 196.

WORK,
  literary, may be criticised, 95.
  of art may be criticised, 96.
  printer cannot recover for libellous, 60.
  remedy of printer who discovers he is printing libellous, *ibid.*

WRIT,
  application for leave to serve, when defendant is out of jurisdiction, must be to judge in Chambers, 71, *et seq.*
  how indorsed, 211.
  of *certiorari, precedent of statement of claim* in action of libel removed by, 220.

WRITERS FOR THE PRESS,
  defences open to, 80, 200–202.
  duties of, 86, 89–93, 117.
  liability of, 59, 61, 202, 203, 204.

www.ingramcontent.com/pod-product-compliance
Lightning Source LLC
Chambersburg PA
CBHW032359230426
43672CB00007B/759